Build Your Own Web Site

Louis Kahn
& Laura Logan

Microsoft Press

PUBLISHED BY

Microsoft Press
A Division of Microsoft Corporation
One Microsoft Way
Redmond, Washington 98052-6399

Library of Congress Cataloging-in-Publication Data
Kahn, Louis Marc, 1967-
    Build your own Web site / Louis Marc Kahn, Laura Anne Logan.
      p.   cm.
    Includes index.
    ISBN 1-57231-304-8
    1. World Wide Web (Information retrieval system)   2. Microsoft
Windows NT. 3. World Wide Web servers.   I. Logan, Laura Anne,
1964-   . II. Title.
TK5105.888.K34   1996
    005.7'13--dc20   96-17525
                                                    CIP

Printed and bound in the United States of America.

1 2 3 4 5 6 7 8 9 MLML 1 0 9 8 7 6

Distributed to the book trade in Canada by Macmillan of Canada, a division of Canada
Publishing Corporation.

A CIP catalogue record for this book is available from the British Library.

Microsoft Press books are available through booksellers and distributors worldwide. For
further information about international editions, contact your local Microsoft Corporation office. Or contact Microsoft Press International directly at fax (206) 936-7329.

Acquisitions Editor: Casey Doyle
Project Editor: Kathleen Atkins
Technical Editor: Dail Magee Jr.

To Mark, Keith, and Anya.

Table of Contents

Foreword

When the telephone was first released commercially, it was used for years in a way that seems ridiculous from today's viewpoint. An executive would dictate a memo to his or her secretary, who would take the dictation to the telephone room. A call would be placed to the receiving company's telephone room where the memo would be transcribed and then delivered to the receiving party. It took time for telephones to become common enough, and for people to think of them as common enough, to be used the way we use them today: to call a specific location directly and, with cellular phones, to call a specific person directly.

Today, computers are still used mostly as tools to create or analyze information, which is then typically consumed through existing media forms (paper, for example). But now, with the widespread adoption of the Internet, and with computers commonplace, people for the first time can use their computers to communicate in very rich ways with other people *through* their computers. We've obviated the need for print to carry our computer-generated communications the same way we removed print from our telephone conversations. What we're experiencing today with the Web is comparable to the time when people stopped transcribing their phone conversations: Computers (together with the interconnection between them—the Internet) are common enough, and people think of them as common enough, that we're beginning to use them in fundamentally new ways. The Web is the beginning of the way computers will *really* get used as communication devices. In my view, having access to the Internet is as important as everyone having a telephone.

The Internet offers a level of access to information that is unprecedented. Anyone with access to the World Wide Web has access to all the information published on it as well as the powerful tools for searching through all that information to find what they need. The opportunities for learning, for fairer exchange of goods, and for increased understanding between people are mind-boggling. Moreover, Web technology offers a way of making information widely available with an ease that is unparalleled in our history. The need to own or buy space in a newspaper or a magazine, or time on a television or a radio station, to make your views, services, or products known is diminishing. The Web levels the playing field between individuals and governments, between small and large businesses, between consumers and producers, between charities and political action committees. The World Wide Web on the Internet is the ultimate democratic medium where everyone can have their say and everyone can hear what they're saying without intermediate interpretation, distortion, or censorship. (Of course, laws do apply on the Internet too, but I believe the vast majority of people are good and will use this medium toward good ends.) The Internet makes freedom of expression and freedom of information available in ways not thought possible before.

Just as companies have telephone systems for employees to communicate with each other as well as with the outside world, the Web has applications for communications within organizations as well as between organizations and their customers, constituents, or partners. The same Web technology that makes it possible for a small business to hang its shingle on the Internet can be used by a larger company to communicate project status on its internal intranet so that its people can stay informed and responsive in the face of small, nimble competitors. The use of intranets within organizations to make information more accessible to its members is again a shift away from the usage of the past. Now, rather than being stored away in the computer version of inaccessible file cabinets, documents can be (securely) searched for, described, referred to, and indexed in a readily accessible form. Web technology can make our businesses more effective.

These changes in the way we produce, find, and publish information will change the way we do business, govern, express ourselves, and learn. I can't think of anything more important than having everyone participate in these changes. It's long been my belief that the best way to predict the future is to invent it. With this book, Laura and Louis empower you to step into this exciting arena and to help invent the future of the Internet or the future of your company's intranet.

Jim Allchin
Senior Vice President,
Desktop and Business Systems Division
Microsoft Corporation

Acknowledgments

One evening, after enjoying a nice meal and having a most pleasant conversation, two good friends decided it would be a great idea to collaborate on a book. That was the easy part. The rest was difficult, sometimes tedious, and always time-consuming work that would never have been completed without the assistance of many people and significant sacrifices from those close to us. We would like to express our sincere gratitude to everyone who helped make it possible for us to complete this project.

For support through countless hours at the computer and away from home, for technical assistance, chapter reviews, endless encouragement, and faith in everything we do, we thank our partners in life, Keith Logan and Mark Walter. Laura also thanks Anya Logan, even though she can't really understand it yet, for being as patient with her mommy through this project as a two-year-old can possibly be.

We gratefully acknowledge everyone at Microsoft Press who contributed to this book and guided us through the process. We were surprised and delighted by your enthusiasm! Special thanks to our terrific editor, Kathleen Atkins, as well as to Jim Brown, Casey Doyle, and Dail Magee Jr.

For their encouragement and enthusiasm for this project, and for listening to us talk about it endlessly, we thank our family and friends: Lesa Berec, Pamela Fury, Lisa and Dale Howie, Cindy and Tom Kahler, Eric Kahn, Joanne Kahn, Michael Kahn, Allan and Bernice Logan, Stuart Logan, Steve and Debbie Madigan, Michael O'Rourke, Kevin Phaup, Karin and Dan Plastina, Miriam and Jeff Rasco, Karen Roper, Shari and Ramon and Erica-Marie Sanchez, Cindy and Haydn Tanner, Terry Ward, and Cathy Wissink.

Many thanks to Steve Jackson, Chris Peters, and Eli Shapira who supplied us with software for the CD-ROM.

And last, but certainly not least, for their advice, encouragement, and contributions to this book, we thank the following people from Microsoft: Jim Allchin (for amazingly squeezing a press deadline into an impossibly busy schedule), J. Allard, Bob Muglia, and Todd Warren.

Louis Kahn and Laura Logan
Redmond, Washington
June, 1996

Introduction

Anyone who hasn't been in hibernation for the last couple of years has certainly noticed the recent hype surrounding the Internet. Internet references have been haunting you everywhere: at the movies, in magazines, in books, on television, in advertisements. You can't help but notice politicians throwing out the buzzwords "Information Superhighway" at every opportunity. It's likely that your local newspaper now includes a page devoted to Internet news and happenings. In fact, you can probably even subscribe to your paper on line if you want to. Suddenly, it's apparent that every company that expects to make it into the next century is scurrying to develop an Internet business plan.

It's not difficult to conclude that the Internet is becoming entrenched in our culture and is changing the way people communicate and do business worldwide. Perhaps you've even gone so far as to hook up with an online service to use the Net. You might use e-mail to communicate with people, subscribe to an online news service, and browse the World Wide Web. But now you're wondering just what it would take to be a more active participant on the Internet, to actually put something up on the Net for other people to look at. Or you're interested in using a private intranet to improve communication within your organization. You have recognized Internet technology as a significant new method for reaching people, and, essentially, you want to know what would be involved in having your own Internet presence.

Building an Internet Site

The project of building an Internet or an intranet site can be divided into two primary jobs. The first we call content creation. It includes the development of the presentation of the content or resources that you want to publish and make available to your intended audience. Content creation usually involves the use of a simple "programming language" for getting your information into a form that computers on the Internet can read. Frankly, there is already a lot of really good material available in the form of books and courses for you to learn content creation, so we do not cover content creation in depth in this book. The software provided with this book, however, contains templates to help you set up some basic Web content, and our recommended reading section points you toward some good books on the subject.

The primary purpose of this book centers around the second task: getting the resources on line. In other words, making that information available on an Internet server so that people can have access to it.

The process of setting up Internet servers is complex. This book walks you through all the steps. We start with a brief section on Internet basics, including definitions of terms, for those of you who are really new. Then we help you to consider some preliminary issues—what your site will consist of, hardware requirements, communications links, and service providers. Once you have these issues

resolved, you can move through the steps for installing and configuring your system. We also discuss in this book security issues, content creation, maintenance of your system, and future Internet technologies that you might want to investigate.

While you can find quite a few books about content creation, you can't find so many on the market that deal with setting up Internet servers, and the books that are out there are technical and not very easy to use. One reason these books are so complicated is that they assume you will be using a UNIX platform. Since our goal is to make it as easy for you as possible to build your Internet site, we have written this book specifically for the use of the Microsoft Windows NT Server operating system as your Internet platform.

The Internet UNIX Myth

When you start researching and talking to people about setting up your Internet site, some people might discourage you from using any operating system other than UNIX for your Internet platform. You will probably be confronted with the Internet UNIX myth. There is such a huge UNIX bias in the Internet community that some people believe UNIX is the only operating system that you can use to set up an Internet server. This is untrue. Many operating systems today make very good Internet platforms. We happen to think that Windows NT Server is the best and easiest operating system to use for the Internet, so we have chosen to write specifically about the Windows NT platform. We want to make it easy, even for those with very little experience with networking, to successfully set up a presence on the Internet.

Platform

In computer terminology, a *platform* is the foundation that other technologies run on top of. A software platform is usually a core piece of software such as the operating system. For example, Windows NT Server is a platform for running Windows-based applications. Hardware can also be referred to as a platform.

So, if the UNIX myth is untrue, then why do so many people stick with UNIX on the Internet? The short answer to this question is history. UNIX had a long run as the first and only operating system available for use as an Internet platform and, as a result, became fixed in people's minds as *the* Internet platform. Also, UNIX has its roots in the same places that the Internet does—in academia, research, and government, where UNIX is still in widespread use. The domination of the Internet by different flavors of UNIX is an unfortunate legacy, especially since the development of more powerful and easier-to-use operating systems like Windows NT Server.

What Makes Windows NT Server a Better Internet Platform than UNIX?

It is not really possible to do a complete feature-for-feature comparison of UNIX and Windows NT Server because the UNIX community is internally inconsistent. The source code for UNIX is available to anyone; therefore, many, many different vendors offer variations (flavors) of UNIX. As a result, you cannot pick a feature from one flavor of UNIX and assume that it is a feature of UNIX systems across the board. We will, however, draw some general comparisons between the two operating systems to illustrate our enthusiasm for Windows NT Server as an Internet platform.

Probably the most important feature that puts Windows NT Server miles ahead of UNIX is simply its ease of use. Most UNIX operating systems have a command line interface, whereas Windows NT Server has a *graphical user interface* (GUI), which is generally easy for people to learn. Also, Windows NT Server shares the look and feel of the Windows 95 operating system, which many people are already familiar with.

Ease of use extends to other areas of the operating system. Installation of Windows NT Server is nearly trivial. Most people can install it without ever having to read the documentation, and setup is usually complete in a matter of hours. Most of the installation is automated, and hardware is autodetected. UNIX has no automated installation and no autodetection of hardware. In fact, UNIX installations assume you have intimate knowledge of your hardware, such as interrupt settings; I/O memory addresses; the number of heads, cylinders, and sectors on your hard disk; and other gory details that can make a UNIX installation arduous. It can literally take days and the assistance of experts to set up a UNIX system.

Administration of a Windows NT–based server is also much easier than with most UNIX systems. The administrative utilities use a GUI, and a large suite of wizards walk you through common functions such as adding users, installing and configuring printers and modems, creating groups, setting security, and many of the other usual tasks involved in administrating a server. Figure I-1 (on the next page) shows you a Windows NT Server User Manager screen. Administration of a UNIX system is usually a matter of editing text files and then running a program that processes the file. This is time-consuming, complicated, and clunky work.

Scalability of Windows NT Server is another important feature that makes it better than UNIX as an Internet platform. Windows NT Server is compatible across multiple hardware platforms, so if you want to scale up, you just buy bigger hardware and load the same operating system. (See Figure I-2.) Scaling up with UNIX might require a change of UNIX vendors, making all your old software incompatible.

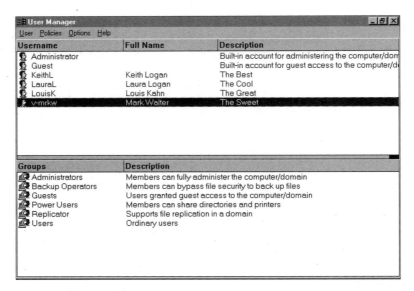

Figure I-1. *The Windows NT Server User Manager makes administrative functions easy.*

As a scalable system, Windows NT Server can be used by businesses of all sizes. Therefore, as your Internet presence grows, and your needs change, you can still rely on the same operating system. Windows NT Server can run on computer systems with as little as one processor and 16 megabytes of memory as well as on machines with 32 processors and 4 gigabytes of memory. Additionally, a Windows NT–based server can support mass storage of up to 32 terabytes (a terabyte is a thousand gigabytes) of disk space.

SCALABILITY

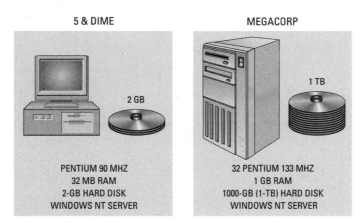

Figure I-2. *Windows NT Server can be used by businesses of all sizes because it is scalable.*

Windows NT Server is hardware independent. There are virtually unlimited options in your choice of hardware, which gives you a great deal of flexibility. Some versions of UNIX are completely dependent on hardware from specific vendors. Hardware independence allows you to change your hardware architecture without losing your investments in your operating system, applications, and training.

Here's a list of other features that make Windows NT Server a strong Internet platform:

◆ Reliability: the ability to set up fault tolerance is built into the system.

◆ Security: Windows NT was designed from the ground up to be able to provide high security, with built-in security protocols, and the ability to be certified for C2-level security.

◆ The Internet technologies built into Windows NT Server include connectivity software, routing, RAS (Remote Access Service), FTP, Gopher, WWW, and DNS.

What You Will Find in This Book

Now that we've talked a little bit about what it means to have an Internet or an intranet presence and have given you all the good reasons to use Windows NT Server as your Internet platform, it's time to tell you about the contents of this book and how it will help you to put your site together.

The first chapter contains mostly background information and is intended for people who are relatively new to the world of the Internet or as a reference for people who are more familiar with it. In general terms, we introduce you to the Internet, briefly explain how it works and where it came from, and describe the various services and technologies you will need to understand.

Once you are introduced to the Internet, you can go on to thinking about your own Internet site—what it is for, what it may include, and how it will run. Chapters 2 and 3 are intended to help you plan and design your Internet site. First we deal with the conceptual parts of this process. We discuss potential applications for your Internet site, show you some example sites from a variety of Internet hosts, and then discuss how to select the services that you will use for your Internet presence. Chapter 3 deals with the more tangible preparations you will need to make in designing your Internet site—specifically, hardware requirements and options for establishing your physical links to the Internet.

After your preparation work is complete, you will be ready to get down to the nitty gritty of actually setting up your server. Chapter 4 walks you through all the steps necessary to make your Internet presence work and, if necessary, get your connection established, from installing and configuring all of your hardware and software to making your connection to the Internet and testing it.

At this point you will have an Internet server running; the next step is to make sure it is secure. You will want to consider protecting the information that's stored on your servers as well as the information that you and your users are sending out over computer networks. In Chapter 5, you learn how to set up basic security for your Internet presence and how to monitor for security breaches.

The remainder of this book covers issues that are related to the creation and maintenance of your Internet presence. Chapters 6 and 7 gives you some guidelines and suggestions for creating and managing content, particularly Web content, and discusses the various resources that you can use for this purpose. Chapter 8 talks about what it would take to establish yourself as an Internet service provider and goes through the steps necessary to set up this kind of Internet business. Chapter 9 addresses the ongoing maintenance of both your server and your content.

Now, on to some more exciting stuff. For those of you who are interested in cutting-edge technology, Chapter 10 discusses new technologies related to Internet authoring, and Internet services that are in their infancy but will soon make an impact. Included here is the future direction of scripting languages, authoring tools, and video and telephony over the Internet.

The appendixes at the end of the book include a glossary of terms; a recommended reading section; a case study of GUIware, a growing Internet presence provider; and a guide to the software that comes with this book.

If you're new to the world of the Internet, we congratulate you for jumping in with both feet! If you're not new to the Internet, well, congratulations to you too for taking the next logical step—hosting your own Internet site. Like the printing press and the desktop publishing systems that came before it, the Internet (particularly the World Wide Web) allows information to be distributed quickly, efficiently, and in a virtually unlimited number of formats. Abbott Joseph Liebling said, "Freedom of the press is guaranteed only to those who own one." If you have a computer and access to the Internet, you now own a potential printing press. We're here to show you how to use it.

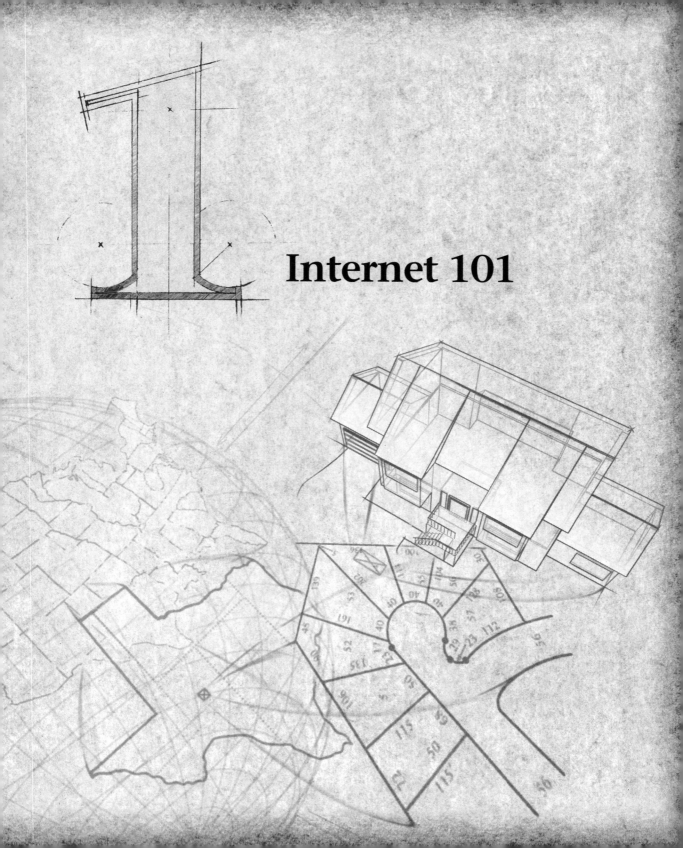

Internet 101

This chapter is a crash course in the basics of the Internet. Topics include what the Internet is, how it works, what you can find on the Internet, and where it came from in the first place. Several sections discuss some of the more popular Internet services and technologies, including the World Wide Web, and some of the more commonly used search engines. Some of you may already be old hands at all this stuff. Feel free to proceed directly to Chapter 2 if this is the case. You can always use this chapter as a reference if you need it.

What Is the Internet?

Providing a definitive answer to this question is next to impossible. Because the Internet is constantly changing and evolving, it's possible to have only an approximate idea of the number of computers connected to it and the number of people that use it at any given time. You can't pin down an exact location for the Internet either, and, depending on who you talk to, you can hear different definitions and ideas floating around about what the Internet actually includes. One good way to think of the Internet is as a very large, worldwide computer network that consists of many smaller networks and individual computers all connected together so that they can communicate and exchange information with one another.

The Internet can be seen as both a technology and a form of communication, comparable to the telephone system. (In fact, in some places the Internet *is* the phone system, but we'll get into that later.) Both the telephone system and the Internet are very large networks. As with the Internet, the purpose of the telephone system is communication. Both systems have hardware that you use, specifically telephones and computers, and they both have a mess of wires and other components that link them behind the scenes. To use the Internet or the phone system, you don't have to know very much about how they actually work. With the telephone system, the end result is that you can exploit all forms of audible communication. With Internet communication, you can exploit all of the capabilities of computers, which includes the exchange of information in textual, graphical, audio, and video formats.

The Internet has been very successful because it works as if it were a single entity. You can access information on a remote computer as though that information were right there on your own computer. In most cases, nothing changes about the operation of your computer; everything works the same way, even though you may be connected through your own network to another network thousands of miles away. This ability to access information from all over the world as if it's in your very own computer is one of the features that makes the Internet such a powerful new tool for information exchange and communication.

What Makes the Internet Work?

Just as two people need to speak the same language to have a conversation, computers connected in a network need to have a common language in order to communicate. And for multiple networks to be able to exchange information, all the computers and networks that connect to them must use the same rules for communicating with one another. A "language" that lets computers or networks interact with one another is called a *protocol*.

Protocols

In noncomputer terms, a protocol is a formalized and agreed-upon set of rules for behavior. When you establish communication with someone over the telephone, you use a kind of communication protocol. It usually goes something like this:

"Hello, Bigtime Computer Corporation."

"Hello, could I speak to Mr. So-and-so, please?"

In computer terms, protocols are essentially the same thing: a well-defined set of procedures for interacting that all the computers use. On the Internet, protocols make it possible for each computer to communicate with every other computer.

Two primary protocols make it possible for computers on the Internet to communicate and exchange data. They are called *Transmission Command Protocol (TCP)* and *Internet Protocol (IP)*. Because these protocols are both essential in making the Internet work, they are usually referred to together as *TCP/IP*. Even though the various networks attached to the Internet might work differently, TCP/IP provides them with a language to talk to one another and a way to exchange information.

TCP/IP takes information destined for the Internet and breaks it into smaller pieces (*packets*), making it possible for the data to be transferred across the electronic connections. The packets are then routed from the originating computer to the receiving computer and reconstituted as information once the packets have arrived at their destination. Occasionally, packets get lost in transit; in such a case, TCP/IP tells the originating computer to resend that specific packet to the destination.

The TCP/IP protocols are responsible for specific jobs. TCP is the protocol that divides the information into packets so that they can be sent over the connections between the computers and which then puts the packets back together when they get to the receiving computer. IP is the protocol that actually transmits the information and finds the best route to take from one computer to the other. Between networks on the Internet are individual computers called *IP gateways,* or *routers*. They receive packets from one network and send them on to another network in the right direction. This keeps happening until the packets reach their destination. Figure 1-1 shows an IP gateway between two networks.

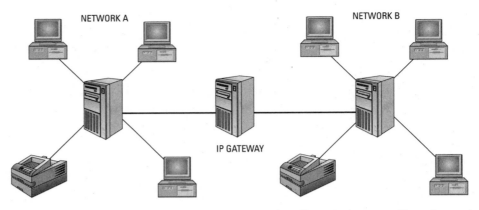

Figure 1-1. *IP gateways, or routers, are servers that direct Internet traffic to its destinations.*

What Can You Find on the Internet, and Who Uses It?

If you've been exploring the Internet, you know you can find an amazing amount of information on it. You can reach millions of computers through different services, and new services emerge daily to enable you to get the information you want. You can, for example, transfer or download information into your own computer, browse through multimedia pages, search through postings on electronic bulletin boards, exchange electronic mail with friends and colleagues, read electronic newsfeeds, join in chat sessions, shop electronic storefronts, and make airline reservations. On the Internet, you can find information available concerning virtually any topic. You can obtain information from government agencies, universities, nonprofit organizations, political organizations, commercial enterprises, and the Web pages of private individuals. The breadth and depth of content on the Internet is astounding—and growing at an almost inconceivable rate. The number of users accessing content on the Internet is also growing at a remarkable rate. Although the exact number of Internet users is difficult to gauge, a research organization called Matrix recently concluded that 26 million people in North America use the Internet.[1] CyberAtlas averaged this number with those from other research outfits and estimated that there are 23 million users. Regardless of the actual numbers, there is little doubt that the user base of the Internet is increasing rapidly.

The market for Internet-related services and products is currently around 1.2 billion dollars and could increase to 23 billion by the turn of the century. Within the United States, recent data from various research agencies show that in 35 percent of all homes (around 32 million) is a personal computer, and, of these homes, 6.9 million have access to the World Wide Web. By the year 2000, IDC expects that 59.1 percent of home computers and 31.8 percent of business personal computers worldwide will be on the Internet.[2] Figure 1-2 graphs these projections.

---

1. Unless otherwise noted, all facts and figures in this chapter regarding the size, market, and growth rate of the Internet come from CyberAtlas: The Internet Research Guide. CyberAtlas can be found on the Web at *http://www.cyberatlas.com.*

2. IDC can be found on the Web at *http://www.idcresearch.com/idc.htm.*

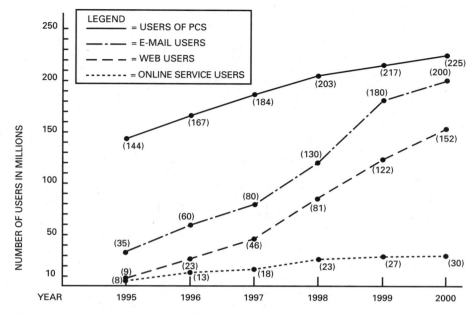

Figure 1-2. This graph depicts the projected growth in numbers of users of selected Internet-related products and services from 1995 to the year 2000.

Evolution of the Internet

What is now commonly referred to as the Internet, or simply "the Net," evolved from technology developed in the mid-1970s by the Defense Advanced Research Project Agency (DARPA), an organization closely related to the United States military. DARPA built the technology in order to connect military organizations with defense contractors and university researchers, enabling them all to have quick and reliable information transfer and access to limited high-cost resources such as supercomputing centers. The network they built, called ARPANET, was a wide area packet-switched network and formed the basis of the technology that has become the Internet. As the technology matured to its current form between 1977 and 1979, greater numbers of universities and private organizations became involved with government research and were added to the network.

Actual implementation of the connected Internet began around 1980, and in 1983 the basic infrastructure that exists today was completed. At that time, many more commercial enterprises hooked up, and the amount of traffic across the network for purely military purposes was dwarfed by other communication. As this happened, the military, because of budgetary constraints, decided it had to stop funding the Internet, but its nonmilitary users didn't want to lose this valuable method of communication. Because of the large number of educational organizations using the Internet, the primary responsibility for the Internet was transferred from the Defense Department to the National Science Foundation (NSF). The NSFNET then became the backbone of the Internet.

Backbone

A *backbone* is a high-speed connection between networks, capable of carrying large amounts of data traffic.

Very recently, responsibility for the Internet has moved to commercial enterprises. The old backbone, NSFNET, is now controlled by SprintNet. One result of this change is that the content on the Internet is becoming increasingly commercial. What was once the domain of defense contractors, researchers, and professors gradually became a sounding board for university students and has now become commonplace in many homes and businesses.

Few people anticipated the incredibly rapid growth the Internet has sustained, especially the use of the Internet by home users. The facts that personal computers are quickly becoming essential at home and that accessing the Internet is becoming both affordable and easy are at least partly responsible for the Internet's mainstream popularity. With this growing segment of consumers, we are seeing a new marketplace with incredible potential.

The World Wide Web (WWW)

The World Wide Web, also called simply "the Web," is a very large Internet service and, since 1993, the most popular of the services available. In fact, many people think of the Internet and the WWW synonymously, and some don't realize that the Web actually is an entity that runs on the Internet. Most of you will find the Web the best place to set up your Internet presence. Current estimates attribute 85 percent of Internet traffic to the WWW, and setting up a Web server is a primary focus of this book. The Web contains a virtually unlimited number of documents that are presented using a variety of media, from plain text documents to those with multimedia capabilities.

The truly compelling feature of WWW documents is that they are linked to other documents by means of a technology known as *hypertext*. Hypertext allows you to get from one related document to another by simply clicking your mouse to select a word or a graphic that has been set up as a *link*. A link is normally indicated by a word or a graphic set apart from the usual text by the use of a different color or boldface text. Usually, the linked document that you call to your screen defines or elaborates on the term or graphic used as the link in the original document. For instance, a catalog might have hypertext links to product specification sheets, allowing potential customers to easily access more detailed information about products of interest to them. Hypertext makes the Web truly interactive. When browsing Web resources, *you* decide how to navigate through a specific document. In other words, you do not have to read a Web resource in the linear way you read most books. You can jump around from one place to another in a document, pursuing your specific interests. The Web also supports other protocols such as FTP, Gopher, e-mail, and NNTP. Figure 1-3 shows you two related Web documents, connected by means of a hypertext link.

Welcome to Wakeboarding Online:

The source for wakeboarding on the Internet. Wakeboarding Online will bring you the latest insane action from the sport of wakeboarding.

Featuring...

- WakeBoarding Magazine's Team Challenge - Here's the complete online coverage of the first-ever team challenge, complete with final results and sick photos

  NOTE: The above links are really graphic-intensive; you may want to disable auto-loading of images if you're on a slow link. Also, be sure to use a table-aware browser, such as Netscape 1.1N (or later) or Microsoft's Internet Explorer 2.0, as some of these pages contain tables.

Darin Shapiro-Bud Tour Champion
Lake Billingham, Washington

WakeBoarding Magazine's Team Challenge - *Results*

Photos by Tom King

For the first time ever WakeBoarding Magazine hosted a team challenge putting today's top riders against each other in a "freeriding" style contest. Riders were encouraged to go out and do whatever they want. No attack sheets, no set trick runs, no rules, no penalties for falling.

Congrats to **Team Hyperlite** for winning the Team Challenge!
Also congrats to **Shannon Best** for winning the Individual Title.

Above: The scene at the dock

- Coverage
- Photos
- Comments from the Pros

Figure 1-3. Two Web documents, linked.

The WWW project was developed at CERN (the European Laboratory for Nuclear Physics) in Switzerland. *Hypertext Transfer Protocol (HTTP)* is the protocol that forms the foundation for the Web. Originally intended as a means for physicists to share information, the HTTP protocol was soon incorporated into the Internet when people figured out how widely they could apply the technology.

Web Browsers

A *browser* is a program that provides an interface to access and view files on the Internet. Before the advent of browsers, you needed to know a bunch of complicated commands to view resources on the Internet. Browsers basically make the Internet friendlier and easier to use.

In order to view WWW resources, you need to have a Web browser on your computer. If you happen to know the location of a specific document, you can type its Internet address (called a *URL*) into the Web browser and it will call up that resource for you and display it on your screen. Additionally, Web browsers allow you to navigate through hypertext documents and to go back and forth between documents. Microsoft's Web browser is called Internet Explorer and runs on Windows NT Server and other platforms. Many different browsers are available, all with their own various characteristics (such as look and feel) but with essentially the same capabilities. Figures 1-4 and 1-5 show you examples of what you can call up using a browser.

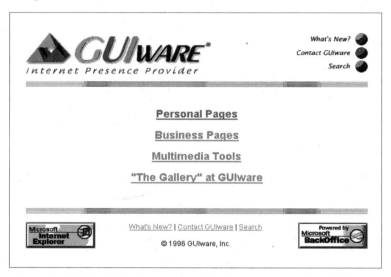

Figure 1-4. *This is the home page of GUIware as seen though Microsoft's Web browser, Internet Explorer.*

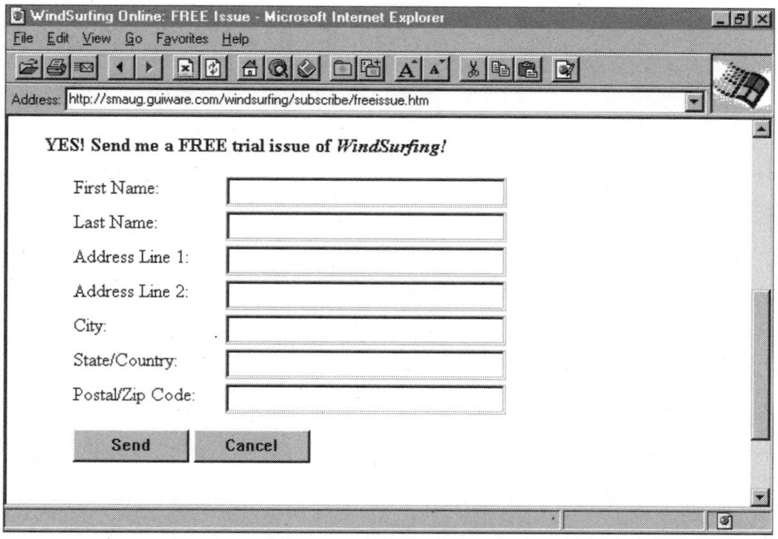

Figure 1-5. *This is what it looks like when you access a form on the Internet using Internet Explorer.*

Client/Server Technologies

Client/server technologies make it possible to distribute work among computers. Essentially, a single job splits up and is processed by more than one computer. Computers referred to as *servers* are usually used for storage of resources that many users might want to access. Servers wait passively to service requests from client computers that access them. A *client* makes a request of the server for information or for a specific resource. The server retrieves the information and sends it to the client, and the client displays the information to the user.

Just as the actual computers that perform client/server tasks are called client or server machines, the software that runs on these computers is referred to as client or server software. Hence, Web browsers are actually client software programs used for accessing and viewing Web resources.

The Internet is based on the use of client/server architecture. In this way, you can look at the Internet as an enormous, global network of networks of servers that are being accessed by millions of clients. Depending on the type of information that they store, Internet servers are optimized with different characteristics. For instance, Web servers handle requests for Web resources. Internet servers can also handle more than one type of Internet service. For example, you can set up a computer to act as a Web server, an e-mail server, and an FTP server (described in the next section) all at the same time.

Finding Resources on the Internet: Services and Technologies

Let's look briefly at some of the more popular services and technologies other than the WWW that are used on the Internet. The Web is gradually replacing many of these legacy technologies on the Internet, but they are not yet redundant. Depending on the needs for your Internet site and the type of resources you want to make available, you might want to consider these technologies. Also included in this section is a quick description of the services and technologies that help you to find resources on the Internet. While there are many other services and technologies besides those mentioned in this section, the services described here are some of the more popular Internet services—those that we think are the most likely candidates for your own Internet site.

File Transfer Protocol (FTP)

FTP is a legacy service on the Internet, but it is still much used and valuable for making some types of information available. Basically, FTP is an Internet protocol used for transferring documents or files from one computer on the Internet to another. Dedicated FTP servers on the Net exist solely so that you can search around inside them and then FTP files back to your own computer. The term *FTP* is used to describe the technology itself, the act of transferring files, and the type of server those files reside on.

FTP sites are useful when you have large amounts of information that you want to make available for your clients to download onto their own computers. Suppose you have a company with a number of products, and you want to make your product specifications available to potential customers on the Internet. Each product specification consists of multiple pages of information. In this case, you might choose to have this information on an FTP site so that your customers can download it and read the information at their convenience. This gives your customers the benefit of having to pay for their connection to the Internet for only the amount of time needed to download the information. If they had to stay connected to view this, they could rack up large connection charges. Figure 1-6 shows you an FTP session.

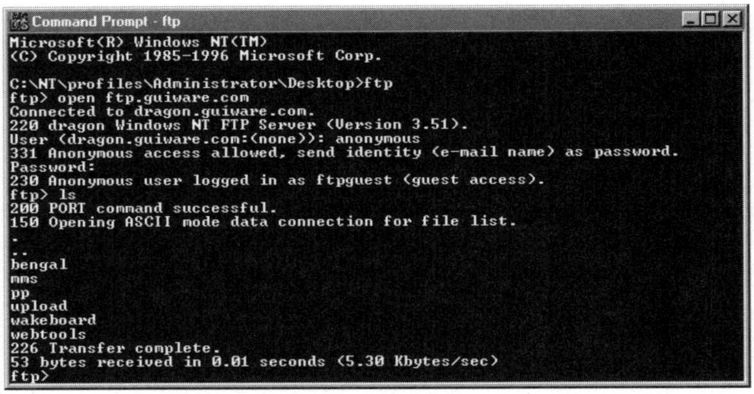

```
Command Prompt - ftp

Microsoft(R) Windows NT(TM)
(C) Copyright 1985-1996 Microsoft Corp.

C:\NT\profiles\Administrator\Desktop>ftp
ftp> open ftp.guiware.com
Connected to dragon.guiware.com.
220 dragon Windows NT FTP Server (Version 3.51).
User (dragon.guiware.com:(none)): anonymous
331 Anonymous access allowed, send identity (e-mail name) as password.
Password:
230 Anonymous user logged in as ftpguest (guest access).
ftp> ls
200 PORT command successful.
150 Opening ASCII mode data connection for file list.
.
..
bengal
mms
pp
upload
wakeboard
webtools
226 Transfer complete.
53 bytes received in 0.01 seconds (5.30 Kbytes/sec)
ftp>
```

Figure 1-6. An FTP session from the client perspective.

Gopher

Before the explosive growth of the WWW on the Internet, Gopher was the fastest growing and most popular Internet service. Gopher is a menu-based system for finding resources on the Internet. When you begin a Gopher session, you find yourself at the main menu of the Gopher server. You look through the list of menu items and then choose either another menu or a specific resource. You can then search, view, download, or e-mail the Gopher resource that interests you. The entire Internet-wide collection of files on Gopher servers is commonly referred to as *Gopherspace*. Gopher servers contain a large amount of information that is not necessarily related. Figure 1-7 shows a Gopher menu.

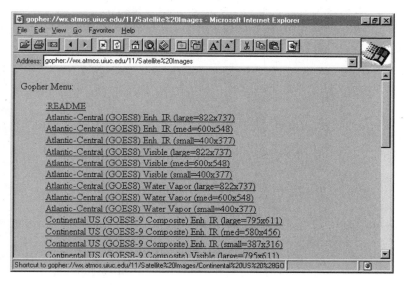

Figure 1-7. *This is what it looks like when you make a search request from Gopher.*

WAIS (Wide Area Information Service)

WAIS and Gopher are virtually identical in terms of functionality. WAIS is differentiated because it is the protocol that the United States government has chosen to standardize on for its enormous collection of data. If accessing government data is key to a business, then an interface with WAIS would be mandatory.

Electronic Mail (SMPT, POP 2/3, E-mail)

It's hard to find anyone anymore who isn't at least familiar with the idea of e-mail. If you use it yourself, you know that e-mail is a great way to communicate with other people electronically. E-mail can exist on a network of any size; therefore, it is not surprising that you can send e-mail over the Internet. After the World Wide Web, e-mail is probably the most popular service on the Internet.

The two protocols most commonly used for e-mail over the Internet are Simple Message Transport Protocol (SMTP) and Post Office Protocol (POP). SMTP is the protocol that delivers or transports mail from one server to another on the Internet. It also determines and implements the best route for your mail to travel. POP is the protocol that handles the delivery of e-mail between server and client.

In order to process e-mail, it is necessary to have an electronic mailbox that resides on an e-mail server. If you are interested in having e-mail, you have the option of renting a mailbox from a commercial provider or you can set up your own e-mail server. Figure 1-8 shows you what Microsoft Exchange looks like.

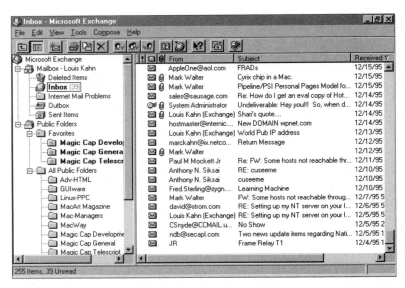

Figure 1-8. *This is the client side of Exchange, Microsoft's e-mail program.*

Network News Transfer Protocol (NNTP, Usenet, News)

NNTP is used to post public messages (articles) on a particular subject in a particular area. You can think of these collections of postings as being like bulletin boards in grocery stores, company break rooms, schools, clubs, and anywhere else a public forum is useful and usual. More than 18,000 NNTP topics are currently on the Internet, with more being added daily. Most topic areas are open to anyone to post or read articles. Figure 1-9 shows a list of such topics.

You can use an NNTP site as a public feedback, customer testimonial, or complaint forum. Companies might also find it useful for research purposes to monitor NNTP topics others have created about their product or their competition.

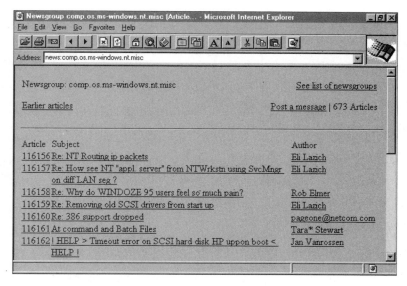

Figure 1-9. *An example of an NNTP client.*

Internet Relay Chat (IRC)

IRC is an interactive, real-time, text-based, person-to-person form of communication over the Internet. When you are using IRC, you are essentially having a conversation with someone, or a group of people, but, instead of talking, you are typing the words. IRC channels are topic-specific, meaning you choose a group that is talking about a specific, common subject. Figure 1-10 shows a chat in progress.

Figure 1-10. *An IRC conversation.*

There are many possibilities for using IRC in connection with your Internet presence. It could be a good tool for handling product support, for teaching people how to use certain products, for customer service, and even for special lectures by guest speakers.

Uniform Resource Locator (URL)

A URL essentially refers to the location of a specific document or file on the Internet. One of the features that make it possible for the Internet to work with the same characteristics as a smaller network is that URLs provide a standard way of referring to specific data. They can be compared to street addresses for all the documents and resources available on the Internet.

After you've seen enough URLs, you begin to notice some patterns. If, in your experience with the Internet, you have looked only at Web resources, then all the URLs that you have encountered have begun with *http://*. The first part of a URL refers to the protocol that the resource uses. If the resource you were after was located at an FTP site, the URL would begin with *ftp://*. The second part of a URL specifies the server where that resource is located. It will probably look something like *www.some-random-company.com* or *www.university-of-someplace.edu*. The third part of a URL points you to the directory structure, and the URL ends with the name of the specific file or document. The directory path and filename usually look something like this: *directory/subdirectory/filename.html*. Figure 1-11 below labels the parts of a URL.

Figure 1-11. *Anatomy of a Universal Resource Locator.*

NOTE: If you want to look for, say, Web resources at a certain company but you don't know the URL, it is usually worth trying *http://certain-company.com*. In most cases, this will get you to the right place. You can try the same approach to look for sites using other protocols if you know the URL indicator for that service. For instance, *ftp://* refers to FTP sites, *gopher://* to Gopher sites, and *news://* to NNTP.

Domain Name Service (DNS)

Computers and people don't remember information in the same way. People like to remember words, while computers need to remember and store information numerically. Sometimes you need a translation program. DNS is one such service. It can be thought of as the Internet version of a telephone directory. DNS simply translates text names of servers into the numeric names that computers recognize so that servers can find one another on the Internet.

In the previous section, you learned that a URL is an address for locating a specific document on the Internet. In order for your computer to be able to find a document, it must be able to find the server where the document is located. You, of course, recognize that server by its text name in the URL, type it in, and expect your computer to happily find that server for you. Your computer, however, identifies servers (including itself) with numeric addresses called IP addresses. DNS sits somewhere in between. It is a vast, distributed (meaning that parts of it are located in more than one place) database, representative of all published machines, and it is responsible for converting machine names into IP addresses.

If you've used the Internet before, you've used DNS, possibly without knowing it. For example, when you send e-mail, DNS converts the recipient's e-mail address into its specific IP address for proper routing. Figure 1-12 shows you DNS.

Anyone with an Internet presence will use DNS to provide friendly names to the services they make available to their customers. For a WWW site, the friendly name might be *www.company.com*. *User@company.com* would refer to an e-mail address at an e-mail server, and *ftp.company.com* would refer to an FTP server, even if all of these services are on the same computer.

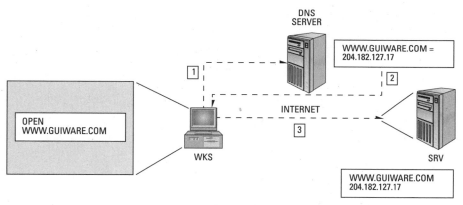

1. THE CLIENT REQUESTS TO OPEN *WWW.GUIWARE.COM*; THAT NAME IS THEN AUTOMATICALLY SENT TO THE CLIENT'S DNS SERVER FOR RESOLUTION.

2. THE DNS SERVER LOOKS UP THE NAME *WWW.GUIWARE.COM* AND RETURNS ITS ADDRESS, 204.182.127.17, TO THE CLIENT.

3. THE CLIENT THEN TALKS WITH THE SERVER POINTED TO BY THE DNS SERVER.

Figure 1-12. DNS is used to translate a computer's people-friendly name to the numerical IP address that another computer can understand.

Search Engines

As good as the Internet is in providing information, one of the biggest problems yet to be solved is how to find the resources you are looking for. If you are looking for a specific document or file and have an Internet address for it, then finding the file is as simple as typing or copying the address into your browser. The problems start when you are looking for information on a particular topic and don't have a specific address to begin with. The Internet can bring you a vast amount of information, but it can be difficult to decide where to start looking for particular instances of it, especially since the Internet has no central indexing system for all resources.

Searching for resources on the Internet can be compared to doing a search at the library in the card catalog, except you find many card catalogs to explore and they all work slightly differently from one another. To find all the documents that pertain to a specific topic, you might have to use multiple search engines.

When you set up your own Internet site, you will probably want people to be able to find your site and the resources it has to offer. This entails getting your site listed on the various search engines.

WEB SEARCH ENGINES

Web search engines do basically the same thing that you do when using the Web: they look at documents and follow links. The difference is that these technologies actually store the information about each link they go to. They build up databases that are searchable, and you can do complex queries against those databases. When you set up an Internet presence, the new site you create should be cataloged in the search engine databases so that users can find it. Figure 1-13 and Figure 1-14 show you search service home pages.

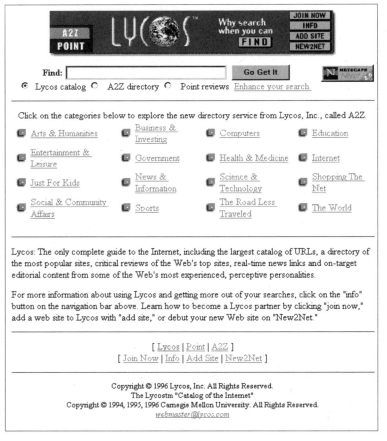

Figure 1-13. *The Lycos front end.*

Yahoo and Lycos are two of the many Web search engines that have *front ends* for searching. This means that they have nice interfaces that allow you to make a request for a search with various criteria. For example, you could request all the links that contain a certain word or phrase and that have been updated in the past six months. The search engine would rummage through its database and then show any matches that it finds. Different Web search engines have different characteristics. Lycos actually stores the whole document when it finds a match, whereas Yahoo stores only the first paragraph. Other popular Web search engines are Alta Vista, InfoSeek, WebCrawler, Excite, and Magellan. If you set up a Web site, you should get your site listed on these services so that people can find you. There will be more information on how to go about this task later in the book. Figure 1-13 shows you Lycos's home page, and Figure 1-14 shows you the Microsoft Network search service.

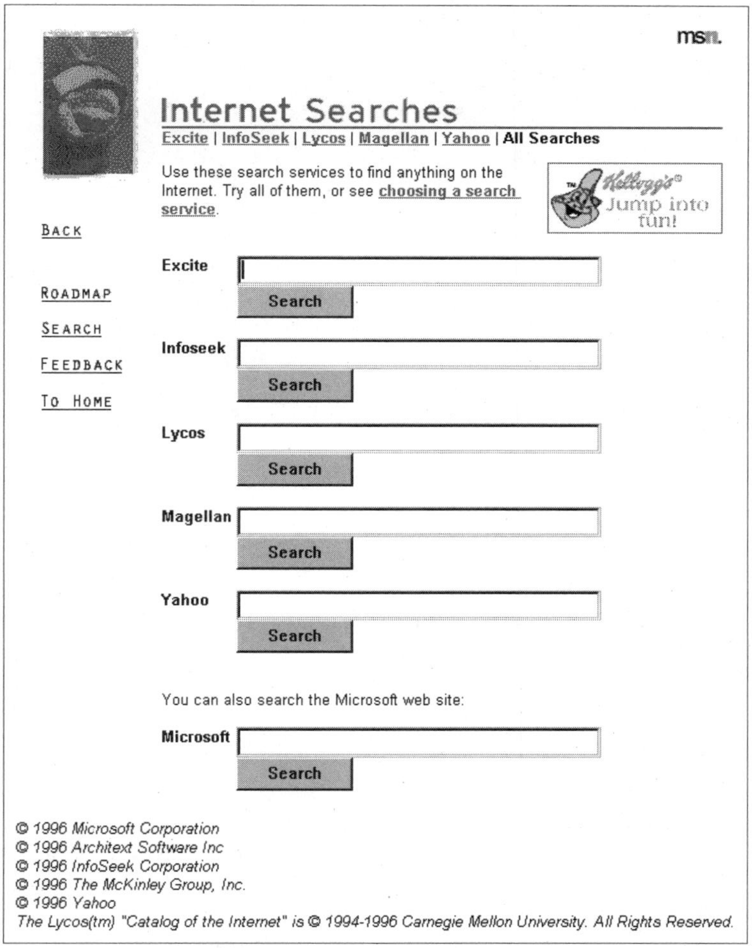

Figure 1-14. *The Internet searcher on The Microsoft Network.*

ARCHIE

Archie is a search engine specifically for finding resources on FTP sites. An Archie server is basically a distributed database that contains a list of machines that you can query. Archie is used for finding specific files or documents when the server that they reside on is unknown. A key word in the document is used to make the request. The Archie server will continue to pass the request along until it comes up with a result. Figure 1-15 shows you an Archie search request.

If you are going to set up an FTP server, you will want to register your site with the Archie service so that others will be able to find your content.

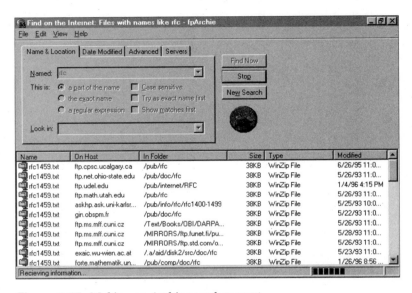

Figure 1-15. *Making an Archie search request.*

VERONICA

Veronica is an acronym for Very Easy Rodent-Oriented Netwide Index to Computerized Archives, and it is a utility for searching Gopherspace. Basically, Veronica contains an index of menu items from Gopher sites that you can search. Veronica clients are usually installed along with Gopher clients, and Veronica appears as one of the menu items when you start a Gopher session.

Course Summary

You have now finished cramming Internet 101. In a nutshell, you know that the Internet is a vast, global network of computers that is able to work as if it were a single network because of the protocol suite TCP/IP. You can find an overwhelming amount of information on the Internet in many different forms. Of the variety of client/server technologies used for making information available on the Internet, the WWW accounts for the majority of Internet traffic seen today. Many different tools are available to assist you in searching for resources.

What's Next

If our Internet 101 was, in fact, your introduction to the world of the Internet, we encourage you to get connected to the Net and start exploring. It's difficult to really get the feel of the various technologies until you actually see and use them yourself. It's also a good idea to take a look at other people's Internet sites. If you have a business, you might want to check out your competitors and see what their sites include.

In the next chapter, we discuss options for your Internet site. At this point, you want to start thinking about your own site and the resources that you want to make available in relation to the services or technologies that you might want to use.

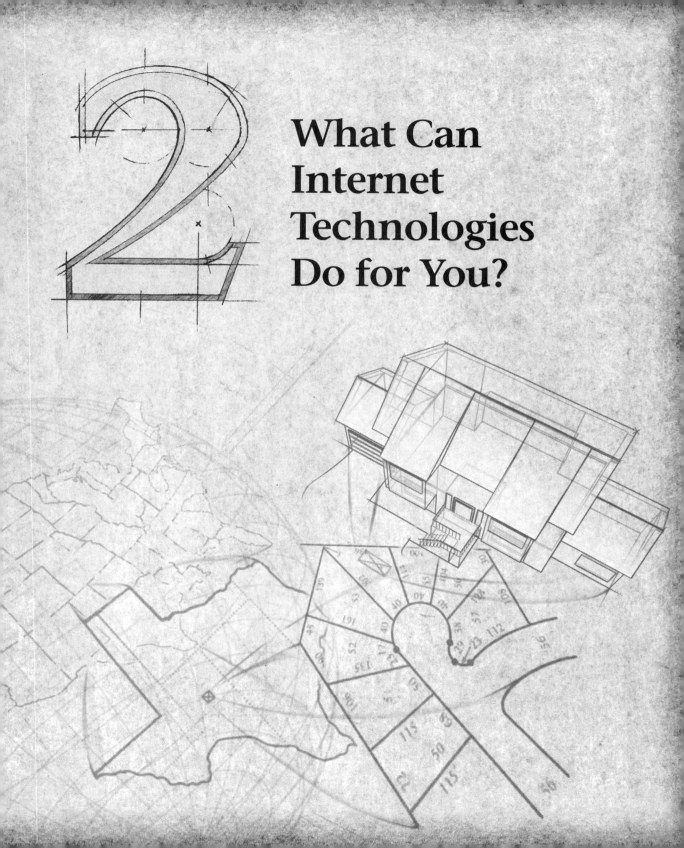

2

What Can Internet Technologies Do for You?

To make effective use of Internet technologies, you need to think about how you can best use the technology and the Internet. You need to consider what you want to accomplish, your potential audience, your reasons for using a particular technology, and the amount of time and money you want to spend on the project. If you're a computer hobbyist, perhaps you want to set up a Web site for the fun and challenge of it. If you have a business, you might want to establish a presence on the Internet to enhance service to your customers or you might want to set up a corporate intranet to improve communication within your organization. Or maybe you want to start a business based entirely on the Internet, providing Internet-related services. Whatever your motives, you need to develop your own Internet business plan and decide which services and technologies make sense for you to use.

Our intent in this chapter is to introduce you to a variety of uses for Internet technologies and suggest how you might apply these to your goals. The next chapter moves on to hardware and bandwidth requirements; in order to make practical use of the material in Chapter 3, you'll need to have formed a fairly solid idea about what your Internet presence will do and include.

What Does It Mean to Have an Internet Presence?

In the simplest sense, having an Internet presence means making your ideas and the services you might provide known and available on the Internet. Of course, how this is achieved depends on your interests and goals and is likely to be different for each person setting up a new site. You need to consider other, more practical matters as well. Besides thinking about what your ideal Internet site would include, you need to think about the amount of time and money you are able to spend—not just setting up your site, but maintaining it. The investment of your resources in an Internet presence can be considerable. But there are definite advantages to developing and maintaining your own site as opposed to publishing on "rented" server space.

From the perspective of maintenance, keeping the responsibility for your own server gives you complete control of your site. If you need to make any changes or updates to your site or if you have hardware difficulties, you can change and repair whatever you need to immediately. If you used a third-party provider, you would be at the mercy of their schedule. Also, when you maintain your own server, you can take advantage of new technology as soon it's available, without having to wait for an Internet service provider other than yourself to supply it.

Having an Internet site definitely means added expense. There is no way around that, but if you are planning to run a site long term, it will be cheaper to handle your own. Once you have established your connection to the Internet and after you account for production and maintenance costs, reaching your audience via the Internet costs appreciably less than traditional methods of communication, like mail, fax, telephone calls, or personal visits.

Ways to Use Your Internet Presence

Primarily what you will be providing to people over the Internet is information: information about you, your company or organization, your products, or anything else that you want people to know about. In this sense, establishing your Internet presence will make you an Internet publisher. You might also want to offer people the opportunity to do more than simply access information. You might want your site to be interactive, allowing for exchanges of information between you and your users. Or maybe you want to go one step further and actually run your entire operation on line with a virtual storefront. It is possible for you to have any of these levels of involvement with your Internet site, but they naturally require corresponding levels of resources. The virtual storefront is a complex type of Internet site and might not be an area that a beginner to the Internet wants to jump into. You might want to begin with a simple site, publishing resources, and then let your Internet presence grow when you are ready to devote more time and money.

This section discusses some of the more common uses of the Internet. Nothing is cut-and-dried here. Ways to exploit the Internet that we list for businesses might also be great for other kinds of organizations. You can use your imagination to decide what would work for your own Internet presence.

Supporting Your Current Business with an Internet Site

If you are setting up an Internet site as part of your current business, then you can do most of your business on line. Following is a list of some common business practices performed at Internet sites. (This is by no means a complete list; you can probably think of more ways to do business from an Internet site yourself.)

- Advertisement and promotion, notices of special sales

- Product information of any kind, including specifications, pictures, announcements, price lists, performance results, catalogs

- Sales transactions

- Warranty registration and recall notification

- Communication with an established customer base through newsletters, brochures, and online magazines

- Interactive customer service and product support

Publishing Information on the Internet

People who have sites on the Internet are, in effect, Internet publishers by virtue of the fact that they make information available to a large audience. The Internet makes publishing cost-effective and accessible. Consider the expenses you incur by sending out a newsletter: paper, printing, and postage, at least. Once you have a connection to the Internet, you can send out all the news you want to your customer base, just for the cost of the connection. This might let you pay for things like surveys and brochures that in the past have been impractical or too expensive.

ONLINE MAGAZINES

Some magazine publishers have of late been going on line as a supplement to their current publications, while others are forgoing ordinary print publication altogether and publishing their magazines only on the Internet. Besides the obvious advantages of being able to reach additional customers and not having to deal with the expenses and delays associated with printing and distributing paper, an online magazine is able to take advantage of the multimedia capabilities of the Internet. For instance, in addition to having the usual graphics, an online magazine can include video clips, as you see indicated in Figure 2-1.

Welcome to Wakeboarding Online:

The source for wakeboarding on the Internet. Wakeboarding Online will bring you the latest insane action from the sport of wakeboarding.

Featuring...

Darin Shapiro - B wl Tow Champion
Lake Billingham, Washington
Photo by Heather Lee

- WakeBoarding Magazine's Team Challenge - Here's the complete online coverage of the first-ever team challenge, complete with final results and sick photos.

  NOTE: The above links are really graphic-intensive; you may want to disable auto-loading of images if you're on a slow link. Also, be sure to use a table-aware browser, such as Netscape 1.1N (or later) or Microsoft's Internet Explorer 2.0, as some of these pages contain tables.

- 1995 Wakeboard Worlds - November 11 & 12 - Altamonte Springs, Florida Complete online coverage coming soon! Check here for info about the '95 Worlds - the final big pro event of the season. All the best riders will be there.

- Wakeboarding Trick List WakeBoarding Online Exclusive - Check out the point-by-point breakdown of the latest moves in wakeboarding in this HTML-3 table. Are you doing these? (Provided by the World Wakeboard Association).

- Video Reviews - Editors Tom James and Heather Lee give their take on the latest videos. You can download clips from Spray, HO Expression Session, How to Ride a Wakeboard, and Wake The Beast.

- Latest ramblings from our editor - Read our version of what contests should be like.

- What's New? - New links and things to think about from WakeBoarding Online.

- Video Tips WakeBoarding Online Exclusive - Download these videos to get a frame-by-frame breakdown of some of the hottest moves in wakeboarding. Tips presented by Eric Perez and Jeff Heer showing videos of Brannon Meek and CC Roberts.

Figure 2-1. *The online version of* WakeBoarding *magazine includes video clips.*

PUBLICATIONS FOR NONPROFIT, CHARITABLE, POLITICAL, OR SOCIAL ORGANIZATIONS

The Internet is a great venue for a group of this nature to reach and communicate with a large audience that is sympathetic to its cause or has similar interests. This type of organization could use Internet publishing for press announcements, newsletters, public relations, calls to action, fundraising efforts, and more. See Figure 2-2.

Top Row
Greenpeace International: Homepage The Shelf: Search | Gopher | Site Statistics | Other sites | Mirrors
Bottom Row
Campaigns: Toxics | Nuclear | Atmosphere | Biodiversity Services: Archives | Marine | National Offices | Hot Pages
Interactive: Membership | Information | Mail | Chat

Figure 2-2. The home page for Greenpeace.

A PERSONAL OR FAMILY HOME PAGE

Having your own personal WWW page can be something fun to do, but it can also be a great way to keep in touch with faraway friends and family. For instance, you could put up a Web site with your family's latest news, pictures of the kids, and the vacation photos that everyone loves so much. A personal home page can be a great way to keep everyone updated without having to send tons of mail. Do keep in mind that, unless you set up some sort of logon security, anybody can visit your personal home page. In other words, it's not a good idea to publish your vacation itinerary in advance. For an example of a personal home page, see Figure 2-3 on the following page.

Creating an Interactive Site

Having an interactive Internet site goes beyond content publishing, giving you the capability for interactions with those who access your site. You might want them to be able to hit a link in a Web page in order to send you e-mail, or you might want them to be able to fill out a form on line, or perhaps you want to be able to communicate with them in real time. These things are all possible. Of course, they take more of your time and energy for maintenance than simply posting documents does.

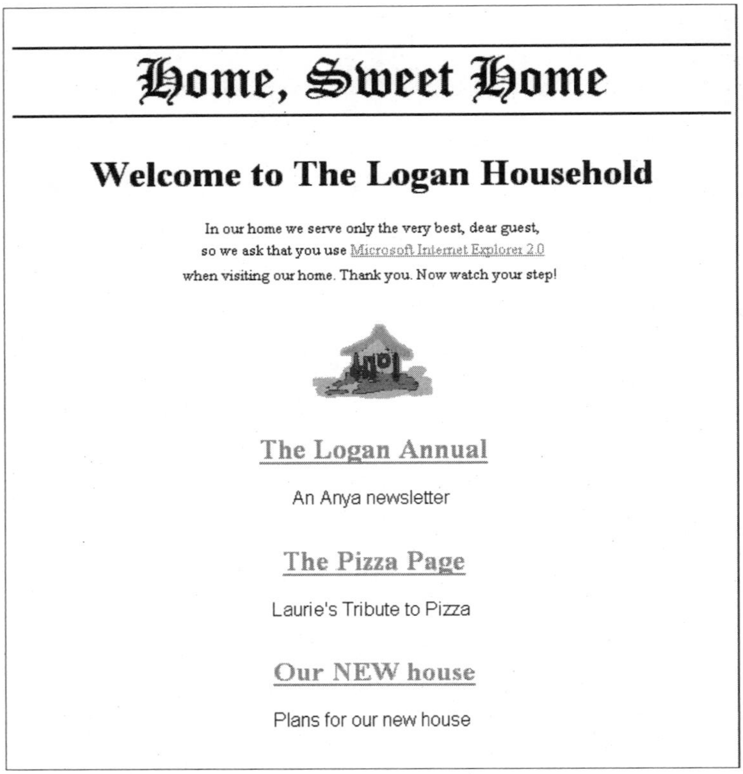

Home, Sweet Home

Welcome to The Logan Household

In our home we serve only the very best, dear guest,
so we ask that you use Microsoft Internet Explorer 2.0
when visiting our home. Thank you. Now watch your step!

The Logan Annual

An Anya newsletter

The Pizza Page

Laurie's Tribute to Pizza

Our NEW house

Plans for our new house

Figure 2-3. *The family home page of one of the authors of this book provides a way to communicate with distant family and friends.*

FOR MANUFACTURING COMPANIES

An interactive site could be of great benefit to a manufacturing company. As well as being a place to publish product specifications, news of product shortages, production problems, future product plans, product designs, dealer location, and usage tips, an interactive Internet site could be used for online product registration, recalls, surveys, and warranty claims. An Internet site could even provide a manufacturer a channel for direct sales, bypassing the retailer. Figure 2-4 and Figure 2-5 show you what interactive sites might look like.

FOR SERVICE-ORIENTED BUSINESSES

A business that provides services rather than tangible goods can use the Internet in much the same way as other kinds of organizations, with the added benefit of being able to deliver its actual goods over the Internet. A company providing information services or consulting services can provide information to clients without physically going to the clients' places of business. A consultant can go global.

Figure 2-4. Intel uses its Web site to communicate with customers.

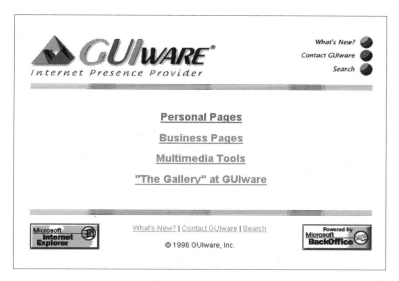

Figure 2-5. GUIware is a service-providing business that offers Internet content creation and Internet publishing.

Creating a Virtual Storefront

The Internet could generate for some organizations a substantial part of their revenue. To build a virtual storefront where customers could get information about products and purchase them on line might be an excellent business decision. But a site like this requires a great deal of maintenance, and it also brings up the issue of security, especially if you are planning on doing financial transactions on line. At this point in the evolution of the Internet, some people are still wary of the Internet's ability to provide privacy and are unwilling to buy things this way for fear that a hacker will be able to access their credit card numbers. Many companies are developing ideas for secure transactions, and we will discuss security in much more detail in Chapter 6.

A retail or mail-order sales operation is a natural business for an electronic storefront, creating the potential to sell products, advertise and promote goods, and provide customer service over the Internet. Pretty much everything you can do in a physical store or on the telephone you can do through the virtual world, with the exception of actually handling the merchandise. In some cases, the Internet provides a more enjoyable shopping experience for the customer. It provides the same benefits as catalog shopping—namely, no lines to wait in and shopping at a convenient time with no pressure from salespeople. The Internet, though, has the potential to provide the customer with much more detailed information than most catalogs can offer, such as video demonstrations and detailed product specifications.

Any catalog publisher will find benefits in publishing on line. Updates can be posted immediately, mistakes can be corrected at any time, and last-minute changes can be made without sacrificing a publication deadline. These activities are often not possible when you are dealing with traditional publishing. See Figure 2-6 for an example of a virtual storefront.

Figure 2-6. *Egghead has a virtual storefront on the Internet.*

So Then, What's an Intranet?

The use of Internet technology is not limited to the connected Internet. Many companies are now implementing private corporate internets using TCP/IP and other Internet technologies, such as HTTP, to foster better communication among individuals and groups within their organizations. These private networks are now commonly referred to as *intranets* and are making a whole new level of communication possible within large companies. Microsoft, for example, has adopted the use of an extensive intranet as a venue for dissemination of information within the company. Employees can access the corporate intranet to see the details and status of various projects across the company, the weekly newsletter, employment opportunities, the employee handbook, internal server status, and many other documents. Also available over the corporate intranet are such things as internal software tools, employee personal Web pages, HR and benefits information and forms, information about social clubs, and even the current price of Microsoft stock.

As a general rule, any information that you want to share within your organization but don't want to publish outside your company is suitable material for your intranet site.

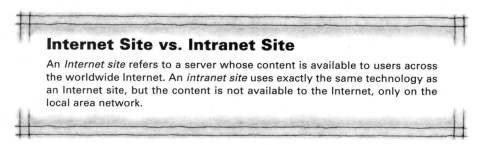

Internet Site vs. Intranet Site

An *Internet site* refers to a server whose content is available to users across the worldwide Internet. An *intranet site* uses exactly the same technology as an Internet site, but the content is not available to the Internet, only on the local area network.

Setup and maintenance of an intranet is much easier than an Internet site because you don't have to make the connection to the Internet. Each group or individual who contributes to your intranet will maintain the content, reducing the staff needed to maintain the intranet and leveraging resources across the company rather than concentrating demands within a single department. Because your intranet is not viewed outside your organization and because you typically have high-speed connections between the server and workstations, you can publish content that might not be appropriate on the Internet for reasons of performance or corporate image.

Lately, many companies have realized the value of intranets and have been rapidly implementing them. One of the reasons for the rapid increase of numbers of intranets is that any organization that has a network in place already has the infrastructure for setting up an intranet. This makes intranets a very cost-effective and relatively easy means of improving and enhancing companywide communications. Setting up and maintaining an intranet can also provide a good training ground for an Internet presence. We highly recommend setting up an intranet site if your organization already has a network.

Turning Your Internet Site into an Internet Business

Up to this point, we have discussed setting up your Internet site for your own use only. This level of involvement in Internet publishing is referred to as a *private content publisher*. As a private content publisher, you have resources that you want to make available over the Internet and you have the responsibility for creating and maintaining your own Internet presence. Private content publishers have recognized the Internet as a significant new method for reaching people and are willing to make the investment in time, equipment, and possibly staff to run a site.

Once you have made this investment, you might want to consider the idea of making a business or a side business of your newfound expertise. You might be able to fund your own Internet presence by using your knowledge and server space to publish other people's resources for them. Two sorts of businesses on the Internet set up Internet servers: the *Internet presence provider* and the *Internet service provider*. We will discuss both of these kinds of businesses in the following sections and throughout the rest of the book.

Internet Presence Provider (IPP)

As an IPP, your business would be to publish other people's content on the Internet, in effect, to "rent" out space on your servers. You would need to have both a connection to the Internet and Internet servers with plenty of disk space. Anyone who wants to have an Internet site but does not want to set up and maintain the system himself or herself could contract with you to do this work. The business of IPP is a good startup business for entrepreneurs interested in the Internet. It's possible to set up an IPP business literally in the basement of your own home and run it single-handedly. It could be a part-time or full-time venture depending on how much you wanted to put into it.

Many IPPs also get involved in the business of Web page design and creation. This job involves taking someone's raw content before it goes up on the server and creating polished Web content that can be read by Internet clients. An IPP that handles content creation basically creates a customer's Internet site. Web design and creation can be a lucrative part of an IPP's business for those who are adept at online graphic design or who are willing to learn the skills necessary. Offering content creation as an IPP will give you a competitive advantage over an IPP that doesn't offer this service, and it can actually generate more revenue than the rental of server space.

Internet Service Provider (ISP)

The core business of an ISP is to provide dial-up Internet access to its customers. In addition, ISPs can offer all the same services as an IPP, including the rental of server space and content creation. Figure 2-7 diagrams what an ISP can do. The biggest difference between an ISP and an IPP is the level of investment and overhead required to start up the business. ISPs have extensive hardware requirements. They need large banks of modems for inbound communication, powerful terminal servers to connect to the modems, multiple phone lines, and routing software and hardware. This is a huge investment but gives you the potential for a much greater volume of customers and consequently more potential income. As an ISP, you can also expect to have a large customer service burden, and administration of the system can be difficult. The business of being an ISP is not typically a home business, although it's possible for your IPP home business to grow to this level.

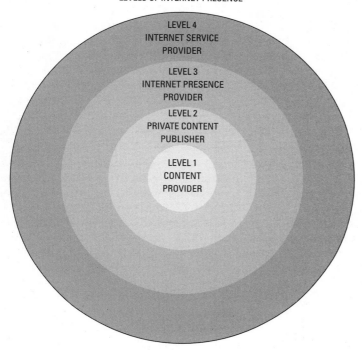

Figure 2-7. *The concentric circles show that an ISP, located in the outermost ring, can do any of the jobs described in the inner rings of the circle.*

Selecting Services for Your Internet Presence

In Chapter 1, we introduced you to some of the basic technologies and services that are used on the Internet, such as WWW, FTP, e-mail, Gopher, and others. Of these services, you need to decide which ones you are going to include in your own Internet site. The services you choose will naturally be dependent on the kind of resources you will want to make available, the kind of site you will have, and your level of involvement with the Internet. Some preliminary questions to ask yourself are these:

- Can the site be supported completely by the WWW?

- What do my customers want?

- What is my competition providing?

- What are the costs of the services I want to provide?

The WWW Is Taking Over the Universe

OK, so we're just slightly prone to exaggeration. The point we want to get across to you here is that the Web is gaining tremendous popularity. In fact, the Web is gradually supplanting legacy systems on the Internet such as FTP and Gopher and making them obsolete. Just about everyone setting up a new Internet site will implement the WWW due to its ease of use and ability to provide multiple services with a common interface. The Web can support all the functions that you might want to have on your Internet site, from publishing to interactive sites to virtual storefronts. In addition, the WWW supports many of the legacy services that it is supplanting, such as Gopher, NNTP, FTP, and e-mail.

The WWW is very compelling to people because of its graphics capabilities and hypertext links. On an FTP site, you can handle the transmission of graphics, but FTP sites are not as accessible as WWW pages are. For people accessing your site, there are some other significant differences between FTP and the WWW. An FTP site allows information to be downloaded into the client's computer before it can be viewed, and, furthermore, it is not interactive. On the other hand, WWW pages allow clients to view them, interact with them, and then decide whether they want to download the information. The choice between WWW and FTP is somewhat dependent on the type of information you want to provide and how much time and money you have to prepare your content. In the event that you have a very limited amount of time or no expertise in Web content authoring, FTP is a better choice.

Do I Need Anything Other Than the Web?

The answer to this question is "yes," but only if you are going to be an IPP or ISP. Most of your clients will want to publish their content on WWW servers, but you might also want to offer FTP because the server is easy to maintain, no special skills are needed for content authoring, and it comes with most operating systems.

Additionally, offering DNS (Domain Name System) to your customers allows them to have personalized domain names. Otherwise, when customers contract with you to service their WWW pages, they will end up with addresses based on the name of your domain, and each customer name will be a directory attached to your URL. Your customers might want to use DNS so that they have their own domains, making it easier for their own customers to find them. Offering DNS can be a nice benefit for your customers while allowing you to charge a higher monthly fee for service. It could give you a competitive advantage over other IPPs that don't offer DNS.

More advanced and complicated services you might offer are transactions and databases. This would allow your customers to have online ordering, requests for information, or any other interactive service that requires some process that's not part of the standard WWW service.

As we said earlier, ISPs can offer all of the same services as an IPP, but, in addition, they provide dial-up connection to the Internet. If you run an ISP, you can offer your clients e-mail so they can have mailboxes on the Internet, access to news services like NNTP, and chat services.

Summary

◆ If you are a private content publisher, you should set up WWW, DNS, and e-mail.

◆ An IPP should offer WWW, FTP, and DNS.

◆ An ISP should provide Internet access, WWW, DNS, e-mail, FTP, and NNTP.

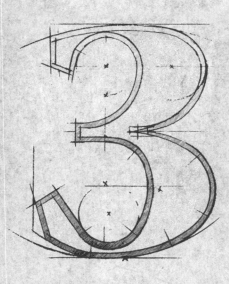

3

Taking Care of Your Physical Needs

Hardware and Bandwidth Requirements

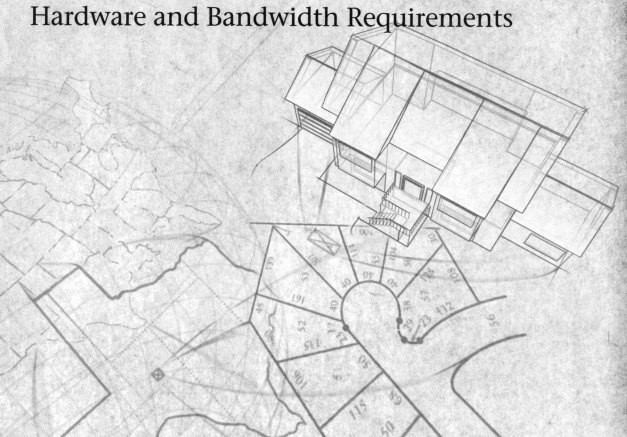

Now that you've done some thinking about what you'd like your Internet site to consist of, it's time to figure out whether your current PC will be up to the job and how you'll be making your connection to the Internet. Choices regarding hardware and Internet connections center on the issue of capacity planning, and, as you will discover, this is far from being an exact science. We will, however, give you some guidelines for hardware and bandwidth requirements and make some general recommendations in this area. Falling under the category of hardware is the issue of reliability, and we will include some suggestions for backup and fault tolerance. Once you have your hardware and bandwidth requirements nailed down, you will need to contact an Internet service provider (ISP) to get your link to the Internet established, so we'll give you a brief rundown on how to find and choose an ISP.

Bandwidth

The term *bandwidth* refers to the amount of information that can be transmitted and received within a given interval of time. A link to the Internet that has higher bandwidth allows more information to be communicated in a shorter time to more people. Bandwidth is measured in bits per second (bps), kilobits per second (Kbps), or megabits per second (Mbps). One Kbps is equal to 1024 bps, and 1 Mbps is equal to 1024 Kbps.

Cost is one of the biggest concerns you are likely to have when you consider hardware and bandwidth. We cannot give you any specific prices to go by as there are just too many variables, but we will make some generalizations as we go along. Naturally, it would be nice to be able to use only hardware that you currently have, but you might find that your current machine (assuming you have one) won't be adequate to run all the services that you had hoped for. If this is the case, you need to think about upgrading your hardware or consider having a less sophisticated Internet site.

Capacity Planning

Capacity planning is at the same time one of the most important and one of the most difficult tasks you undertake in setting up your Internet site. What we'd really like to be able to do in this section is to give you some neat little formulas to use to figure out your hardware and bandwidth needs. Much to our chagrin, this is not possible. A large percentage of what's involved in capacity planning is making some educated guesses. For instance, can you predict the number of people who will be accessing your server at the same time? Do you know how much computer memory you'll need to handle all the activity at your Web site yet still enable you to use your computer for other things? Yikes! These are hard questions to answer. And to further complicate matters, the answers can change over time. Well, don't stress about this. Just get ready to guess and make changes. The best that we can do to help you with capacity planning is to provide guidelines for you to use.

Bandwidth needs depend primarily on the number of simultaneous users of your site. If you are setting up a personal home page, you probably won't need to worry about getting a lot of hits on your site and you can expect relatively low capacity, unless your name happens to be Michael Jackson or Princess Diana. Conversely, if you have a successful small business that has gained popularity with a hot new product, you need to prepare for a busy site. Capacity planning is even more difficult if you are going to be an Internet presence provider publishing other people's Internet sites. If you think it is hard to predict the amount of traffic and content your own site will generate, just imagine doing that for multiple other sites on the same server or across multiple servers. You really need to analyze your audience to make these predictions.

Other factors to take into account when considering bandwidth are the nature of the content you are offering and the type of users who will be accessing your site. Your bandwidth needs will generally increase if your content is graphically intense and if your typical users are advanced. Furthermore, if your site grows in popularity, you might need to readdress your bandwidth requirements to make sure you can handle a surge in use.

Capacity planning also influences your choice of hardware. You must consider the amount of memory and disk space in your computer in relation to the volume of content that you will be making available at your Internet site. There are no hard-and-fast rules here either. Even though you might have a pretty good idea about how much disk space your Internet site will occupy, you need to keep in mind that the act of people accessing your site will affect your machine's RAM and processor, and hence the performance of your system. If you have a computer that is key to the operation of your non-Internet business, you might want to run your Internet site on its own server so that it will not adversely affect the functions of your business computer. Of course, this is probably going to be a problem only if you have a busy Internet site.

The very best that we can tell you in regard to capacity planning for hardware and bandwidth is to take your best guess as to capacity. Then be prepared to upgrade until the performance is satisfactory or as your needs change. You should monitor your site very closely for the first six months and do frequent tests of your Internet site to make sure that everything is running smoothly. The bottom line is that you will need to start somewhere and then make real-world adjustments until the performance is to your own and your customers' satisfaction. The following questions are good ones to keep posted when you're planning the capacity of your Internet site.

◆ Which Internet services will you be using?

◆ What is the nature of your content? Are there many graphics to consider? Do you have large file-storage needs? Will your content fill up your current hard disk?

◆ Do you expect your site to grow in the near future? What hardware will be able to support the growth you project?

◆ Do you have enough business to justify more than one machine?

◆ What type of users do you expect to have? Are they new to the Internet or are they advanced?

The tables that we provide in this chapter show basic hardware and bandwidth requirements, depending on the services you will be using and traffic levels you anticipate. These are the main variables that are going to affect the performance of your system. The tables are based on real-world experience but are by no means accurate for every given situation.

Hardware Recommendations

Table 3-1 lays out our best recommendations for hardware needs and is based on the most likely services that you will be using and your best guess for number of simultaneous users, expressed as low (fewer than 3 users), medium (3 to 15 users), or high (more than 15 users) traffic. Although we refer to these recommendations as minimum requirements, we are referring to systems on which we think your site will run comfortably within the given parameters. These are more than just bare-bones requirements.

You will also see that we give some recommendations for hard disk space, although we do this with a certain amount of trepidation. The amount of disk space you need is directly dependent on the amount of content you have, and content can vary considerably from one site to another, as you might expect. The good news here is that disk space is inexpensive and easy to upgrade.

As a general rule, it is more important to make sure you have adequate RAM. If you are purchasing a new system, RAM is not the place to scrimp because it is both expensive and difficult to upgrade. If you're going to have a more advanced site with services like transactions, search engines, or query databases, then, depending on the amount of traffic that you expect on your site, you might need to get a faster machine and increase the memory.

For future growth there are many options for you to consider. A Pentium-class machine, depending on the manufacturer, can support a maximum of 128 MB RAM at the low end to 1 GB RAM at the high end. Also, using multiple servers and moving to a different server architecture (specifically moving from Intel-class machines to RISC-based machines) are additional ways to increase capacity. If you really like having the very latest technology, don't want to worry about having growth problems for awhile, and cost is not a big issue for you, then consider Intel's new Pentium Pro high-end processor from the start. All of these platforms will run Windows NT Server very nicely.

	Low Traffic (fewer than 3 simultaneous users)	Medium Traffic (3 to 15 users)	High Traffic (more than 15 users)
WWW	486/66 32 MB RAM 1-GB hard disk	486/100 32 MB RAM 1-GB hard disk	586/90 48 MB RAM 2-GB hard disk
FTP	486/66 32 MB RAM 1-GB hard disk	486/66 32 MB RAM 1-GB hard disk	486/66 32 MB RAM 1-GB hard disk
E-mail	586/75 48 MB RAM 1-GB hard disk	586/75 48 MB RAM 1-GB hard disk	586/90 64 MB RAM 2-GB hard disk
For all services	586/75 48 MB RAM 2-GB hard disk	586/90 64 MB RAM 1.5-GB hard disk	586/90 64+ MB RAM 2-GB hard disk

Table 3-1. *Minimum hardware requirements.*

Hardware for Reliability and Fault Tolerance

If the Internet is going to be an important part of your business, you should protect yourself against lost information or system failures. The term *fault tolerance* refers to technologies that duplicate critical systems of your computer and allow for automatic switchover from the failed system to the healthy system. If you invest in fault tolerance, your system can continue to operate in the event of a major hardware failure without interrupting the operation of your Internet presence. The main drawback to adding fault tolerance to your system is that it requires the expense of additional hardware and, in some cases, software.

Most of you starting out on the Internet don't need fault tolerance. But if you are really concerned about the possibility of downtime, *disk mirroring*—cloning your hard disk in real time—is an inexpensive option.

Computers have few moving parts, but they do have some in critical areas. Disk drives are generally reliable, but if something is going to go wrong in a computer, a disk drive is a likely candidate. When you set up disk mirroring, you are equipping your computer with another hard disk that contains exactly the same data as your first one. If something goes wrong with your primary disk, the clone or "mirror" disk then takes over. With Windows NT Server, configuring disk mirroring is built into the Disk Administrator tool and is easy to set up. Figure 3-1 diagrams disk mirroring. Figure 3-2 shows you the Windows NT Disk Administrator for setting up disk mirroring.

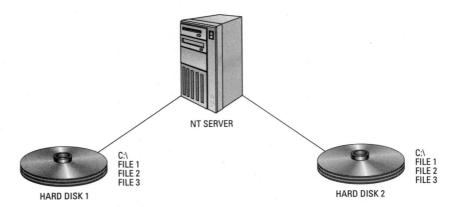

Figure 3-1. *With disk mirroring, if there is an interruption to your system, a second, identical hard disk takes over the operation of the system.*

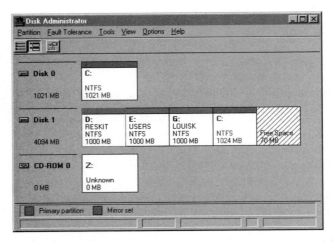

Figure 3-2. *Windows NT Disk Administrator makes it easy for you to set up disk mirroring.*

Even if you use disk mirroring, but especially if you don't, you'll want to have a backup system. You can use the files stored in a backup system to recover in the event of a crash, but, more important, you can recover files that might have been mistakenly or maliciously deleted. If you don't have a backup system, we recommend that you purchase a tape backup drive, preferably a SCSI (Small Computer Standard Interface) backup device. Windows NT Server has built-in software for backup, but you will need to run a backup procedure. You can also schedule backups to happen automatically with third-party backup software that you can purchase for Windows NT Server.

Another consideration for the reliability of your system is how your system will handle interruptions to the power supply. Your computer cannot operate for a split second without power, and if the power is interrupted, you could experience a loss of data. If you want to protect yourself from this kind of event, you should purchase an uninterruptible power supply (UPS). This is basically a big battery and an inverter that allows your system to run long enough for you to cleanly shut down the system, thus protecting your data. Windows NT Server has built-in UPS software.

What Does It Mean When Your Operating System Crashes?

A *crash* is a condition in which either an application or the hardware fails to perform as expected and results in the operating system not knowing how to handle the situation. When a crash occurs, your server will be, at best, unusable; in the worst case, important data can be lost. Crashes are usually a result of hardware failures or bugs in the software, both of which leave the operating system unable to access critical information.

Options for Connecting Your Site to the Internet

Those of you who access resources on the Internet probably do so with a modem connection or, if you're really lucky, a speedy ISDN (Integrated Services Digital Network) line. Modems and ISDN links can also be used to host your Internet presence, but there are also more options than these to consider. In the following sections, you can read about the most common and cost-effective methods for making your connection.

Link speed and cost will be your basis of comparison for the connection types. Link speed is measured in terms of the number of bits per seconds (bps) the link can handle. Not surprisingly, the cost of a connection increases with the link speed.

As you are probably already aware, the hardware you buy for your communications link depends on the kind of link you choose. We highly recommend that you consult the Windows NT Server Hardware Compatibility List (HCL) before choosing any specific brand names. Getting a brand that is not on the list to work properly can be very difficult, so choosing from the HCL will likely save you some irritation.

Modem

A modem connection to the Internet costs relatively little. It runs over a standard telephone line and offers link speeds of up to 28.8 Kbps. Modem connections are, however, considered to be unreliable and are not generally used for a permanent Internet presence. Although 28.8 Kbps is a pretty good speed for surfing the Internet, this is a slow connection for hosting an Internet presence. Your users will find it slow to access your site. But because of their ease of setup and their low cost, modem connections are good for low traffic Internet sites, for personal Web pages, or for the hobbyist. Modem connections are also valuable for testing a business site prior to installing a faster, more expensive line and provide a reasonable connection for low- and medium-traffic e-mail.

If you choose to set up a modem link, you will need a modem and a phone line. You can use either an internal or external modem, but there are some advantages to choosing an external modem. External modems are easy to transport between machines, and they are not tied to any specific hardware platform. And you can connect up to 256 modems to a single machine. An external modem, therefore, will give you more flexibility in setting up your system than an internal modem.

ISDN (Integrated Services Digital Network)

An ISDN line is very similar to a standard phone line except that it is entirely digital and offers a much higher speed of connection, up to 128 Kbps. Although ISDN connections offer higher speeds than modem connections, like modem connections, they are not permanent, meaning that you have to dial in to make the connection. For this reason, you should use ISDN lines for the same conditions as modem connections—specifically low-traffic connections, testing, and low-to-medium–traffic e-mail. If, however, you find that acquiring a permanent connection to the Internet is prohibitively expensive, but you want higher speed than modems can offer, then ISDN would be the best choice for lower-end e-mail, FTP, and WWW sites.

If you choose ISDN, you need to get either an ISDN modem (technically a misnomer, but one that is likely to stick) or an ISDN adapter. You might also need an NT-1, which is the equivalent of the phone jack that you plug your device into, and an ISDN line from your telephone company. Remember, it will be to your advantage to choose hardware listed in the Windows NT Server HCL.

ISDN modems hook up to your computer through a serial port, much the same way that regular modems do. This means that, since a serial port can go no faster than 115 Kbps (which is lower than the total effective bandwidth of the ISDN line), some throughput will be lost if you are using the maximum ISDN bandwidth.

For this reason, we generally recommend ISDN adapters, which go at bus speed, a rate higher than ISDN needs. With most ISDN modems and adapters, you will also need an NT-1. Please note, though, that some ISDN equipment comes with the NT-1 built in. For your ISDN line, it will be much more economical for you to order a flat rate or nonmetered ISDN line if available. Figure 3-3 shows you how ISDN connects you to the Internet.

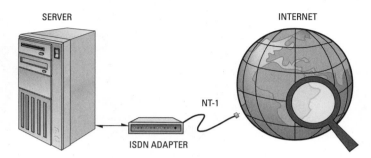

Figure 3-3. *ISDN hardware connections.*

Frame Relay

A frame relay connection makes a dedicated permanent communication link between two locations. Your computer connects directly to the frame network, which acts as a backbone where your ISP is also connected. This establishes your connection to the Internet. Because the backbone is shared by all customers using the frame network, it's possible for your total bandwidth to be temporarily unavailable when you need it. For this reason, your throughput may be slower than if you were using another permanent connection such as a leased line. When buying frame relay, you must specify a speed of connection. Frame relay link speeds can range from 56 Kbps to T1 (1.5 Mbps). These links get significantly more expensive as they get faster.

Since frame relay is a permanent connection to the Internet, we recommend it as a reliable link to the Internet for your site. Specifically, frame relay is a good choice for all medium-traffic sites and for high-traffic e-mail.

To set up a frame relay connection, you need a frame relay card for your computer and a frame relay line from your telephone company. You could also choose to use an external router for frame relay, in which case you would need only an Ethernet card in your Windows NT server. If you expect to have high-traffic volume, we recommend external routing instead of using Windows NT Server as a router because routing takes significant processing resources away from your Internet server. If you choose external routing, you might also need a CSU/DSU, which is, in effect, a phone jack for this kind of line that sits between the line from your telephone company and your equipment. Check with your router manufacturer. Figure 3-4 on the following page shows you how you can set up a frame relay connection.

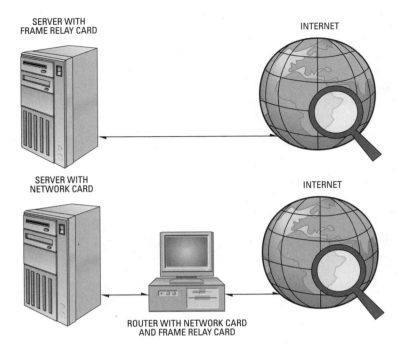

SERVER WITH
FRAME RELAY CARD

INTERNET

SERVER WITH
NETWORK CARD

INTERNET

ROUTER WITH NETWORK CARD
AND FRAME RELAY CARD

Figure 3-4. *You can install a frame relay card in your computer and use Windows NT Server as your router, or you can use an external router.*

Leased Line

A leased line operates in a fashion similar to frame relay technology with the notable difference that the connection is end to end. In other words, there is no intermediary backbone network to go through. This results in faster throughput, fewer possible failure points, and higher security, since you're not going through another channel. Speeds offered with leased lines range from 56 Kbps to T3 (45 Mbps), and the throughput is usually faster than with frame relay because a leased line is dedicated only to your traffic.

If you can afford it, a leased line is the best choice for any permanent connection to the Internet. We recommend a leased-line link for all high-traffic sites with the exception of e-mail, which, with its lower bandwidth requirements in general, shouldn't put you to this expense.

If you choose to have a leased-line connection, you will need an external router, a leased line from your telephone company, and a CSU/DSU. With this kind of investment, we recommend against using the same server to handle both routing and your Internet site because the performance degradation from such high-volume traffic could be problematic.

Bandwidth Recommendations

Table 3-2 contains our recommendations for the type of connection and link speed you will need to host your Internet site depending on the services you will be offering and the amount of traffic that you expect for your site.

	Low Traffic (fewer than 3 simultaneous users)	Medium Traffic (3 to 30 users)	High Traffic (more than 30 users)
WWW	28.8 Kbps modem or ISDN	56 Kbps frame relay	T1 leased line
FTP	28.8 Kbps modem or ISDN	56 Kbps frame relay	T1 leased line
E-mail	28.8 Kbps modem or ISDN	28.8 Kbps modem or ISDN	56 Kbps frame relay
For all services (any combination)	28.8 Kbps modem or ISDN (per single user)	56 Kbps frame relay (minimal needs)	T1 leased line

Table 3-2. Bandwidth requirements.

Choosing an ISP

Anyone making a connection to the Internet must go through an ISP to get the service set up. Even if you are going to be an ISP yourself, you will have to find a higher-tier ISP to make your connection. Top-tier ISPs are generally the big telephone companies such as MCI or Sprint and deal only with high-level, expensive connections. You will need to find a lower-tier ISP.

If you have access to the Internet, it is itself a great guide to ISPs. Otherwise you can try your local telephone directory, classified ads in computer magazines, word of mouth, or the InterNIC (the organization that coordinates Internet addresses). We advise shopping around carefully for your ISP. Switching to another company after you have been established can be costly to you and confusing to your customers.

A very important factor in your choice is proximity of your ISP to your location. Regardless of which type of link you use, cost goes up as the distance increases; therefore, having your ISP geographically close helps keep your expenses down. Other considerations are reliability of service, the particular services offered (such as DNS and NTTP), the number of redundant connections an ISP has, the speed of the connection, the availability of support personnel, and cost. Customer service is going to be very important to you. If you have a problem with your connection on a Saturday afternoon, for instance, you want to make sure someone will be available to help you so that your server is not down the entire weekend.

When you contact an ISP to establish your service, you will need to tell the ISP what services you want and what your expected bandwidth needs are. Once you have contracted with the ISP, they supply you with your IP addresses, subnet mask, DNS server names, instructions about how to actually hook up to their network, and advice regarding any additional hardware you will need. Once you have this information, the ISP will either refer you to the telephone company or deal with the telephone company on your behalf. If your ISP deals directly with the telephone company, you might want to check on pricing yourself to verify that quotes from your ISP are accurate.

Summary

◆ Capacity planning is important in choosing your hardware and bandwidth needs yet difficult to do. You will have to base your choices on educated guesses.

◆ Your main considerations for choosing your hardware and Internet link will be the number of simultaneous users you expect to have and the services you will offer.

◆ Fault tolerance is not necessary for most small Internet sites. But if your site isn't going to be small and you are concerned about reliability, you should consider disk mirroring, a backup system, and UPS.

◆ Location, price, reliability, and services offered are the main criteria for choosing an ISP.

◆ Your ISP will provide the information you need to configure your Windows NT server.

Coming Up Next

Finally we will be getting to the good stuff. Chapter 4 walks you through the installation and configuration process of Windows NT Server and the services for your Internet site.

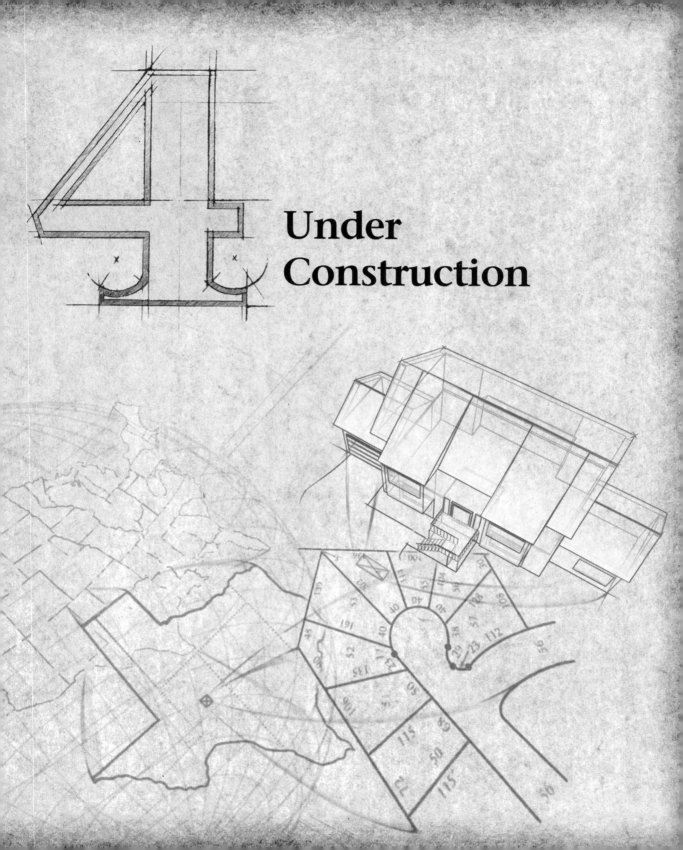

Under Construction

It's time to get your Internet server up and running. You have some big jobs ahead of you. If you've already contacted an ISP, you know that you need to choose and register a domain name and set up your network hardware. Then you need to make sure your operating system is installed and configured properly, depending on the services that you choose for your Internet site. Once all this is accomplished, the big task that remains in getting your Internet server operational is setting up your link to the Internet and testing it for connectivity. Doesn't sound too bad, does it? Well, none of this is difficult, but to be truthful, some of the steps might try your patience.

We will walk you through all processes as best we can to get your Internet server in working order. Once we're there, we'll show you how to test your connection and set up backup and basic fault tolerance, and we'll discuss additional software that you can use to expand the range of services on your site. When you get through all the steps in this chapter, the skeleton of your Internet presence will be up and running and just waiting for you to add your content. It will be like having a whole bunch of empty bookshelves waiting for you to set up your library.

NOTE: About time: We want to warn you that it might take you longer than you expect to get your server running. Setting up an Internet presence is a complex process, and even experts cannot accomplish it overnight. If you've already contacted an ISP, you might have learned that just the lead times for ordering your communications link could be weeks or months, and this is only one small part of setting up your server.

Registering a Domain Name

Most domains on the Internet are on a lower level of a hierarchy of domains. For example, in the domain *guiware.com*, *guiware* is a second-level domain and *com* is the top-level domain. In order to have a domain on the Internet, you must register it with the naming authority that is responsible for the top-level domain where your domain name will be included. An organization called the *InterNIC* is the naming authority for the top-level domains *gov* (government), *edu* (education), *com* (commercial), *org* (organization), and *net* (for ISPs). As you probably noticed, the top-level domains classify different kinds of organizations. Most of the domains have strict qualifications for you to meet before you can be approved for that domain. Most people fall into the *com* domain because there are no qualifications to meet to be included in this domain, but you still need to decide which top-level domain you properly belong in.

In this chapter, we discuss the process of getting a domain in the *com* domain. If you think that your organization belongs in a different top-level domain and would like to see the qualifications for domains other than *com*, you should consult the InterNIC at *http://www.internic.net*.

Once you have decided which of the top-level domains you belong in, you should choose a name for your own domain. This can be more challenging than it sounds. You need to choose a name that has meaning for you, serves as a marker for your Internet site, is easy to remember and type, and is not already in use by another organization on the Internet. If you have a trademark on a name and find that someone is already using it as a domain name on the Internet, you must go through legal channels to get the name released to you if that organization does not want to give it up.

After you have picked an available name, you need to register the name. The most common way to do this is to connect to the InterNIC's Web page at *http://www.internic.net*. Go to the Registration area, and choose either to download a text-based template file or to use a WWW form. If you choose the text-based template file, you will fill in the required information using a text editor or a word processor. If you use the WWW form, you answer the same questions, but you fill in the blanks using your Web browser software.

The InterNIC needs to know the following details: first, who will be the contact for your domain? The organization recognizes three official contacts—an administrative, a technical, and a billing contact. These can be different people or all the same person. Second, you need to supply the InterNIC with names and IP addresses of the DNS servers that will maintain your domain. The InterNIC requires that registered domains have at least two DNS servers. If you are handling your own DNS (which we don't recommend), then you should be able to supply that information yourself. Otherwise, your ISP will give you the DNS address information. Finally, the InterNIC wants to know how you want to be billed. The current fee registration for a domain name is $100.00. Half of this fee is a one-time setup fee, and the other half is the first payment of a recurring maintenance charge payable every two years to keep the domain name.

E-mail the completed form to the InterNIC at the address *hostmaster@internic.net*. Typically, you receive two e-mail notices from them, the first being a confirmation that they received your request, and the second being the approval of your domain name. See Figure 4-1 on the following page.

For more information on how to register a domain name and to check for any changes that might have occurred in the process since this book was written, you should check the InterNIC's Web page at *http://www.internic.net*.

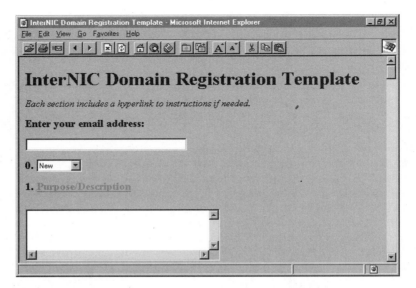

Figure 4-1. *The first page of the InterNIC domain registration form.*

> **NOTE:** We've seen it take from as little as one day to as long as three weeks for the process of registering your domain name to be completed. Certain kinds of domains take longer to get because of the qualification process. Normally, registering within the *com* domain is fast.

Setting Up Network Hardware

It is important that you consult the Windows NT Hardware Compatibility List (HCL) before you choose network hardware and components for your Internet site. Hardware that is on the HCL has been tested to work with Windows NT Server, and, in many cases, the driver for that particular hardware will be included in Windows NT Server, making it easier to install. If the driver for your hardware is not included in Windows NT Server, then the drivers come with the hardware, and you will have to install them separately, either during the installation process or later.

After you have purchased your network hardware, be it modems, ISDN adapters, frame relay or network cards, you will have to install it in your machine. Of all the things you need to do to get your Internet site set up, installing network hardware for frame relay or leased line is likely to be the most difficult task you will encounter. Our advice to you here is to get professional help if you need it.

Because so many different brands are available and the steps for setting up this hardware vary greatly depending on the make, we are going to have to punt this topic and tell you to consult the documentation that comes with your hardware for the installation instructions. It would take us volumes to go through the steps for setting up this hardware for each and every brand. If you have a good ISP, you should be able to rely on their help in both choosing the network hardware and setting it up. If your ISP cannot provide these services, we strongly recommend that you hire a network consultant.

Preparations for Installing Windows NT Server

Whether you will be doing a fresh installation of Windows NT Server or configuring the settings of a previously installed server, in order to set up your Internet site you'll need the following information. You must consider such issues as which protocols to install, which file system to use, what role your server will play within Windows NT Server terminology, and which additional services will be applicable to your Internet site. Windows NT Server setup is comparatively straightforward, but taking the time to prepare for some of the questions that will come up in the installation will be of benefit to you.

What Protocols Should I Install?

To set up a server for the Internet, you must use the TCP/IP protocols. Windows NT Server also supports several other protocols for networking. Two of the most common protocols are built into the operating system. They are IPX and NetBEUI. If you do not have a LAN and are setting up only a single machine to be your Internet server, you should not load any protocol other than TCP/IP because each additional protocol you load uses memory and processing resources. If you do have a LAN, you can use TCP/IP for your entire network unless you are concerned with the potential security risk of having all your machines accessible via the Internet. If you don't want to use TCP/IP on all your computers, you should load whichever protocol is necessary to communicate with your other computers. We recommend that you use IPX as your first choice after TCP/IP.

Which File System Should I Use?

Windows NT Server supports two file system types on hard disks, NTFS (Windows NT File System) and FAT (File Allocation Table). A *file system* describes the way a hard disk is formatted and the way it interacts with the operating system. You need to choose which file system you will use on your server.

The FAT system is an old file system with limited functionality. The only advantage to using FAT is that if you *dual boot* your server, which gives you the option of loading either MS-DOS or Windows NT Server, you will be able to see the hard disk when you are in MS-DOS. FAT can't support file-based security, does not have the fault tolerance capabilities that NTFS has, and doesn't handle block allocation as well as NTFS does on large drives.

What Is Block Allocation?

Block allocation refers to the way in which a computer divides a hard disk into discrete chunks where the data is placed. A file can span more than one block, but a single block can't have more than one file in it. Smaller blocks mean less wasted space for very small files.

The main advantage to NTFS over FAT is that it provides you with significant security enhancements. If you use NTFS, security can be set on files, directories, and drives by user and by group, allowing significant security flexibility. Also, an NTFS drive is secure if someone moves the drive to another machine, reinstalls Windows NT Server, or boots into another operating system, because without the proper user accounts, the system will not let anyone in. Because of its security capabilities, we strongly recommend that you use NTFS as the file system for your Internet server.

What Role Should My Server Play?

Windows NT Server can function and be installed in one of three possible roles: primary domain controller, backup domain controller, and stand-alone server. In addition, a stand-alone server can be either a member of a domain or a member of a workgroup. A *domain controller* is responsible for logon security for all the machines within a given domain. The *primary domain controller* has the master copy of the user database. A *backup domain controller* has a copy of the user database and helps authenticate users for the domain when the primary one is busy. You can assign only one primary domain controller per domain, but you can have any number of backup domain controllers. A *stand-alone server* doesn't have a copy of the domain's user database and doesn't handle authentication for the domain, which gives the server a slight performance advantage over a domain controller.

If your Internet server is your only computer, you should make it the primary domain controller. If you plan to connect your Internet server to a network that already has a Windows NT domain, you can install Windows NT Server either as a backup domain controller or as a stand-alone server in the domain. You could also choose to make the Internet server a stand-alone server in a workgroup, but being outside a domain makes some of the security options that we discuss in the next chapter unavailable.

What Additional Services Do I Need On My Server?

Each additional service you install on your Internet server will consume system memory and processing time. As the volume of traffic on your Internet site increases, you'll find that you need every bit of memory and processing power you have. Therefore, as you consider the following additional services, make sure that you install additional services only if you absolutely need them.

DNS

To refresh your memory, DNS is the service that translates your machine's IP address into a domain address. You can set up your domain name several ways. You can either maintain your own DNS server or have your ISP maintain DNS for you.

If you decide to maintain your own DNS server, you need to install the DNS server that comes with Windows NT Server. This would give you the advantage of being able to make immediate changes to your domain as opposed to having to notify your ISP and wait for the ISP to make the changes. One warning before you proceed: maintaining a DNS server on the Internet is complicated. DNS has a specific file format that it uses for its database. This format can be very difficult to understand, and it is beyond the scope of this book to show you how to create DNS databases. Because of its complexity, we recommend that you use your ISP's DNS server. If you would like more information about DNS, refer to our recommended reading list in Appendix C.

So, if you don't want to spend the time to maintain your own DNS, you can get DNS service from your ISP in one of two ways. One option is to have a third-level domain name off your ISP's domain. For example, if you wanted to use the domain name *kahn* and your ISP was GUIware, your domain address would be *www.kahn.guiware.com*. Your ISP probably charges a small fee for the service. Another option is to have your own second-level domain name hosted on your ISP's DNS server. In this case, your domain address would be *www.kahn.com*. Besides having a second-level domain name, this has the advantage of passing the administration of your DNS server to your ISP. Your ISP probably charges a higher fee for this, but it may well be worth it if you don't know how to manage a DNS system.

DYNAMIC HOST CONFIGURATION PROTOCOL (DHCP)

DHCP is a service that you will need to consider only if you are going to configure TCP/IP on a large number of workstations. DHCP dynamically assigns TCP/IP settings, such as IP address, subnet mask, and default router to workstations as they are needed. If you have a network connected to the Internet, you would configure a *scope,* which consists of a range of TCP/IP addresses and their respective settings. When one of the computers connects to the network, it asks the DHCP server for an available TCP/IP setting. DHCP can be useful with the management of TCP/IP addresses for a large network, but it is not necessary. For a small number of workstations, setting up DHCP is probably not worth the effort. If you have only one computer that will communicate with the Internet, you should not install the DHCP server.

WINDOWS INTERNET NAMING SERVICE (WINS)

WINS is another name-resolution service like DNS, which has a distinct advantage if you are using DHCP. In a Microsoft networking environment, WINS doesn't require the administrator to enter TCP/IP information for each workstation in the database. As a workstation boots up on the network, it will register itself with the WINS server. If you are using DHCP to configure your TCP/IP properties, it's possible that the IP address for a computer might change from day to day. If this happens, a DNS server would have to be manually updated to track the new IP address. WINS, on the other hand, gets the new IP address from the workstation when it acquires a new IP address. If you have only a single computer or a small network of computers, you might not want to install WINS. If you have a large network, you should use WINS. You should definitely use WINS if you are using DHCP.

ROUTING

If you have a LAN that you want to connect to the Internet, you need to have a router to direct traffic from the Internet to the individual computers on your network. You don't need a router for a single computer connecting to the Internet.

If you need to use routing, you can do it two ways. You can use the router built into Windows NT Server, or you can set up a dedicated router. The router in Windows NT Server is an economical routing solution for low-traffic situations. If you are expecting a high volume of traffic, you probably want to buy a dedicated router.

FTP SERVER

If you decide to have an FTP server, you can take two approaches. You can install the FTP server that is included in Windows NT Server, or you can use the FTP server that comes with the Internet Information Server. If you plan to use any of the other pieces of IIS, such as WWW and Gopher, we recommend you use the FTP service in IIS. The FTP service included in IIS provides more functionality, better security, enhanced logging, and superior performance to the FTP service in Windows NT Server's TCP/IP. If you plan to use the FTP server that is part of IIS, it will be automatically installed along with IIS. If you decide to use the FTP server that is included in Windows NT Server, you will select it from the list of additional network services you see during installation.

NOTE: If you are installing the IIS FTP server, don't select the FTP server that is part of Windows NT Server.

Checklist: What Do You Need Before Installing Windows NT Server?

Let's make sure you're ready to proceed. Here is a checklist that includes all the steps you should already have taken to be ready to set up your server.

◆ Your computer hardware is ready, and the communications hardware is installed in it.

◆ You have chosen the services you want to have on your site.

◆ You have contracted with an ISP and have been given your IP address or address range, subnet mask, default gateway, DNS server names and their IP addresses, and any other information you will need to set up your site.

◆ If the ISP didn't contact the telephone company on your behalf, then you have contacted them yourself and made sure that you have the actual communication line set up and the information you need to configure the connection.

Installing Windows NT Server

If you are going to do a fresh installation of Windows NT Server, you can configure a good percentage of the settings for your Internet site during that process. In the following section, we'll walk you through Setup for Windows NT Server. We don't intend this to be a replacement for the Windows NT Server documentation— merely a supplement that contains advice specifically for setting up your Internet server. For complete details regarding the Windows NT Server installation process, refer to the documentation that came with the operating system.

We have divided Windows NT Server Setup into smaller sections to make it more manageable and easier to talk about. The initial setup processes occur in text mode, and these include all the procedures necessary to set up your disks. When the text mode part of Setup is complete, the server software will have been installed to a point where it reboots the computer and then switches to graphics mode. Within graphics mode, three primary areas of Setup need to be completed: gathering information about your computer, installing Windows NT Networking, and finishing Setup. Installing Windows NT Networking is the most critical section of the installation for someone setting up an Internet server. This is also the most complex part of the installation process.

Before you set up Windows NT Server, you might want to read through this section and take a look at the figures of the Setup screens before you actually start the installation. Anything that is not covered here you will be able to find in the documentation for Windows NT Server. If any of the steps produce results different from what we tell you here, consult the documentation for Windows NT Server installation.

Setup in Text Mode

1. Boot Windows NT from the boot disks. At the Welcome To Setup screen, press Enter.

```
Windows NT Server Setup


     Welcome to Setup.

     The Setup program for the Microsoft<R> Windows NT<TM>operating system
     version 4.00 prepares Windows NT to run on your computer.

         · To learn more about Windows NT Setup before continuing, press F1.

         · To set up Windows NT now, press ENTER.

         · To repair a damaged Windows NT version 4.00 installation, press R.

         · To quit Setup without installing Windows NT, press F3.




 ENTER=Continue   R=Repair   F1=Help   F3=Exit
```

2. Follow the prompts for detection of SCSI devices such as hard disks and CD-ROM. If Setup is unable to detect your SCSI devices, you should make sure that your SCSI adapter is configured properly and is on the HCL for Windows NT Server. Press Enter to continue.

3. Verify that the machine-specific information displayed is correct for your computer, and press Enter.

```
Windows NT Server Setup

     Setup has determined that your computer contains the following hardware
     and software components.

                 Computer: Standard PC
                  Display: VGA or Compateble
                 Keyboard: XT, AT, or Enhanced Keyboard (83-104 keys)
          Keyboard Layout: US
           Pointing Device: Microsoft Serial Mouse

               No changes: │The above list matches my computer.│


     If you want to change any item in the list, press the UP or DOWN ARROW
     key to move the highlight to the item you want to change.  Then press
     ENTER to see alternatives for that item.


     When all the items in the list are correct, move the highlight to
     "The above list matches my computer" and press ENTER.


 ENTER=Select    F3=Exit
```

4. Follow the prompts to partition and format your hard disk. Our recommendation is that you create one partition for the entire hard disk and format it as NTFS.

5. Specify the directory where Windows NT Server will be installed. We recommend that you accept the default of WINNT.

6. Setup will check your hard disk for disk errors that might cause problems during setup. We recommend that you allow Setup to do this.

7. Setup will then start copying the system onto your hard disk. Have fun watching the yellow bar get longer.

8. When the system has finished copying, it will prompt you to restart. The system automatically restarts when you press Enter. After the system has restarted, you will be in graphics Setup mode.

NOTE: The boot loader will appear for a few seconds at the beginning of the restart. No action is necessary on your part.

Setup in Graphics Mode—Gathering Information About Your Computer

1. The first screen you see is the Software License Agreement page. You must accept the agreement in order to proceed with installation. Choose the Yes button.

2. Setup then initializes and copies some files. When the copy process is complete, you will be in the Setup wizard. Choose the Next button.

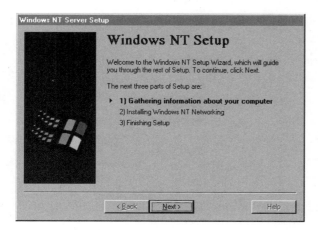

3. At the Name And Organization page, enter your name and your company name. This information is displayed in most of the administrative tools in Windows NT Server. Choose the Next button.

4. At this point, you need to determine the licensing mode you want Windows NT Server to operate in. Please refer to online Help for more information. Select your licensing mode, and choose the Next button.

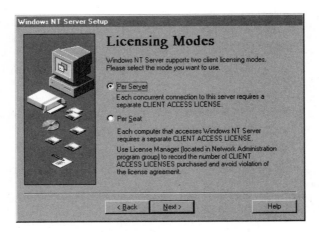

5. Windows NT requires a unique name for your computer. This name is used only by computers on your LAN and not on the Internet. Type a computer name, and choose the Next button.

6. You must select the role for your Internet server. For more information about roles, refer to the section on this topic on page 52 of this book and to the Windows NT Server documentation. Select the role, and choose the Next button.

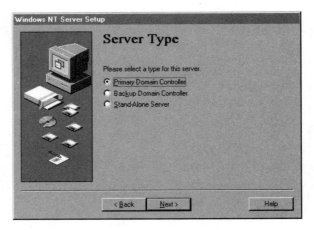

7. If you selected Primary Domain Controller or Stand-Alone Server, you will be prompted for a password for your Administrator account. Every Windows NT Server machine you install has a local administrator. The password being asked for here is for that user. Type in a password and keep it safe. Choose the Next button.

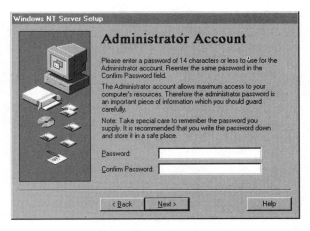

8. An emergency repair disk can be used in the event your hard disk is corrupted. You don't need to create an emergency repair disk during setup because you can do this at any time using RDISK as noted in the dialog box. Although your screen recommends Yes, we recommend that you create an ERD at a later time. Select No and choose the Next button.

9. At this point, Windows NT Server Setup prompts you for additional components to install. We recommend that you accept the default components. You might want to install additional ones later. Refer to your documentation for further information. Choose the Next button.

Network Installation

Congratulations! You have just completed the easy part of the installation process. Welcome to the Network Installation informational screen. You now enter the part of Setup where you will configure settings for your networking components.

1. Choose the Next button to continue.

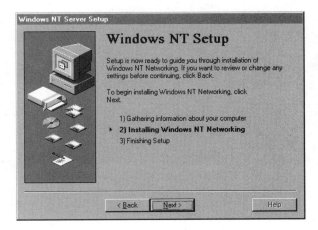

2. Setup needs to know how this computer will communicate with both the Internet and any LAN you might have. If you plan to have your Internet server connect directly to the Internet using anything other than a dial-up connection, you should select the Wired To The Network option. Additionally, if you have a LAN, you should select Wired To The Network. If you plan to use dial-up networking, either to connect your site to the Internet or to have people connect to you, you should select Remote Access To The Network. These options are not mutually exclusive, so you can select both. Choose the Next button.

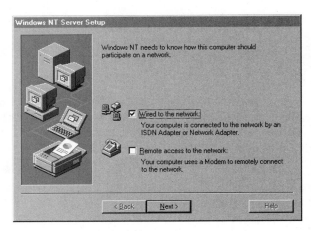

3. Now Setup asks you whether you want to install Microsoft Internet Information Server. This is the heart of your Internet server, so we recommend you select this option. (No kidding!)

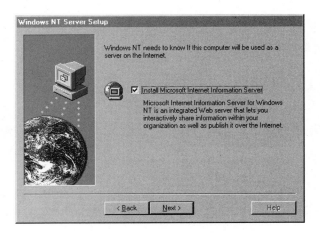

NOTE: If you checked the Wired To The Network option, continue with Step 4. If not, proceed to Step 7.

4. Setup needs to determine what kind of network adapters you have in your computer. In many cases, Setup can automatically detect these devices. But if you are using a device that is not on the hardware compatibility list or is older and therefore doesn't support autodetection, you might need to select it manually. You should choose the Start Search button to see whether Setup can find your adapters.

5. If Setup finds an adapter, it will list it. If you have more than one adapter, you should choose the Find Next button until Setup has found all of your adapters.

6. To manually select an adapter, choose the Select From List button. If the adapter is shown in the list, choose it; otherwise, you need a disk from the adapter's manufacturer with the Windows NT drivers on it. If you have the disk, choose the Have Disk button and follow the prompts.

7. Now you get to choose your Network Protocols. Assuming that you installed the IIS, TCP/IP will automatically be selected in this dialog. Any other protocols should be selected only if you need them. Choose the Next button.

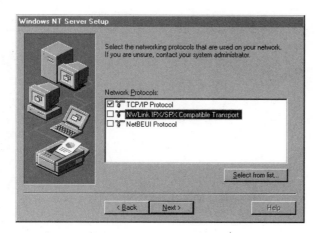

8. Setup now needs to know what additional network services you want to install on your Internet server. It shows you a list of the services that are currently included.

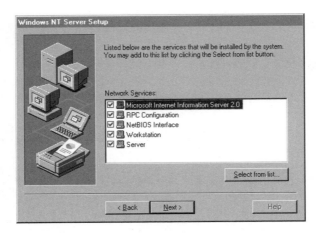

9. To install additional services, choose the Select From List button and then select the specific service you want to add. If you want to install more than one additional service, you must repeat this process. When you finish, choose the Next button.

10. You see another informational screen that tells you that you are ready to install networking components. Choose the Next button.

Install Networking Components

Depending on the type of network cards you have in your computer, you might see additional dialog boxes that ask you to select specific options for those cards.

1. Follow the prompts, and refer to your network adapter's documentation if you require assistance. When you are done, choose the OK button.

2. At this point, Setup will ask you how you want to configure your TCP/IP settings. The first question it asks is whether you have a DHCP server on your network. If this is your only machine, or if you know you don't have a DHCP server, click No. Otherwise, if you have a DHCP server and it is configured to give out valid Internet IP addresses, select Yes.

NOTE: If you checked Dial-in Networking, proceed with Step 3. If not, go to Step 8.

---

3. At this point, Setup attempts to configure your dial-in and dial-out capabilities. If Setup is unable to find compatible communications hardware,

you'll be asked to invoke the modem installer. If you have a modem, you should click Yes and follow the prompts from the Install New Modem wizard.

4. If Setup detects your communications device, or if you manually select it, Setup then prompts you to select the RAS-capable devices you want to use. Once you have done this, click the OK button.

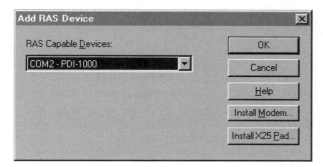

5. In the Remote Access Setup dialog box, you should select the Configure button for each communications device that you have.

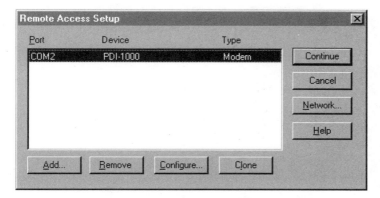

6. A communications device can be configured one of three ways. *Dial Out Only* means that the specified device will be used to connect the server to some other network such as the Internet. *Receive Calls Only* means that the specified device will be used to allow other people to connect to your server. *Dial Out And Receive Calls* allows the specified device to be used for both dialing in and dialing out. Select the appropriate option for each communications device that you have.

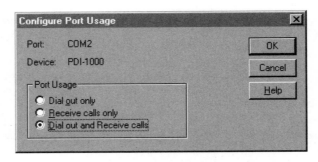

7. After configuring your devices, click the Network button in the Remote Access Setup dialog box. In the Network Configuration dialog box, make sure that at least the TCP/IP protocol is selected. Other protocols should be selected only as needed. When you get back to the Remote Access Setup dialog box, click the Continue button. Setup now installs the networking components.

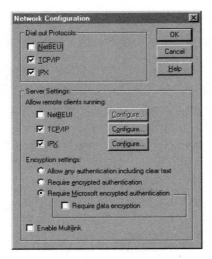

8. If you don't have DHCP, Setup prompts you for TCP/IP configuration information. You need to enter the IP address for your Internet server along with its subnet mask and default gateway. If you have more than one IP address you want to assign to this machine, you should click the Advanced button to enter them.

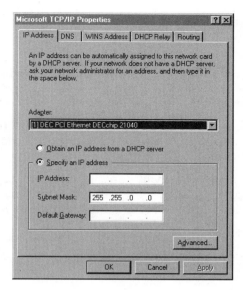

9. In the Advanced IP Addressing dialog box, type in the IP address and subnet mask and click the Add button for IP addresses for each IP address you want to include. When you finish, click OK.

10. Select the DNS tab of the TCP/IP properties dialog box. Enter the host name you want to use for your server on the Internet. This name doesn't have to be the same as your machine name, but it will default to the machine name. Then enter the Internet domain name for this server. Click the Add button for DNS Service Search Order, and enter the IP address for your DNS server. Either your ISP will have provided you with this address or it will be your own IP address if you set up your own DNS server.

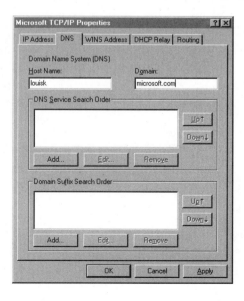

11. If you are using your Internet server as a router, select the Routing tab in the TCP/IP Properties dialog box and check the Enable IP Forwarding box.

12. If you have WINS installed on your network, configure the WINS Address tab of TCP/IP Properties as well. You don't need this for your Internet server so we will not go into detail describing this service.

13. When you have finished configuring the TCP/IP properties, click the OK button. If you didn't configure WINS, Setup will ask you to verify that this is OK. Click the Yes button. Some processing will occur.

14. Setup displays the network bindings about to occur. A binding connects a protocol to a service and to an adapter. We highly recommend that you accept the default bindings as Setup configures them. Click the Next button.

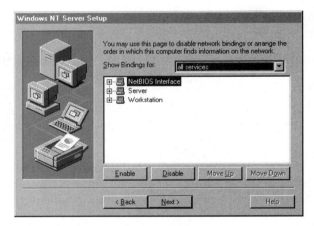

15. Setup is now ready to start your network services. Click the Next button.

16. Twiddle your thumbs for a few moments while Setup does some processing.

17. Depending on the role you selected for your server, you see a dialog box that either creates a new domain or joins a backup domain controller into an already existing domain. Or, if you chose to make yours a stand-alone server, you choose from options to join a domain or a workgroup. You should either create or join a Windows NT Server domain. Click the Next button.

Finishing Setup

You are almost through the setup process.

1. Click the Finish button to continue the process. Watch the system do some more processing.

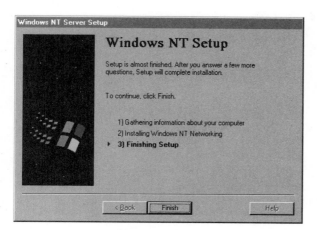

2. Setup will now walk you through the installation of IIS. Select the services you want to provide on the Internet from the list shown. By default, all services are selected. You need Internet Service Manager and Help & Sample Files. ODBC Drivers & Administration is necessary if you plan to offer any database connectivity to your Internet server. You can choose to remove the FTP, Gopher, and WWW services if you don't need them. Then click the OK button. Confirm the creation of the directory where IIS will be installed by clicking Yes.

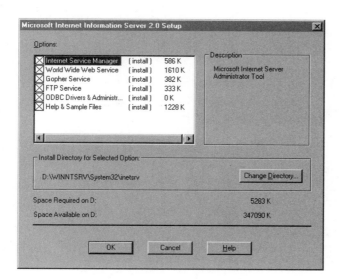

3. The IIS needs a location for the content of the different services that you plan to offer. Lists of contents like these are known as *publishing directories*. Setup suggests default directories, or you can choose your own.

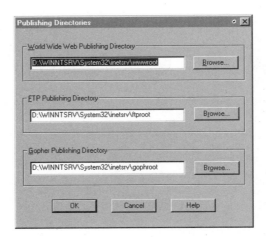

4. Click the OK button once you have specified the directories. If these directories don't yet exist, confirm their creation by clicking Yes. Watch the system do some copying. Stretch your legs. Get a cup of coffee.

5. If you selected ODBC, Setup now prompts you to install drivers for ODBC. Select the appropriate driver for your database. For example, if you have Microsoft SQL Server, select SQL Server from the list. Click the OK button. See even more copying!

6. Select your time zone from the list. Select the Date/Time tab to verify the correct time and date. Click the Close button.

7. Setup automatically identifies the kind of video card that you have and now prompts you to configure the settings you want to use. Click OK in the Detected Display dialog box, and choose the settings you want. Follow the prompts to set your video settings. Click OK when you're done. Now see some more delightful processing. Isn't it fun watching those bars go by? This is a good time to take up a new hobby, say knitting.

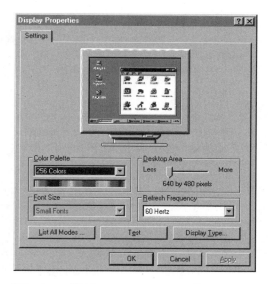

8. Windows NT Server is now installed. Choose the Restart Computer button to reboot, and take a well-deserved break. When you get back, you'll be ready to configure your system.

Modifying a Previously Installed Windows NT Server

If you have Windows NT Server installed but not set up for communication with the Internet, you need to reconfigure some of your current settings. You should be using Windows NT Server version 4.0 or later for your Internet site. If you have an older version, the first thing you should do is upgrade to 4.0. If you need to upgrade, refer to the documentation that comes with the upgrade. The following describes the process for getting a previously installed Windows NT 4.0 Server ready to configure for the Internet.

Checking Your Network Configuration

1. The first thing you should do is determine whether TCP/IP is already installed and properly configured. You need to be logged in as Administrator or as a user with administrative privileges to configure these areas.

2. Launch the Network control panel found inside the Control Panel.

3. Select the Protocols tab.

NOTE: If you find that TCP/IP has already been installed, continue with Step 4. If you need to install TCP/IP, proceed to Step 6.

---

4. If TCP/IP is in the list, that protocol is already installed. You should check its properties by clicking the Properties button.

5. Compare your TCP/IP properties with the setting your ISP gave you. Make any changes as necessary.

6. If TCP/IP is not in the list, click the Add button and select TCP/IP Protocol from the list. Click the OK button.

7. The system asks whether DHCP is used. Unless you actually have set up a DHCP server on your network, click the No button.

8. Next you need to insert the installation CD for Windows NT Server. TCP/IP will then be listed as one of the protocols. Click the Close button.

9. Processing happens, and then you will see the Microsoft TCP/IP Properties dialog box. At this point, you must enter your IP address, subnet mask, and default gateway.

10. If you have DNS server information, you should click on the DNS tab and choose the Add button under DNS Service Search Order. Enter the IP address of each DNS server, and click the Add button. If you have more than one adapter in your server, you must enter this information for each adapter. Make sure that you enter the right information from the right adapter. Click the OK button when you're done.

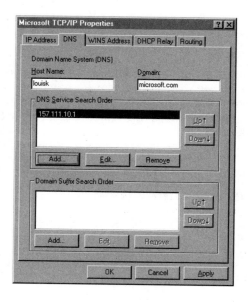

11. You might get a message that tells you the primary WINS address is empty. Click the Yes button to continue.

12. Setup now requests that you reboot your computer for the changes to take effect. Do it.

Install the Internet Information Server (IIS)

You need to install the Internet Information Server Version 2.0, which is Microsoft's Web, Gopher server, and FTP service.

1. To install IIS, insert the Windows NT Server CD.

2. Open a command prompt, and change to the CD drive.

3. Change directories to the INETSRV subdirectory.

4. Execute the INETSPT.EXE program by typing *Inetstp*. When you see the IIS informational screen, click the OK button.

5. Make sure that all the services you want are installed. Refer to the Fresh Install section under Finishing Setup for information about the services and the steps to complete the installation of IIS.

Check for Your Communications Devices

You must make sure Windows NT Server can communicate with the Internet.

1. Launch the Network control panel from inside the Control Panel.

2. If you plan to use a modem or ISDN, select the Services tab and add Remote Access Service if it's not already installed. To configure Remote Access Service, follow the steps in the Install Networking Components section on page 62.

3. If you plan to use frame relay or a leased line with an adapter in your Windows NT Server, select the Adapters tab and click the Add button to install the driver for your communications card. Refer to the documentation that came with your adapter for more information on installing the drivers.

NOTE: For ISDN, you may also have to go to the Adapters tab and add the ISDN card. See your ISDN documentation for more information.

Configuring Your Internet Server

Once you complete a fresh installation or modify a previously installed server, you need to do some additional configuration in order to complete the setup and establish your Internet link. In this section, we will walk you through the steps to configure IIS and DNS and to connect to the Internet. When you have completed this, the only areas left for consideration will be security configuration and directory layouts.

Configuring IIS

Setup installs IIS with default settings that might not be appropriate for your Internet site. Before going live on the Internet, you should go through the Internet Service Manager to check the settings and make any changes that you need. Internet Service Manager can be found in the Programs/Microsoft Internet Server group.

If you have enabled all the services on IIS, specifically WWW, FTP, and Gopher, you need to configure settings for each of these services. We'll go through the complete process of configuring Web for IIS, meaning that we discuss in this section each option for each tab. When you configure FTP and Gopher, you'll notice that many of the options are the same. We discuss only the settings that are unique to FTP and Gopher; you can refer back to the WWW section for information regarding the rest of the settings. Unless we tell you otherwise, the settings on each of the service's tabs are specific to that service even if they have the same name. This means that you must configure the setting separately for each service.

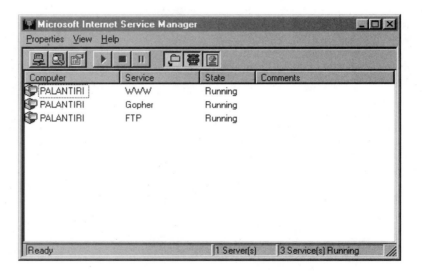

WWW SETTINGS

If you installed WWW, double-click on the line for your WWW service in the Internet Service Manager to get to the settings. This dialog box has four tabs, which are for Services, Directories, Logging, and Advanced settings. You should step through each tab to ensure that you are happy with the default setting and change anything that you want to work differently.

On the Services tab, you can change the following settings:

◆ Connection Timeout refers to the amount of time a connection can remain idle before the server disconnects it. The default of 900 seconds in most cases is fine. You might lower this number if your server has heavy traffic.

◆ Maximum Connections is the total number of simultaneous connections that the server can handle. The proper setting for this depends greatly on the speed of your hardware and the amount of memory you have. The default setting is 1000 simultaneous connections. If you find users complaining about the speed of the connection at certain times, you might lower this number.

◆ Anonymous Logon has two items: Username and Password. This is the user ID and password that IIS uses to access the files on your Web site for your Web users. You should not change the default of *IUSR_machinename*.

◆ Password Authentication has three options: Allow Anonymous, Basic (Clear Text), and Windows NT Challenge/Response. These are the methods by which users can connect and identify themselves to the IIS server. Allow Anonymous means that users don't have to identify themselves to the server. Basic means that users will be asked for their user IDs and passwords and that information will be transmitted to the IIS. Windows NT Challenge/Response allows Windows 95 or Windows NT Workstation clients running Microsoft Internet Explorer 2.0 or later to identify themselves to the server automatically. For more information regarding security, refer to Chapter 5 of this book.

◆ The Comment box is used only for identification purposes via the Internet Service Manager. You can put any identifying information you want in here.

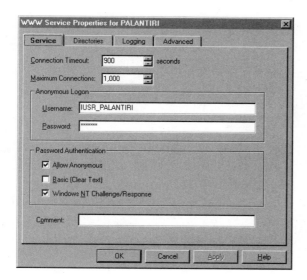

Under the Directories tab, you can change the following settings:

◆ The directory list names the directories and virtual directories that the IIS can access. The default directories are WWWROOT and SCRIPTS subdirectories. Chapter 6 covers options for configuring your directory structure for your Internet site.

◆ Enable Default Document means that if a user connects to your Web site without referencing a specific WWW file, the specified document will be sent to the user. By default, the Enable Default Document check box is checked, and the Default Document Name is DEFAULT.HTM. (We get a bonus for each time we use the word *default*!)

◆ If enabled, the Directory Browsing Allowed option lets the user see all documents on your Web server in a file list and select from it. The default setting for this option is disabled, and we recommend that you leave it that way to prevent unintended access to files.

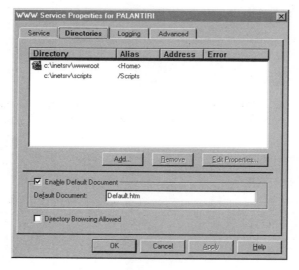

Next select the Logging tab. Logging is the process the server uses to track use of your Internet site over time.

◆ The first option is Enable Logging, which is turned on by default. If you don't want to track your server usage or potential security problems, you can disable logging—it does use up both disk space and processing power. Most site builders, however, will probably want this feature.

- If you have enabled logging, you must choose between logging to a file or logging to a database. If you want to log to a database, refer to the documentation. We recommend logging to a file because most of the IIS log analysis tools work only against files.

- The Automatically Open New Log option allows the IIS to create a new log file based on the criteria you select; otherwise, one log file will be created. By default, this option is enabled to create daily log files. We recommend that you accept the default.

- Log File Directory refers to the location in which log files should be placed.

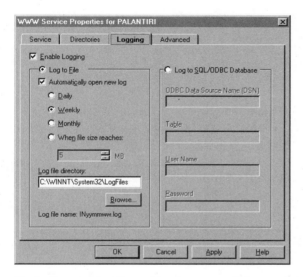

Typically, you don't need to change anything on the Advanced tab unless you have specific IP addresses to which you want to grant or deny access to your site.

- You can choose to grant or deny access to all computers. The default is to grant access, and we recommend that you accept this setting. For more detailed information, refer to the online help and documentation.

- Limit Network Use By All Internet Services On This Computer applies to FTP and Gopher as well as the WWW service. It enables you to throttle the bandwidth that the Internet services use. We recommend you don't enable this option.

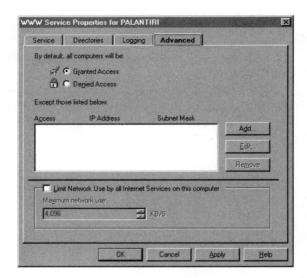

When you finish reviewing and making any necessary changes to your WWW settings, click the OK button.

FTP SETTINGS

If you chose to have an FTP site on IIS, double-click on the entry that corresponds to FTP in the IIS Manager. You see tabs for Service, Messages, Directories, Logging, and Advanced settings. Some of these tabs have settings similar to those in the WWW settings. We're walking you through only the exceptions, here.

◆ On the Service tab, you find two items that differ from the WWW settings. Allow Only Anonymous Connections prevents users from identifying themselves to the system; they can connect only as anonymous users. If you want to provide special access to certain users, you might want to change that default setting from enabled. The Current Sessions button displays the currently logged-on FTP users on your IIS. You can disconnect individual users or all users from the FTP service.

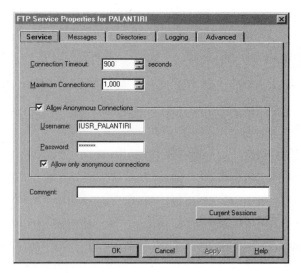

◆ The Messages tab is unique to the FTP service and allows you to specify messages to be displayed to your users at logon, logoff, and when your server is busy. Type in any messages that you want. If you leave these blank, no message will be displayed.

◆ Under the Directories tab, you find Directory Listing Style. The two options are UNIX and MS-DOS. Each option refers to the way the contents of a directory (names, dates, and size of files, for example) are displayed to the user. The default is MS-DOS; this setting is a personal preference so we make no recommendations.

When you finish reviewing and changing the settings, click the OK button to return to the Internet Service Manager.

GOPHER SETTINGS

If you enabled Gopher service, double-click the Gopher entry in the Internet Service Manager. The four tabs for the Gopher service are Service, Directories, Logging, and Advanced.

The Gopher service has only one unique setting, and it can be found on the Service tab. You need to type in the name and e-mail address of the Service Administrator whom users can contact when they have problems and questions.

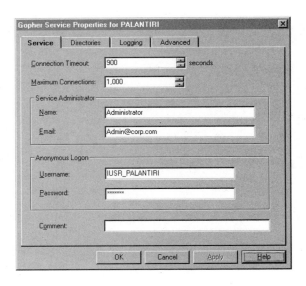

Tweaking Your System

When you have an Internet site, two of your main concerns are that your system perform adequately and that it be available 24 hours a day. By configuring certain system and network properties, you can improve the performance and availability of your server. If you want a truly thorough discussion of how to optimize your Internet server, you should refer to the Windows NT Resource Kit. But we'll give you *some* guidance here.

CONFIGURING SYSTEM PROPERTIES

System settings control general behavior of Windows NT Server. By changing some of the system properties settings, you can improve the performance of certain applications and provide your server with default actions to take when certain conditions are met.

1. Launch the Systems control panel from the Control Panel.

2. Select the Performance tab, and change the Application Performance Boost setting to None. When Application Performance Boost is set to Maximum, the system gives the priority for system resources to the foreground applications running on your server. Since your Internet-related services are considered background applications, changing the setting to None means that the foreground applications are given no priority over background applications.

3. Click the Change button for Virtual Memory, and verify that Initial Size for Page File Size For Selected Drive is set at the minimum recommended page file size.

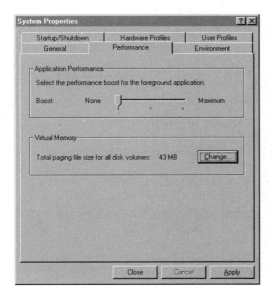

4. Select the Startup/Shutdown tab in the System Properties dialog box.

5. Reduce the number of seconds in the Show List For option to 10 seconds. This decreases the amount of time the system waits while rebooting before loading Windows NT Server.

6. Choose the Automatically Reboot option to enable Windows NT Server to reset itself in the event of an operating system failure.

7. Click the OK button to close the System Properties dialog box.

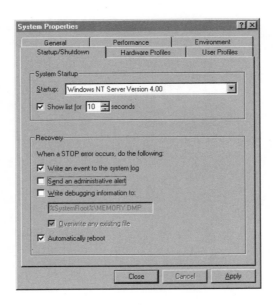

OPTIMIZING NETWORK PERFORMANCE

If you installed more than one protocol, you can get a slight performance boost for your Internet traffic by setting the TCP/IP protocol as your top-level protocol.

1. Launch the Network control panel from the Control Panel.

2. Select the Bindings tab, and make sure that the Show Bindings For option has All Services selected.

3. Click the plus signs to open the protocol order list for each service. If TCP/IP is not the first protocol listed, highlight it and click the Move Up button until it is.

4. Repeat this process for each service listed.

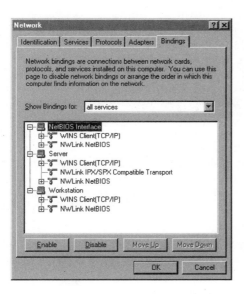

Configuring Your Internet Connection

Without a working connection, everything you have done up until now is point-less. Depending on the type of connection you are using, you might need to do some additional configuration to get the connection up and running. Getting your connection to work reliably can be one of the most challenging steps you make in this journey.

ASYNCHRONOUS (MODEM AND ISDN)

If you are connecting to the Internet via modem or ISDN, you need to give Windows NT Server the appropriate phone number and logon credentials to use.

1. Double-click the Dial-Up Networking icon found on your desktop.

2. Click the New Entry button to create the connection to your ISP, and enter a name for this connection. Click the Next button.

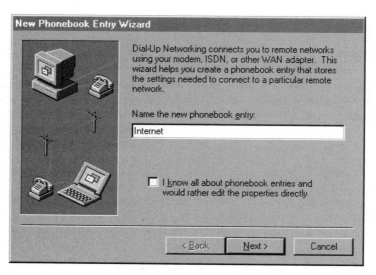

3. Click the I Am Calling The Internet check box. You might need to select the other two options on this screen depending on your ISP. If you are connecting via PPP, you shouldn't have to select any additional settings on this screen. Send My Plain Text Password If That's The Only Way To Connect refers to the ISP's ability to support encryption of your password. The ISP will tell you if you need to select this. You use the third option when a SLIP connection is required.

4. Click the Next button, which takes you to the Modem Or Adapter selection screen. Select the device you plan to use to connect to the Internet.

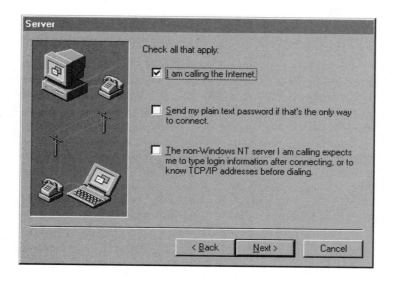

PPP and SLIP

Point-to-point Protocol and SLIP are communication protocols used for asynchronous communication to a network. SLIP is a much older and less advanced protocol that very few ISPs still support. You should make every effort to use PPP when connecting to the Internet.

5. Click the Next button, which brings you to the Phone Number page. Enter the phone number your ISP gave you for your account. If you have more than one number, click the Alternates button and add them to the list.

6. Click the Next button and then the Finish button, and your entry is saved.

7. In the Dial-Up Networking dialog box, select the dial button to initiate the connection. You probably want to click the More button and choose User Preferences. In the User Preferences dialog box, you want to set the number of redial attempts to a high number, such as 1000, the seconds between redial to 3, and the idle seconds before hang-up to zero. This is because a phone connection is not as stable as a dedicated connection and could drop the line, thereby cutting you off. With these settings operating, your server will automatically redial if it loses connection.

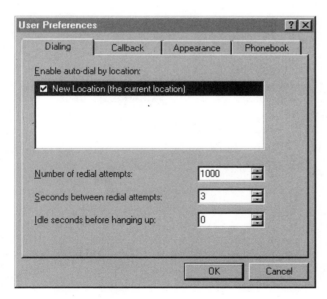

8. Repeat this process for logon preferences.

SYNCHRONOUS (FRAME RELAY AND LEASED LINE)

If you installed a frame relay or a leased adapter in your server, you already configured the settings for these connections during the installation process or when you modified your server. If you plan to use a dedicated router to connect your network to the Internet, you will need to refer to the documentation that came with your router and talk to your telephone company to configure your connection.

A couple of common problems could prevent your connection from working properly. First make sure that the phone company has activated the link, sometimes referred to as "turning up the link." Then ensure that you have the correct parameters set on your system for the type of equipment the phone company uses. For example, the link-management protocol must be configured properly and the routing structure must be configured to support the encapsulation that is required by your ISP. Many different settings must be correct for frame relay and leased lines to work properly. You will have to depend on help from your phone company, your ISP, and the manufacturer of your communication equipment to configure your specific setup.

Checking for Connectivity to and from the Server

Once your server is operational and connected to the Internet, you should test the connectivity prior to announcing your server. One way to test your server is to use it as a client to surf the Web. Using Internet Explorer, you should attempt to connect to other Web sites, FTP sites, and Gopher sites, and you should try to "ping" other Internet servers from your Internet server. Ping is a utility that attempts to make a connection with another computer by sending a packet of information and keeps track of the amount of time it takes to make the connection. If the ping is successful, you will receive a message to that effect on your command-line prompt. In order to ping, you should go to a command prompt and type the command PING *hostname*; for example, PING *www.guiware.com*.

The other method for testing connectivity is to attempt to connect to your Internet server from the outside. Use a friend's computer, or find some other way to get outside access to the Internet, and then try to ping your server and get access to your Internet services.

Setting Up Backup and Basic Fault Tolerance

In Chapter 3, we recommended that everyone use backup and that you purchase a SCSI tape drive as your backup device. Once again, to avoid the possibility of massive frustration, we advise that you acquire a backup device that is on the HCL. Follow the directions that come with this device in order to hook it up to your machine. Then install the drivers within Windows NT Server.

We recommended previously that only those who are really concerned about the possibility of downtime use fault tolerance, specifically disk mirroring. Disk mirroring maintains a redundant copy of your data on a separate disk to protect you from the possibility of losing your data due to disk failure. You must have two disks to set up disk mirroring, and the disk that is to act as the mirror must have at least the same capacity as the original disk.

Installing Backup

1. Open Tape Devices in Control Panel.

2. Choose the Detect button. The system will attempt to detect your tape device. If successful, you will see the name of your device in the dialog box.

3. If for some reason the system is unable to auto-detect your device, you can install it manually. Select the Drivers tab, choose Add, and select your tape device from the list. Choose Have Disk if you have a vendor-supplied driver disk.

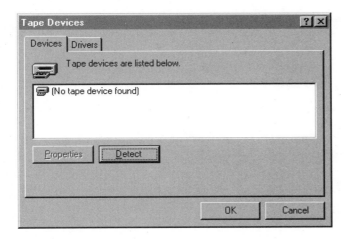

Running Backup

1. Launch Backup from the Administrative Tools program group. You will see all the drives that you are connected to.

2. If you want to back up an entire drive, select the check box that corresponds to that drive.

3. If you want to back up only specific directories or files, double-click on the drive where the directories or files are found and use the disk tree to select the resources that you want to back up.

4. When you have finished selecting the resources that you want to back up, choose the Backup button.

5. Follow the prompts to name the backup set, and choose the OK button to start the backup.

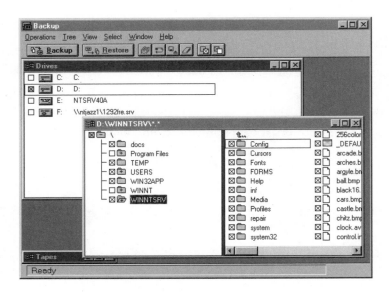

NOTE: The built-in backup software for NT can reliably back up only the local machine and not multiple machines on your network. If you want a network backup solution, you should look at one of the several third-party backup solutions for Windows NT Server.

Creating a Disk Mirror

1. To establish a mirror set, launch Disk Administrator from the Administrative Tools program group.

2. Highlight the partition you wish to mirror.

3. Hold down the Control (Ctrl) key, and highlight free, unpartitioned space on the second disk.

4. Select Establish Mirror from the Fault Tolerance menu.

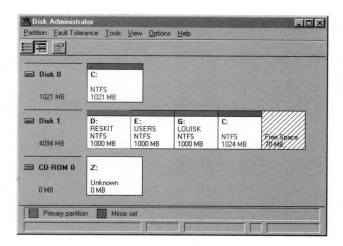

In the Event of a Disk Failure

To make use of the mirrored partition, you must first break the mirror set that you created.

1. Launch the Disk Administrator from the Administrative Tools program group.

2. Highlight the mirrored partition, and choose Break Mirror from the Fault Tolerance menu.

3. Exit Disk Administrator, and reboot Windows NT Server.

Mirroring Your Boot Partition

Your boot partition is a special case because, in order to activate a mirrored partition, you must be able to run Disk Administrator, which would require Windows NT Server to boot. There is a process to create a boot floppy to handle this situation. Refer to the Concepts and Planning Guide in the Windows NT Server documentation for more details.

Additional Internet-Related Software

Installing IIS and configuring Windows NT Server for the Internet gives you a limited number of Internet services that you can have on your site. If you want to expand the functionality of your Internet presence with the addition of databases, e-mail, WAIS, or other Internet services that are not included in IIS, you need to install additional software for those services.

Microsoft SQL Server

If you want any kind of forms, surveys, transactions, or dynamic data shown to your WWW users as part of your Internet site, you need to have a database to act as a repository for the information. The best choice for your database needs would be Microsoft SQL Server. Since IIS is designed to interface with SQL Server, it is the most reliable database that you can use for your Internet needs. IIS is able to access data in a Microsoft SQL Server database without requiring that you write code. It is also fairly easy to install if you follow the documentation that comes with it. We highly recommend the use of SQL Server to extend the functionality of your Internet site.

E-mail

In addition to the other services you have installed on your Internet server, you might also want e-mail so that you can communicate with users and customers. Your users could want to send you e-mail regarding any problems that they have with your Internet site, or you might use e-mail as a way for users to order products or ask you questions. As your site becomes more advanced, or if you become an IPP, you might want to rent e-mail boxes to other users or provide feedback accounts for your WWW customers.

Several e-mail systems are available for Windows NT Server. Shop around and ask some questions about different features and the way that they operate. The two e-mail systems that Microsoft has available are Microsoft Exchange Server, which is the most advanced e-mail system, and MAILSRV.

In addition to standard e-mail functions, Microsoft Exchange Server provides a rich set of features, including public folders, workgroup productivity, and links to other applications, such as Microsoft SQL Server. If you are looking for a high-end mail system that can handle a lot of traffic and provide more than simple mail services, you might want this system.

MAILSRV, which is part of the Windows NT Resource Kit, is a very basic mail system that lets you send and receive mail only. It uses POP3 and SMTP as its communication protocols and requires the use of a POP3-compliant client such as the Exchange Inbox that is found in the Windows family of operating systems. In order to send and receive mail on your Windows NT Server, you should use the Exchange client with the Internet mail service that comes with Windows NT Server. MAILSRV is very easy to install, and almost no maintenance is required.

We won't go through the installation process for setting up e-mail because the installation routine depends on the e-mail server you use. Refer to the documentation that comes with the e-mail system that you choose.

Windows NT Resource Kit

The Windows NT Resource Kit is a collection of books and software that provides detailed technical information and utilities to support and enhance Windows NT Server. Besides MAILSRV, the Resource Kit also includes a Telnet service; a WAIS (Z39.50) search engine and the WAISTOOL used to create the index for searching; and a new tool called dbWeb that allows you to quickly publish SQL Server databases on the WWW. This is just a smattering of what you'll find in the Resource Kit. We highly recommend that you purchase Windows NT Server Resource Kit version 4.0 and any updates; it's the most comprehensive body of work available about Windows NT Server.

What's Next

Now that the construction of your Internet server is complete, you need to address the security of your Internet site. The next chapter walks you through the various security issues and gives you suggestions about how to address them. Security is one of the most important aspects that you need to consider for your Internet server.

5 Hands Off My Hard Disk

Yes, you guessed it. This chapter deals with security. Security in relation to your Internet server is a very complex topic. Not only do you need to think about guarding the information on your server from those who have direct access to it, but you also have to think about safeguarding your information from Internet users. If you are planning on doing financial transactions over the Internet or if you are sending any kind of confidential information over the Net, then you need to secure that information, too.

In this chapter, we discuss some of the possible threats to your system and how to circumvent them. Further, we show you how to implement the security features built into Windows NT Server, along with other security technologies, in order to secure your Internet site.

Do I Really Need to Take Security Measures?

If you have only a single home computer, you might not have thought a lot about the topic of security because you really haven't had to. Maybe you implemented some basic security measures to keep certain confidential information out of the kids' hands, like Santa's Christmas shopping list, but other than that, you probably haven't had to worry too much about protecting the data on your machine. The system is fairly closed, and therefore, no big security risk exists. The more people who have access to your system, however, the more at risk you become. If you have any organization, even a small business, in which a number of people access your server, or if you are connected to a LAN, security then becomes a significant issue. You need to think about the risks posed by all the people who have physical access to your computer. Still, while it is a real concern if someone in your organization accidentally deletes a file, say, the exposure you face is probably limited.

From a security standpoint, the Internet is a hostile environment. The number of people who could access your system and damage it either on purpose or by mistake increases dramatically. The risk of loss is even greater if you want to conduct financial transactions or if you deal with any kind of sensitive or confidential information.

Actually, you can't even install Windows NT Server without enabling some basic security measures, but there are other steps that you should take to provide the best protection you can. Our intent in this chapter is not to instill security paranoia. The odds of someone breaking into your system and wreaking havoc in one way or another are actually quite low. But nonetheless, the risks should not be ignored.

Just Whom Do I Need to Protect My Server from Anyway?

Human risks to your system come in many forms and can be intentional or unintentional. The potential result from any person's harmful actions is the loss of valuable information on your server.

We've all heard news stories about hackers gaining access to important information by breaking through computer security systems. Many hackers can be described as intelligent but bored people who try to break into computer systems for the fun and challenge of it. Most hacking on the Internet results in just plain and simple vandalism. Getting past a security system is like a game for these people—the challenge lies in seeing how far into a given system they can get and, for some, the more difficult the security, the more compelling the game. Once hackers crack your system, they are free to muck about with anything you have on your server. Better-mannered hackers may leave merely a signature file just to let you know they've been there. Others leave more destructive calling cards, like viruses, or in extreme, really pathological cases, they might leave you with nothing left on your server at all. The malice in this is beyond us to explain—we simply want to help you protect your site from it.

Most hacking is done just for hacking's sake, but sometimes hackers turn criminal, breaking into systems for the purpose of theft and financial gain. Hackers that cross this line are referred to as *crackers;* they are looking for specific information, like credit card and bank account numbers. For these thieves, breaking into a secure system is not a game but a serious business, so they may have an arsenal of sophisticated tools and software as a means of gaining access.

You might think you have covered all the security bases by restricting access to your computer from outside your organization. Think again. You must also consider the possibility of enemies within your system. A disgruntled employee can pose an enormous risk. Vandalism of a company's computer can be a great method of revenge for people who feel they have been mistreated or who have been fired from your organization. Less dramatic, but potentially just as devastating, are the risks of accidental deletion of information by trustworthy people or employees. Anyone who has ever worked on a computer has probably had the exhilarating experience of accidentally losing information at some point or another. People are human and mistakes happen. The bottom line is that no matter who has access to your servers, your information must be protected.

How Do They Get In?

Most commonly, hackers study your system and look for any area of weakness. Common security weaknesses include holes in your system from improperly configured software that they can slip through, passwords that can be easily discovered, or information traveling across wires that can be intercepted. Your first job in implementing security is to analyze the weaknesses of your particular system. Let's consider some of the common ways that systems are penetrated.

Improperly configured software can leave holes in your security that a clever hacker can easily discover. If, for instance, you accidentally set up a user account with no password, you are essentially leaving an open door to your system. You should take the time to read the Windows NT Server documentation and really learn how security works.

In rare cases, software can contain security holes that are a result of design flaws or bugs, and hackers make it their business to keep abreast of these. When security bugs are discovered by hackers, that information is disseminated very quickly around the Internet, so it is generally a good idea to keep information about your specific server and software confidential. If a hacker knows specifically what system you are using to run your Internet presence, then the hacker can aim an informed attack at that system.

People commonly protect information and access to their computers by setting up authentication procedures using passwords. This may seem virtually foolproof, and, if used properly, it is. But no system is totally uncrackable. Hackers have methods and tools to discover passwords. For example, a hacker can launch a *dictionary attack* by using software on the hacking computer to try continually to log on to the target server using effectively each word in the dictionary as a password. It could eventually hit on the right word. Another method hackers use to discover passwords is to study any personal information available about you on the network. This often leads to the discovery of a password because many people use personal information, like children's or spouse's names or birthdates, as passwords.

Another tool used to steal information is a *packet analyzer,* also referred to as a *sniffer.* This tool, legitimately used, helps track problems in routing and performance on the Internet. Hackers, however, use packet sniffers to view the contents of packets going across the network, hoping to gain exploitable information from them. You need to be aware that whenever you send information in clear text form over the Net, you face the risk that this information could be intercepted. This is very similar to the risk you take using a wireless telephone. Anyone can be listening at any time, although it is not very likely. Just as some people give out credit card numbers over wireless telephones, you will have to calculate the risk yourself of sending sensitive information over the Internet, or you will have to consider some other way of sending the information.

One of the reasons that Internet security is such a problem is that there is no central Internet authority. This makes it fairly easy for smart individuals to fool the system into thinking they are someone they are not, an attack method known as *spoofing.* Also, it is often impossible to trace hackers on the Internet.

All this said, though, it is our opinion that the media has exaggerated the prevalence of cybercriminals and hackers. Incidents of hackers successfully breaking into computer systems are actually rare and usually occur because of improperly configured security settings.

Managing Security
Using Windows NT Server

Compared to other operating systems, Windows NT Server has one of the best security systems on the market. Microsoft proudly touts the fact that they designed security into Windows NT Server from the ground up, enabling a higher level of security than operating systems that were designed with security as an afterthought. In fact, Windows NT Server takes into account security scenarios that most people won't even think of.

The Administrator Account

To administer Windows NT Server security, you have to either take on the job of security administration yourself or appoint someone within your organization to be the security administrator. The security administrator carries out the security policies that you deem appropriate for your organization. The administrator needs to configure security for Windows NT Server and continually maintain security by tracking and auditing the system.

When you install Windows NT Server, a default account called *Administrator* is created that has full access to the system. You can use this account for security administration, or you can create a separate account with administrative privileges. The structure you choose for administering security depends very much on the size and nature of your organization, as does your security policy. If your organization consists only of a handful of people whom you trust and who all understand your goals for security, you might give everyone administrative privileges. If your organization is larger and you find it is necessary to keep some users out of certain areas of the system, you can have single or multiple administrators and set up other users with appropriately more restricted access. Windows NT Server gives you flexibility in the way you delegate security administration for your organization.

The Administrator account has pretty much complete access to the system, and, for this reason, it can be dangerous if someone compromises the security of this account. We recommend taking the following precautions to protect this account.

First, assign a new user name to it, something that will not make it recognizable as the Administrator account. Don't use the names Admin or Root—pick something unique that other people won't think of. Because of the high degree of access the Administrator account has, it is a likely target of hackers, so you might as well make it difficult for them to find the account in the first place. Second, be just as careful about choosing the password to the Administrator account. Remember the basic password guidelines: don't use your name, birthday, or other personal information as your password. Servers have been broken into because the Webmaster (someone who should know better) used a password that the hacker discovered from the Webmaster's personal blurb on their Web page.

To rename the Administrator account, follow these steps:

1. Launch User Manager For Domains. (You can find it on the Administrative Tools submenu.)

2. Highlight the username Administrator, and then select the Rename option from the User menu.

3. Type in the new name when the Rename dialog box appears. (See Figure 5-1.)

4. Choose OK.

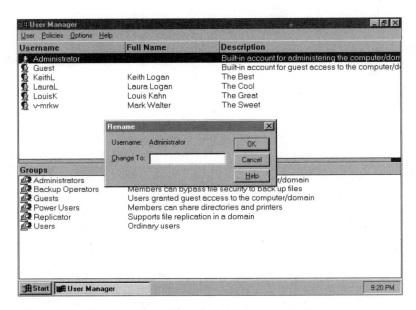

Figure 5-1. *How to rename the Administrator account.*

Managing Multiple Users

If you have multiple user accounts on your system, the best way to manage their security and access to the system is to create user groups. Windows NT Server allows you to group users and apply security to each group. You might want to create groups to represent different departments in your organization or users who need access to a specific directory, but you can use any logical criteria for grouping.

As a member of a group, a user has the same security access as all other members of the group, although a single user can belong to more than one group. Access to files, directories, and other resources can be set for the entire group. To give new users access to a resource, simply make them members of the group that already has access to the resource. It is easier to keep track of the security permissions assigned to a small number of groups than to keep track of those assigned to a large number of users.

To create a group, follow these steps:

1. Launch User Manager For Domains, and select New Global Group from the User menu.

NOTE: Windows NT Server has two types of groups: Global and Local. Refer to the Windows NT Server documentation for more details on the differences between Global and Local groups.

---

2. Enter the name of the group and, if you want, a description. See Figure 5-2.

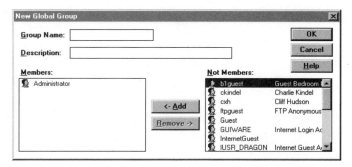

Figure 5-2. *New Global Group dialog box.*

3. Select the user or users you would like to make members of the new group from the list on the right, and click the Add button.

4. Conversely, you can select specific users in the list on the left and remove them from the group by clicking the Remove button.

User Accounts for Access from the Internet

You don't need to set up user accounts for basic access to public information on your Internet server. But if you have areas on your Internet server that you want to restrict access to, such as a subscription service, an employees-only section, or private membership areas, you can create single- or multiple-user accounts. You can either create one user account for this purpose where these special users would all log on using the same user account name and password, or you can give an account to each user, allowing each to log on with a unique account name and individual password. Do what makes sense to you. Keep in mind, though, that the more user accounts you create, the harder it becomes to keep track of who has access to various resources.

You must be absolutely certain when you create user accounts for access from the Internet that you give them security access for only the information that you want them to have. This probably sounds like a no-brainer, but when you allow any access to your server from the Internet, you should be extremely careful.

Individual accounts for Internet users should not be included in the Domain Users group. You should make these accounts members of some other group (perhaps Domain Guests or just Guests) and then set that new group to be the primary group to which individuals belong. After you have set a new primary group, remove the accounts from the Domain Users group. This sounds kind of mixed up, but there is good reason for that. Windows NT Server won't allow the removal of a user from a group if that group is selected as the primary group for that user, so you have to reassign the primary group before you can remove it. By default, Windows NT Server makes the Domain Users group the primary group for all new users.

To create a new user account, follow these steps:

1. Launch User Manager For Domains, and select New User from the User menu.

2. Fill in the requested data for the new user account. See Figure 5-3.

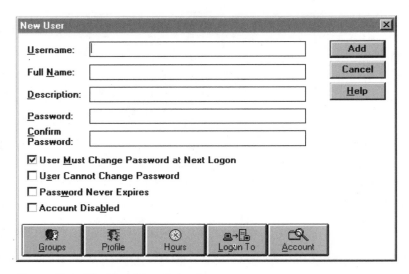

Figure 5-3. *The New User dialog box.*

3. To change group membership, click the Groups button. Make sure you don't put the user in a group that would give him or her more security access than the user needs or you intend.

4. Remove the user from the Domain Users group. Remember, you first have to make the user a member of another group. We suggest choosing Domain Guests, which has very little security access to the system. (The Domain Users group gets some default security settings that you might not want an Internet user to have.)

5. Highlight Domain Guests (or whichever group you chose), and click the Set Primary Group button.

6. Now you can remove the user from the Domain Users group by high-lighting the Domain Users group and clicking the Remove button.

7. Give the user access to any other group you want by highlighting the group name and clicking the Add button.

After you have created a new user account, you might want to set any specific file or folder access for that user. We will discuss security for files and folders later in this chapter.

Maintaining User Accounts

We recommend that you go through User Manager at least once a month to look at both individual user accounts and group memberships so that you can delete or disable accounts that are no longer needed. Keeping the number of accounts on your system down to a bare minimum will help ensure that your system is not left vulnerable to attack and will keep the server easier for you to manage. The more accounts you have on your system, the more likely it is that a hacker will be able to find a poorly secured user account.

Guest Accounts

Windows NT Server creates a default Guest account when you first install the software. Windows NT Server version 4 automatically disables that Guest account. In earlier versions, the Guest account was not disabled, which made it possible for an unknown user to be authenticated as a guest automatically. We recommend that you leave the Guest account disabled. If you want to create guestlike accounts, create a new account instead, to prevent unintentional access through the settings that are automatically given to the Guest user account.

Identification and Authentication

The primary way to control access to your server is by establishing a process for identification and authentication of users on the system. When you use your bank's ATM machine, you follow an identification and authentication procedure: you insert your ATM card into the machine and then enter a secret code or a PIN (personal identification number). This identifies to the ATM who you are and what account you have access to. Identification and authentication for users of your Internet server is not much different.

Windows NT Server automatically implements identification and authentication. When you set up a user account, you are also required to choose a password that will be the user's form of authentication. You can further configure your system to set limits regarding when users can have access to the system, when they will need to change their passwords, how long they can keep a certain password, and other settings.

Windows NT Server supports basic authentication as well as Windows NT Challenge/Response. Basic authentication asks the user for a username and password and transmits that information in clear text format across the Internet. This can cause a potential security problem if someone is using monitoring software to view the packets. Windows NT Challenge/Response, on the other hand, acquires the username and password information from the operating system. The user's computer tells the server which user account the user logged onto at the workstation. The advantage to this method of authentication is that users are not required to enter their usernames and passwords when they try to access a private area. The server checks against information at the workstation to authenticate the user automatically. The drawback to this method is that it does not work with operating systems other than Windows 95 and Windows NT Workstation, and it doesn't work with browsers other than Internet Explorer 2 or later. In addition, many people might find that the user account they log onto at their workstation will be different from the user account on the Internet Information Server (IIS).

IIS allows you to choose the methods by which it will authenticate users. We recommend that you use basic authentication for areas that are private but don't contain sensitive information. Windows NT Challenge/Response should be used in environments where you know the users can log onto their workstations using the same identification as that used on your server.

Setting User Properties

Windows NT Server allows you to set certain parameters regarding passwords on user accounts. By configuring user and machine policies, you can set password restrictions to determine whether users will be allowed to change passwords, how often they will need to change them, and the minimum length for passwords. You can also set a feature called *account lockout* that disables the account after a given number of failed authentication attempts. It is very important to understand the options available before you make choices about the password user properties you will set.

HOW TO SET USER AND MACHINE POLICIES FOR SECURITY

Follow these steps to set your security policies:

1. Launch User Manager For Domains.

2. Select Account from the Policies menu.

3. In the Account Policy dialog box, set the specific Password Restrictions. See Figure 5-4.

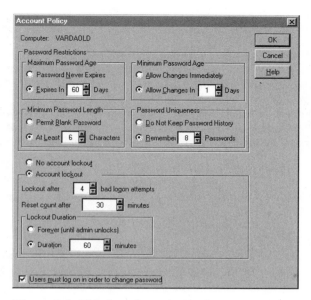

Figure 5-4. *This is perhaps the single most important dialog box for protecting your system from would-be hackers.*

RECOMMENDATIONS FOR USER AND MACHINE POLICIES FOR SECURITY

◆ The Maximum Password Age is the maximum length of time a user may use the same password. We recommend that you allow users to keep a password for no more than 60 days.

◆ The Minimum Password Age refers to the minimum length of time that a user must have a new password before being allowed to change it again. Normally, you can set this to allow changes immediately.

◆ The Minimum Password Length refers to the minimum numbers of characters that a password can have. We strongly recommend against allowing passwords to be blank. A safe minimum length would be six characters, but the more the better.

◆ The Password Uniqueness option can be used to keep people from reusing the same password. This option forces them to choose a password they've never used before for a specified number of times. When a user has changed her password this many times, she can repeat the sequence of former passwords if she chooses. Our recommendation is that you put the Password Uniqueness setting to at least eight.

- Account Lockout is a very important feature, and we recommend that you enable it. This feature monitors the number of invalid logon attempts and locks the account if the number of attempts exceeds the parameters you chose. You must allow for the possibility that from time to time a user forgets a password or types it incorrectly, so we recommend that you set the number of bad logon attempts before lockout to four. You must also choose a length of time to reset the count. We recommend thirty minutes for this option. The lockout duration is the amount of time an account that is locked out remains locked out. You should set this to be at least one hour.

- The final security option is a check box allowing you to determine whether users must log on in order to change their passwords. We highly recommend that you select this option.

Rules for Choosing Passwords

Anyone who has access to your computer should be made aware of some basic rules for creating passwords. The following is a list of guidelines to follow in choosing passwords.

- As a general rule, don't allow password changes over the Internet; they could be intercepted.

- Never allow passwords to be blank. This defeats the whole purpose of authentication.

- Never use as your password your name, your spouse's name, the names of your children, your birthday, anniversary, or any other information about yourself that could be publicly available.

- To foil the hacker who uses the dictionary approach, create passwords that are not real words. Mixing numerals and punctuation marks with letters makes passwords even more difficult to crack.

- The longer the password the better. We recommend that you use at least six characters.

- Change your password frequently, at least every sixty days, even if the security settings for your system don't force you to change it that often.

- Never write your password down, and never give it out to anyone. If you absolutely can't remember your password without writing it down, for heaven's sake, don't label it "password" and don't store it anywhere near your computer.

◆ Never send passwords across the Internet. Someone could always be "listening."

It's a fine line between making user accounts and passwords that no one can remember and making them secure enough that your system is protected, but with common sense (and trial and error), you can protect your system without making it too hard to use.

Choosing User Account Names

Similar rules should apply in choosing user account names as in choosing passwords. Someone trying to break into your system by getting past your authentication will have to choose an account to target, so you don't want your account names to be obvious. For instance, if a hacker knows that a "Bill Smith" has an account on your server, he may start his attack with the username *Bsmith* or *BillS*. If this is the formula you actually use to create names for your user accounts, then a hacker will be one step closer to getting into your system. You may want to give this employee a username like *BillS1*. This might seem like security overkill, but it is an easy way of making your system a little more secure.

More Security Measures for Limiting Access to Your Server

When you install Windows NT Server, certain default security settings are activated that might not be appropriate for someone with a presence on the Internet. One setting that you will need to change is the ability for users to do remote management of your server. Having remote access allows a user to monitor certain functions of the server over the Internet. In the wrong hands, this tool could provide information about the various services running on the server, the processor power and the kind of processor, the amount of memory on the machine, and pretty much all the details about the type of machine and the services it is running. A smart hacker, knowing this much about your system, could use known holes in your software to gain access or could know exactly what it would take to overload your server.

Here's how to remove remote management capabilities:

1. Launch User Manager For Domains.

2. Select User Rights from the Policies menu. See Figure 5-5 on the following page.

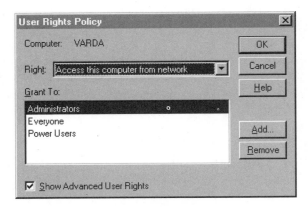

Figure 5-5. *The User Rights Policy dialog box.*

3. Select the Show Advanced User Rights option at the bottom of the dialog box.

4. Using the drop-down list of user rights, select each right, one by one, and make sure that the users who have been given this right do not include Everyone, Guests, or Domain Guests.

5. When you have gone through all the user rights, click the OK button.

NOTE: Pay special attention to the rights about the shutdown commands and accessing the computer from the network. These are very important user rights that very few users should have.

Using Firewalls to Block Access to Your Network

Firewalls apply only to users who have a network of computers rather than just a single server to protect. If you have a network hooked up to the Internet, a firewall is a device that you could implement in order to protect your network from unauthorized access. It acts as a semipermeable barrier that allows only packets of information meeting specific criteria to pass through. The firewall sits in between your network and the Internet and filters traffic to your network. The firewall evaluates all packets coming in and checks them against a list of packet types and source and destination information to determine whether the packet is safe. This effectively blocks potential hackers from accessing anything on the other side of the firewall. The criteria for access are configured by the administrator. If you have an Internet server, it needs to be on the outside of the firewall.

This solution is still not foolproof. There are ways to hack into a firewall. Since firewalls are based on authentication, if someone can crack a password he can get past a firewall. For ultimate foolproof protection, you should not load the TCP/IP protocol on the non-Internet servers on your network, especially if your servers contain sensitive information. That way, if someone actually manages to get past the firewall and into your network, the invader won't be able to access anything on your servers because the machines won't be speaking the same language. See Figure 5-6.

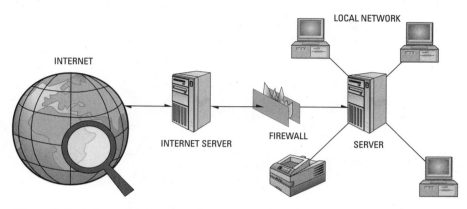

Figure 5-6. *A firewall between an Internet server and a network.*

Event and Audit Logs

Windows NT Server has a logging system that keeps track of all events that happen on your system, including hardware problems, driver problems, network problems, and others. There is also an audit log that, when activated, keeps track of who accessed what files and when. Although the auditing system may sound like a very useful feature, it has a considerable drawback in that it adversely affects the performance of your machine. If you activate auditing, it will slow your system down by approximately 30 percent, so we do not recommend using it.

As an alternative to auditing, the IIS has Web and FTP logs that should provide sufficient information for your needs. The IIS log tracks the IP addresses of all users who access your server, whether they logged on with a user account, and which pages they accessed.

Setting Security for Directories and Files

Windows NT security allows you to set access permissions on files and directories to protect them from unauthorized use by specific users or user groups. When you are authenticated on the server, the procedure creates a *token* that is used to identify you for security purposes throughout the system. The token carries with it a unique identification number for you and a list of all the groups of which you are a member. When you attempt to access a file, the token is checked against the permissions that are set on that file to see whether you or any of the groups that you belong to have access to the file and the level of access that you have. If your token matches the permissions, you will get access to the file.

Setting Permissions

The next few sets of procedures tell you how to set, deny, or change user access to files and folders.

1. Double-click the My Computer icon on your desktop, and double-click the icon of the hard disk to which you want to apply security. See Figure 5-7.

2. Search through the folder icons until you get to the folder or file on which you wish to set security, and highlight that file or folder.

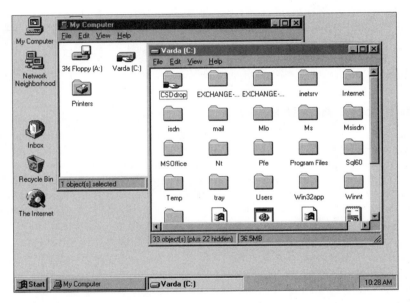

Figure 5-7. *Using Windows Explorer to find a file you want to set permissions for.*

3. Click the right mouse button once to open the context menu for the file or folder, and select Properties from this menu. See Figure 5-8.

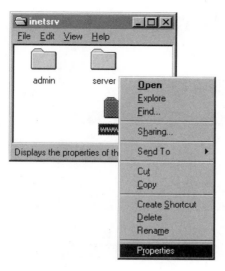

Figure 5-8. *The context menu on a directory.*

4. Choose the Security tab, and click the Permissions button.

5. If you selected a file, you will see a dialog box similar to the one in Figure 5-9. If you selected a folder, you will see a dialog box similar to the one in Figure 5-10 on the next page. Both of these dialog boxes display the current security settings for the file or folder.

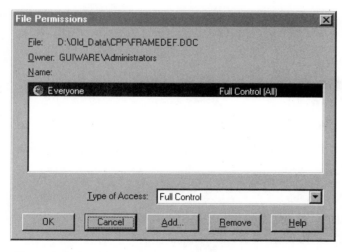

Figure 5-9. *Security permissions for a file.*

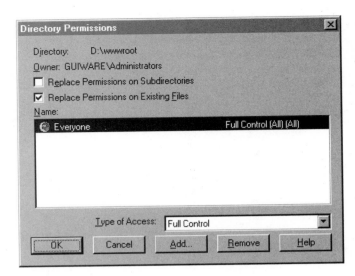

Figure 5-10. *Security permissions for a directory.*

If you want to remove access for a user or a group for this file or folder, then highlight the username in the list shown. Click the Remove button.

If you want to change a user or a group's permission, highlight the username or group name and choose from the drop-down list at the bottom of the dialog box to set the new security for this user or group.

If you want to add a user or a group to those who have access to a file or folder, follow these steps:

1. Click the Add button. This will display the Add Users And Groups dialog box. See Figure 5-11.

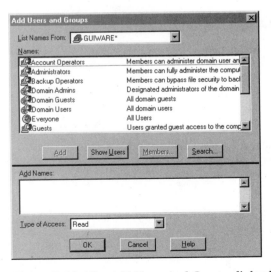

Figure 5-11. *The Add Users And Groups dialog box.*

2. Then select the user or group to whom you want to grant access by high-lighting the group or username. Click the Add button.

NOTE: In order to see individual users, you must click the Show Users button. Otherwise you will see only groups listed here.

---

3. Go to the drop-down list box at the bottom of the dialog box, and choose the security level you wish to provide. This security setting will apply to all the users and groups you selected to add.

If you are changing permissions for a file, that is all there is to it, and you can click OK. But if you are setting permissions for a folder, you need to decide about two more options:

◆ The first option is Replace Permissions On Subdirectories. Choosing this option depends on whether you want this security change to affect all subdirectories that are inside of the subdirectory or folder you are working on now. In most cases, you will choose this option, but you will need to decide that for your individual case.

◆ The second option is Replace Permissions On Existing Files. We recommend that you leave this option checked so that your change affects any other files that already exist in your subdirectory. That way, old and new files will have the same security setting.

Don't Lock Yourself Out

You should be careful about how you set file security so as not to lock yourself out of your own drive by removing all permissions on the file or folder in question. If you do this, it is very difficult to get back in. You will have to reinstall Windows NT Server and reset security on the drive by using the security editor. Of course, if you made backups of your data, you can always recover from this kind of accident.

NOTE: Protect your non-Internet files from the IIS account. When you install IIS, it creates a user account that IIS uses to gain access to your server. Access to files from this account constitute what will be your publicly accessible Web pages. Any areas of either your private Internet site or content that you don't want on your Internet site at all should be protected from this user account.

Setting Permissions on Non-Internet Files

Before you set specific security for files, you should change the security permissions for the root directories of your NTFS drives. By default, Windows NT assigns the group Everyone with Full Control in the root. For a workstation, especially if it's not connected to a network, this setting would likely be acceptable, but for an Internet server or any other network machine, you need to change this setting. Specifically, you need to remove Full Control from Everyone at the root directory. When you do this, make sure you select the option to Replace Permissions On Subdirectories. This ensures that the security you set at the root will apply to the entire drive.

If you set permissions first on directory files and then set permissions on your directories starting at the root, your file permission settings would be overwritten. For this reason, we recommend that you set the standard permissions on directories first, and then set permissions for individual files if you need to.

NOTE: Files or folders on Windows NT Server inherit the security permissions from their parent directory. If you have a folder with a certain level of security, any file that you have in that folder will take on the same permission.

Glossary of Security Settings

Following are the security settings that you can apply to files and directories with explanations of the amount of access that they give. The first seven permissions listed here should meet the security needs for nearly all cases. The last two that we mention are for the advanced user or security professionals.

NO ACCESS This setting removes all access to the selected file or folder for the specified user or group. Normally you would not need to set this permission in order to keep users out of a directory. A user would not have access to a specific resource unless security was configured incorrectly. This setting removes any access to the file/folder that the user might have been granted by virtue of access to the parent directory.

LIST This setting applies to a folder only. When applied, List permission allows the user or group to see the names of all the files and folders that are inside the specified folder. If List permission is turned off, users will not be able to see the contents of the folder. If, however, users know the name of a file within the folder file, they would not be prevented from accessing this file unless another permission has been set to prevent them from seeing it.

READ This setting gives the user or group permission to access the contents of the folder or the files in the folder. If Read permission is not set, the resource is not accessible for viewing.

ADD Add permission can be applied to a folder only, and it gives the user or group the ability to create new files and folders inside the specific folder.

Setting Permissions for Public Internet Files

When you set up IIS, you were asked to pick a directory or folder to act as your root folder. We suggested that you call it WWWROOT. This is the home or root directory for your Internet site. In order for the Web files to be public, IUSR_*machinename* must have access to the root. (This is the user account the system uses to access data when it doesn't have details about the user.) When you installed IIS, you were asked where to place your WWWROOT folder; this is the default root for your Web server. You were also asked where to place Gopher and FTP files, if you selected those services. The setup process by default created the IUSR_*machinename* account and gave it permissions to these default folders. As you create your subdirectories under these root directories and as you add virtual directories to your root, you want to make sure that all areas are also accessible by the IUSR_*machinename* user.

To set up files on your Internet server, we recommend that you design and implement a directory tree structure. See Figure 5-12 on the following page. For example, if you have multiple Web sites, you might have a different directory for each one. Inside each directory would be subdirectories for logical categories like images, HTML documents, and forms.

ADD & READ   Add & Read permission applies to folders only. This setting is just a quicker way to apply the Add permission and the Read permission to a user or group. There is no difference between giving a user add and read rights using this option or using the individual permissions.

CHANGE   This security setting allows the user or group to modify an existing file or the files in a folder. With this permission, a user can overwrite or erase the contents of the file. Extreme care should be given to consideration of who should get this permission, since, in the wrong hands, Change permission can result in loss of data.

FULL CONTROL   This security setting gives the user or group all access rights that are available for the file or folder. Extreme care should be given for this security permission. Only administrators should be given this kind of access. A user with this level of permission can not only change or erase the file or folder in question but also change the security on it and lock out legitimate users.

SPECIAL DIRECTORY ACCESS   This security setting applies to folders only. It allows you to get to a lower level of security than you could get to with the previously mentioned security settings and set more specific rights. We recommend you do not use this option, unless you are experienced with Windows NT Server security, since these settings are easy to interpret. For more details, see the Windows NT Server documentation.

SPECIAL FILE ACCESS   Special File Access is similar to Special Directory Access but, as indicated in the title, applies to files rather than directories. It allows you to set lower level permissions on file access. Please consult the Windows NT Server documentation before applying any of this option's security permissions.

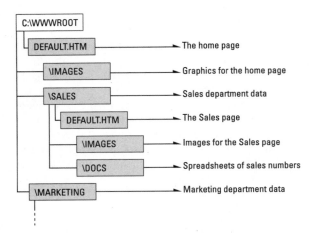

Figure 5-12. *A possible directory tree structure for a Web server.*

To set security permissions for your Internet site, you should go through the directory structure and make sure that all directories that are going to contain public data intended for all Internet users are readable by the IUSR_*machinename* user. For files that you wish to make publicly available, you should make sure that the IUSR_*machinename* user account has at least Read permissions in the areas of the WWWROOT directory tree. If this user account doesn't have Read access to a directory, the IIS treats that directory as a private area and requires additional authentication from the user.

We do not recommend that you give the IUSR_*machinename* account access higher than Read in areas where you would not want the end user to possibly erase, change, or delete files. The only place your users might need to have Write access is in an FTP upload directory or for some kind of form that needs to be written to the disk after the user has filled it out.

NOTE: If you do use forms, we recommend that you send them to a database like SQL Server or Access.

Private Internet Files

Sometimes you might need to create private areas on your Internet site that only certain people can access. This might be for a special pay-for-use area, a members-only area, or some private/sensitive data such as financial or medical information that should be accessible only to the correct user. In order to set this up, you would first verify that the IUSR_*machinename* account has no access to the private data. Then you would create user accounts for the people whom you want to have access to the private areas and give them appropriate permissions.

After you set up your private user account or accounts, you need to provide access to the directories for those user accounts. We recommend that you create a user group to represent each secure file area and either make user accounts members or remove them from the membership in order to control access. That way, you need to set file security only once for the group, and you can manage the membership list of the group rather than the many levels of file security that could come about as time goes on.

An IPP might want to set up private areas to allow users to update their own personal Web spaces themselves. You can create this ability by setting up special directories that the FTP server can access and creating a user account for each Web customer. You would give them Change access to the directory that corresponds to their private Web space. Then create a virtual directory for the Web server and include that private folder in the Web directory space. In this way, Web customers can use FTP to update and add to their own private areas and not be able to change any other areas.

Using a Drop Box

A drop box gives users the ability to send you files without allowing others to view that information. A drop box is like a mailbox: you can put things in, but you can't get them back out, and you can't see the contents of the mailbox. Drop boxes are useful places to privately hand off information from one user to another. For example, a user could send you a new program, but, until you verify that it is virus-free, you don't want to make it available to download. Drop boxes are also useful for an FTP site, where you might want to allow users to send you files without allowing those users to see the contents of the directory where they drop off the files.

In order to set up a drop box, follow these steps:

1. First make sure the directory is in the virtual or physical root for IIS. You can do this by using the Internet Server Manager.

2. In Windows Explorer, right-click the folder that represents the drop box and choose Properties. Select the Security tab.

3. Click the Permissions button. Then remove access to this folder for everyone except administrators.

4. Add the Internet Information Server user account, which is typically called IUSR_*machinename*. Give it Read access.

5. Highlight the username, and select Special Directory Access. Uncheck Read and Execute, and add Write.

6. Select Special File Access, uncheck Read and Execute, and select Write. Make sure that Replace Permissions On Subdirectories is selected, and then click OK.

Scripts and Security

Scripts extend the functionality of your Internet server. Basically, scripts are small programs that you can use to do common tasks such as send data entered on an HTML form to a SQL Server database, or send the latest stock prices to a user. Some common types of scripts are CGI (Common Gateway Interface) programs, ISAPI (Internet Server API) programs, and PERL scripts. Scripting is a very powerful ability, but there are some risks associated with running them. Since a script is actually a process or program running on your Internet server, it is possible that misbehaving code could cause problems. On top of that, if you support a scripting language like PERL, then it is possible that hackers could send their own rogue commands instead of your intended commands to do nasty things to your server, such as erase the hard disk.

Note:

Chapter 7 discusses scripting in more detail.

Windows NT Server and IIS have ways of limiting the exposure to the risks posed by scripts. There is a special permission you must set for a directory in order for IIS to actually execute commands or scripts from it. Without this setting, IIS won't launch these programs. Activating this setting is especially important if you allow users to update their own Web pages on a server. Also, it prevents someone from typing in a command and getting something to launch that shouldn't.

We strongly recommend against using PERL or other free-form scripting languages without serious consideration of the security risks. If you are not well versed in these scripting languages, don't use them on your Internet server.

Security Settings Specific to IIS

Note:

SSL and encryption will be discussed in more detail further on in this chapter.

When you specify directories and virtual directories, you can enable certain IIS security settings for the Web server. These are Read, Execute, and Require SSL. The Read option allows the contents of a specified directory to be transmitted over the Internet and viewed. The Execute option allows scripts and other programs in the directory to be executed by users of the Web server. The Execute setting should be assigned only to directories that contain the scripts you approve and should not be assigned to all directories. The SSL (Secure Sockets Layer) option allows you to specify encryption for a given resource when it is accessed over the Internet.

Unless you have acquired an SSL certificate, you won't be able to select this option. It is highly recommended that you do not give Read and Execute permissions to the same directory. A directory that contains scripts doesn't need Read, and a directory equipped with a Read permission shouldn't contain scripts. This applies an extra level of security to prevent hackers from discovering how your scripts work and trying to use that to help break into your system.

Communications Security

Whenever you send information over the Internet, or any network for that matter, there is a risk that the information will be intercepted. For most people hosting basic Internet sites, it hardly matters if more people see your stuff. If, however, you plan to perform electronic transactions or transmit any kind of sensitive matter over the Internet, be aware that someone might be monitoring and intercepting the data. For this reason, you should consider either implementing encryption to protect information as it is transmitted or using alternative methods for exchanging sensitive data, like the use of a financial clearing house.

Encryption and Certificates

People dealing with highly sensitive information often employ encryption to scramble the data so that it is unreadable unless you have a key to it. This does not prevent the packets from being intercepted and viewed, but it makes them unreadable and therefore useless.

Information is encrypted with the use of complicated mathematical algorithms. When the data is received by the intended recipient, it is reassembled in its original form using the key that deciphers the message. Encryption requires client and server software and requires both parties to have an agreed-upon method of coding the information.

When you send encrypted data, you need to be able to prove your identity to the receiver. One way to do this is to purchase a certificate from a trusted third party. The certificate provides a method to uniquely identify the sender. This is comparable to the certificate received when you purchase something like a rare piece of art. If you resell the art, you use the certificate to prove authenticity. The concept of a certificate has been implemented in the computer world to act as a kind of digital signature.

Certificates are usually assigned by an organization that is known and trusted as a certificate source. Certifiers determine that you are who you say you are and then assign a certificate in the form of a unique set of numbers that are known only to you. These numbers are used in the various encryption formulas to encrypt and decrypt your information and are known as keys. You use a private key to encrypt the data, and a public key is given to the people you communicate with and is used to decipher the information. Certificates provide a highly secure method of identifying the source of the information and protecting the data as it travels over the Internet.

Secure Sockets Layer (SSL)

SSL is a protocol used to encrypt data that is transmitted across the Internet. SSL runs on Internet Information Server. If you enable SSL, you can have a very secure site.

In order to use SSL, the first thing you must do is acquire a certificate. Once you have it, you can enter it into the IIS software by running SETKEY. SSL security slows down the server data transfer rates, so SSL is not usually set for an entire server but rather on specific directories. When you add a new virtual directory to the server, you can enable SSL by selecting the Requires SSL check box. You must make sure that you refer to any links from your nonencrypted data to the SSL-protected area with *https*:// rather than *http*://.

HOW TO GET AN SSL CERTIFICATE

Contact VeriSign to get a certificate. VeriSign is currently the only company that issues certificates for SSL. You will be required to send them some documentation to identify yourself, and you will need to purchase the certificate. At this time, the annual fee is $295.00. Refer to the URL *http://www.verisign.com/microsoft* in order to get the latest instructions for acquiring certificates.

Private Communications Technology (PCT)

PCT is an enhanced protocol very similar to SSL. The main advantage of PCT over SSL is that PCT encrypts your user authentication information with a different and more complex algorithm than is used for the data. This helps ensure that not only is the data protected, but the authentication information, which *must* be kept secret, is protected even more. You might wonder why you don't just apply the more secure encryption to all the data you send. Keep in mind that encryption requires a significant amount of processing power, so the stronger the encryption, the slower the system will become.

Secure Electronic Transactions (SET)

SET isn't so much a security protocol as it is a secure method of handling financial transactions. Some people are uneasy buying goods over the Internet, either because they are uncomfortable sending their credit card numbers and addresses over the Net or because they are unfamiliar with the vendors. When you use SET to purchase something from a vendor, SET sends a packet of information to your credit card company that includes information about the amount of the transaction and the vendor number. The vendor then receives a confirmation from the financial institution that the transaction has taken place and that the bank has a voucher for the money. Using SET, you never have to give your credit card to the merchant. While IIS by itself doesn't support SET, a new product from Microsoft, Merchant Server, will handle this.

Careful That You Don't Catch a Virus

A virus is an undesirable, self-replicating program that gets into your computer system, usually through a floppy disk or through a network. Viruses originate at the hands of people who for some twisted reason think infecting other people's computers is fun. Viruses have a trigger, meaning that when a certain condition is met, the virus activates. They are also designed to spread from one computer to another. Some viruses can be incredibly destructive to your system. They can destroy all your data or do anything else the writer can dream up. Over a network, viruses can spread like chicken pox through a kindergarten.

Your best measure to take against viruses is prevention. This means you must control access to your system. If you have only a home computer and you are careful about the source of the software that goes onto your machine, you probably will not have to worry about viruses getting on your machine. Just make sure that you don't use a floppy disk that has been *anywhere* else. With virus technology becoming more sophisticated and the potential for great damage to sensitive information, some large companies don't permit employees to bring in disks from the outside at all.

Another good measure of prevention, besides controlling access to your computer, is to purchase antivirus software and run it regularly. Of course, you must remember that antivirus software becomes dated. New strains of viruses are being introduced all the time, and the antivirus software you have might not detect a new virus on your system. Besides running the antivirus software regularly, you will have to make sure your antivirus software is up-to-date.

If your computer is connected to a network or to the Internet, your risk factor for contracting a virus increases. One good rule to follow is to never download software from a network or the Internet directly onto your hard disk. Always download new software onto a floppy, and then run an antivirus program before installing it onto your hard drive.

The last measure of prevention is, of course, common sense. Back up your system religiously, not just in case of viruses, but for any of the many problems that can happen.

Physical Security of Your Server

No matter how many measures you take to secure your data with software, this will not protect you from someone who walks into your office with a sledgehammer and lets loose on your computer. Okay, so this isn't a very likely scenario, but you should give some consideration to the physical security of your Internet server. This is really the most basic security for your machine and is based purely on common sense. Like any other important and expensive piece of equipment, your computer is at risk from theft, vandalism, and otherwise prying fingers (like those of curious two-year-olds). If you are concerned with the physical security of your server, you will want to keep it safe from direct attack. The best way to physically protect your server is to keep it in a locked computer room or closet that only you and your trusted employees have access to. You might also want to consider putting a lock on your computer. Most come with locks, but they are about as secure as the locks on your child's diary or your suitcase. You can buy sturdier locks for your computer. Of course, they will not protect you from serious vandals or thieves, but they will keep most people from gaining direct access to the computer. As a theft deterrent, you might consider bolting your computer down to a counter or desk.

Intranet Security Issues

On an intranet site, security is both more of a concern and less of a concern: less of a concern because you are not opening up your system to the Internet, and more of a concern because of potential threats from within your organization and because of the kind of information you might have on your intranet. For the most part, security concerns for an intranet site are identical to those of an Internet site. You just need to consider your audience a little differently and make plans for security accordingly. Some of the main considerations for security on an intranet site follow.

As we mentioned earlier in this chapter, a disgruntled employee who has access to your network can do a considerable amount of damage. One could potentially hack into areas of the intranet that are restricted, such as files that contain your financial data. Most employees have a level of integrity that makes this risk small, but if your intranet includes information of a very confidential nature, the risk factor escalates. Someone could also simply make a mistake by setting improper permissions on a file, thereby making sensitive information available companywide.

Consider using encryption to protect some of the information on your intranet. It may seem strange or unnecessary to think about encrypting information traveling across the network in your own organization, but review the kind of information that could be found on your intranet. As your organization's intranet grows and begins to replace legacy systems for some services such as benefits administration and financial services, you should protect that data as it moves from one computer to another.

If your organization has both an Internet site and an intranet, you will have to be conscious of keeping these two networks separate. Intranet sites often contain content that would not be suitable for public consumption, so make sure that your intranet is not exposed to the Internet. This is even more critical because Internets and intranets use the same protocols to communicate. Having a firewall in place between the Internet connection and your intranet server is mandatory.

Backup, Backup, Backup

Oh, by the way, did we mention backup? Despite all the security precautions that you can take, you still can somehow lose all your information, be it by a hacker, a system failure, a curious two-year-old, or a spilled cup of java. Backup can be an effective security precaution because in many cases when a hacker breaks into your system, the goal is to wipe your system clean. But total losses can also come of accidental disruption to the server by power loss, pulled cables, spillage, or other unnatural disasters. By having regular backups, recovery from such an attack is usually quick and fairly painless. In Chapter 3, we recommended tape backup for those of you who are really concerned with potential loss of information. It is easy to use and to install, not very expensive, and it is supported by Windows NT Server. Of course, any backup system is absolutely worthless to you if you do not use it. It's important that you get into a regular routine of backing up your server, at least once every week, if not every day.

Security Checklist Before Going Live on the Internet

◆ Rename the Administrator account (highly recommended).

◆ Set strong password settings for all user accounts (highly recommended).

◆ Remove the security access for the Everyone group from hard disks (highly recommended).

◆ Set group security according to your particular needs (moderately recommended).

◆ Make sure the user IUSR_*machinename* has at least Read access to all files you want publicly accessible (highly recommended).

◆ For private areas of your Internet server, make sure IUSR_*machinename* has no permissions and that the user or group that can access it has at least Read access (only if needed).

◆ For secure encrypted sites, get and install a certificate for SSL (only if needed).

◆ Verify that IUSR_*machinename* and any other Internet users have no access to files that you do not want published on the Internet (highly recommended).

◆ Verify that only the scripts directory has Execute permission and that there are no scripts that could be used against you (highly recommended).

◆ Verify the physical security of your Internet server, and make sure that it is in a place safe from damage, theft, and vandalism (highly recommended).

◆ Back up regularly—at least weekly (highly recommended).

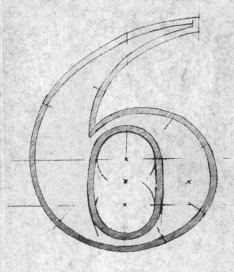

6

Sending Your Message to the World

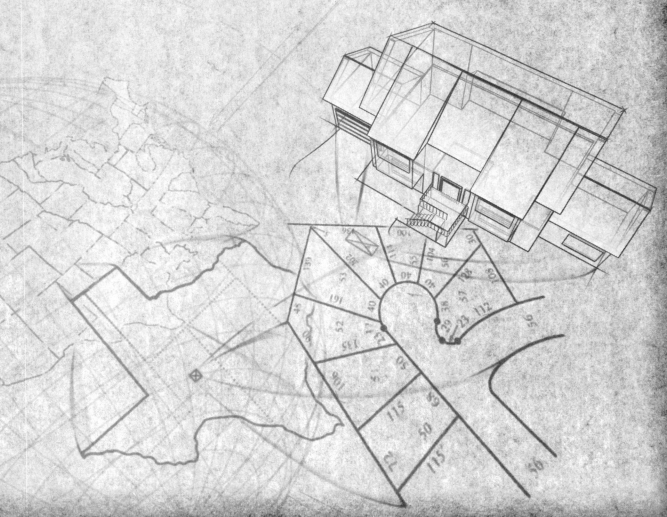

We're finally coming to the whole reason you're setting up an Internet presence in the first place—content. It's safe to assume that if you bought this book, you have something you want to share with the world, or at least with the virtual world. Now it's time to bring this content to your Web server to make your Internet presence complete.

Developing the content for your Web server breaks down into three main jobs: designing your site, programming the content, and organizing that content in appropriate places on your server. First, you need to consider the format and structure of your Web site and decide which is the best way to present the information you have. Once you have a design in mind, you must figure out how to produce the content so that it achieves a form that your users' Web browsers can read. The programming language that is used for the creation of Web content is called Hypertext Markup Language (HTML). To produce your content for the Web, you need to hire someone with HTML expertise to create the pages for you or you need to learn how to create HTML documents yourself. Finally, when you have information ready for the Web, you must figure out the best way to manage your Internet content on your server.

Let's Start with Some Terminology

To this point we have been throwing around terms like *Web site*, *Web page*, and *home page* and just assuming that you know what we're talking about. Now that you're working on the content of your Internet presence, it's probably time to be more precise. Basically, a Web site consists of one or more Web pages plus one or more home pages. Web pages are an organized compilation of the content of your Web site; they can be linked together. A home page is an introductory or main page for your site. So, is that clear? We thought not. Let's take a closer look at the different components of your content so that when we talk about designing and putting together your content, you'll know precisely what we mean.

What Is a Web Page?

In some ways, a Web page is a lot like a printed page. If you want to describe its bare essentials, a Web page is a collection of words, graphics, and other objects organized in a continuous, linear flow from top to bottom. The biggest difference between a Web page and a printed page is that the length of a Web page has no physical limit. Additionally, Web pages have the powerful ability to link directly to any number of other different pages. This means that you don't have to view Web pages in a prescribed order or in a linear fashion as you must do for most books.

What Is a Home Page?

A home page is the particular Web page that serves as the entry point into a Web site; usually it is the introductory Web page. The home page generally welcomes you to the Web site and shows links to all the second-level pages available at the site. Home pages make the first impression a user has of your Web site and hence of your organization. Some small Web sites, like personal pages, consist only of a home page, and some large sites have more than one home page.

What Is a Web Site?

A Web site is a collection of Web pages connected together with hypertext links so that each page is associated with the others. If you think about all the possible links that documents can have to one another, and all the ways that you could cross-reference the material in your Web site, it's easy to see where the name *Web* came from. Hypertext linking allows almost limitless numbers of options for the flow of your material.

Designing Your Web Site

When you consider how you're going to organize information for your WWW site, you'll probably go through a process somewhat similar to that used by the author of a book or a paper. You need to think about the structure and the format of the presentation. The many design questions you might ask yourself include these: What should I talk about first? How will I talk about it? What topics logically follow or suggest each other? What comes next? Do I need graphics of any kind? Depending on the nature and volume of your content, these questions might be easy for you to answer, or you could find that organizing your material is one of the most difficult jobs you have to do. Effectively organizing your content can make the difference between a Web site that people put on their Favorites list and one they leave in frustration after two minutes of not being able to find what they want.

Organizing Your Content

Web sites can range from those having a strictly linear organization to those with almost no apparent structure at all. People commonly organize their pages according to hierarchical, linear, or spiderweblike structures. Instead of imposing a rigid structure on your information at the beginning, you should first make sure that your links are logical and that they'll lead the user to the information he or she is looking for. Above all, you want to make sure it is easy for your user to navigate your Web site. Likely, you will find that a combination of the various approaches to organizing your information will work best.

HIERARCHICAL ORGANIZATION

Web sites that follow a hierarchical or a treelike structure have one point of entry to the site and other pages that branch out from this link. This approach can work very well if you can group your pages easily into categories and subcategories. If the plan of your Web site follows a strict hierarchy, it implies that a lower-level branch appears only on one path, and not on multiple paths. See Figure 6-1.

Having this much structure in your Web site can pose problems for people navigating your site. If, for instance, users follow a path several branches down and then decide they need to be in a different part of the tree, they must retrace their steps back up the tree to find the right branch to go down.

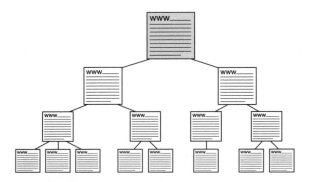

Figure 6-1. *Web site organized hierarchically.*

LINEAR ORGANIZATION

If you want users to read your content as they would a book or magazine, or when you need the user of your Web site to follow a specific flow from the beginning to the end of your Web site, you might choose a linear design. A given page might have links to a few sidebars or notes, but users would need to return to that page in order to go on. They would then select either a Next button to continue through the document or a Previous button to retrace their steps to the top of the site. See Figure 6-2.

The linear approach might not be the best choice if you have a large Web site. Readers looking for specific information might be frustrated if they have to walk through many pages to find what they're looking for. Also, if you use this approach, you might be tempted to write long individual Web pages, which many people find tedious to scroll through.

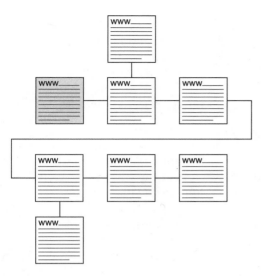

Figure 6-2. Web site organized linearly.

THE WEB APPROACH

A weblike organization of information probably works the best for most people. With this structure, Web pages are linked to each other when they relate contextually. There could be several links to a single page, and every document usually has at least two ways to get to it. Links could lead the user in a circular path. See Figure 6-3.

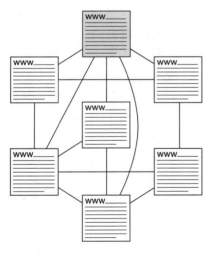

Figure 6-3. A weblike Web site.

From a navigational point of view, this kind of site is very appealing. It allows users to get around the site quickly and enjoy a more freeform experience of your site. The main disadvantage to this approach is that it presents opportunities for your users to miss something on your site by not following all the links.

Guidelines for Creating Great Web Pages

Your users will ultimately be the judges of the content of your Web site, and you'll know what they think either through their direct feedback or as a measure of the number of return visits they make to your site. Just as a store gets most of its business from word of mouth, much of the traffic on your site will also be a result of word of mouth, or, in this case, we should say word of e-mail.

A good Web page should be interesting and fun for people to visit. It should include all the information that your users expect to find and be easy to navigate. You will probably want to include some spiffy graphics, cool fonts, and other eye catchers, but, at the same time, you need to keep the size of your pages small to quicken the download time for your users. Following are some suggestions to keep in mind when creating your Web pages.

MAKE SURE YOUR HOME PAGE STANDS OUT

First impressions really are important. The coolest information in the world will get very little traffic if the home page that points users to the site isn't correspondingly cool. If users make it to your home page and it doesn't keep their attention and invite them to browse through the rest of your site, you have not done a good job designing that page.

KEEP INDIVIDUAL PAGES SMALL AND LIMIT THE SCOPE OF YOUR CONTENT

To make your individual pages enjoyable to read, it's a good idea to limit the scope of what you cover on a single page to one topic. A user can be quickly frustrated trying to find a certain topic and having to sort through a lot of extraneous information. You should also keep individual pages small, which has many advantages: you are less likely to crowd small pages with unrelated information; the user has to do a lot less cumbersome scrolling up and down; and you save download time for the user. If you have more content than will fit on a single, reasonably sized page, you should consider dividing the information between two or more pages and providing links between them.

MAKE YOUR PAGES INTERESTING

Keeping the attention of your audience is not always easy. Some of the ploys that writers of TV commercials use to keep people watching for only 30 seconds confirms this fact. At your Web site, you can't up the volume loud enough to jolt people out of their chairs and you probably don't have the budget to hire a celebrity to endorse your Web site, so you must get and hold your audience's attention in other ways. If you have a hard time thinking of ways to make your Web site compelling, look at other sites on the Web to see what elicits your "Way cool" response. Then think about whether you can transfer any of these ideas to your own site.

Another important way to keep your Web site interesting to your users is to update the content of your pages regularly. People will stop coming back to your site if they repeatedly find the same stuff on it.

DON'T OVERDO THE GRAPHICS

By all means, use graphics in your Web pages if they enhance your content, but remember the trade-off between the number of cool things you can have on a single Web page and the performance of that page. Finding a balance can be really difficult and could be one of the reasons that you might want to hire a professional to create content for you.

The saying goes that "a picture is worth a thousand words," and, certainly, the inclusion of graphics, be it photographs or drawings, can be a valuable addition to your Web site. But a picture is also worth a lot of bytes. Any graphics you use on your site have to be transmitted to the user who views your pages and the more graphics you have on your page, the slower that page will be to download and view. Make sure you have good reasons to include graphics at your site.

FOLLOW THE 14.4 RULE

Sad, but true—we live in a world where people seem to need immediate gratification. Blame it on TV or just plain human nature, but, generally, we have pretty short attention spans and don't like to spend a lot of time waiting for things. Most Web users are no different. If people have to wait eons for your pages to download to their computer, there's a good chance they'll bail out and move on. Even though computer users are used to having to deal with the speed limitations of their machines, when you create a Web page, you should limit the amount of time it takes for your site to download. Our handy rule of thumb is this: If you create a Web page and it takes more than 30 seconds for a person with a 14.4-Kbps modem to load it into their machine, you might as well forget it.

Of course, there are exceptions to this rule. Users of Web sites that are graphically intense in nature, like Internet art galleries, probably will be more patient than most people waiting for graphics to download. You need to decide for yourself whether the nature of your site warrants longer download times. Table 6-1 includes calculations of download times for a 50-KB and 100-KB page for different connection speeds. You can use it as a reference to approximate your user's download time for your Web pages.

Connection speed	50-KB Web page	100-KB Web page
9,600 bps	About 48 seconds	About 96 seconds
14,400 bps	About 32 seconds	About 64 seconds
28,800 bps	About 16 seconds	About 32 seconds
T1 (1,500,000 bps)	Less than a second	Still less than a second

Table 6-1. *Use this table as a reference to download time for your users depending on their connection speed and the size of your Web page.*

BE WARY OF USING GRAPHICS TO REPRESENT OPTIONS

A fancy graphic with a lot of icons for people to click is not going to be a good choice if the average user cannot figure out where the links are. Make sure that if you use graphics instead of words to represent options, the representations of the options are clear to the users. Test such graphics on your friends and see whether they understand the icons before you put them on your site.

DON'T FILL THE ENTIRE SCREEN WITH A SINGLE GRAPHIC

It's a good idea to give your users some text to look at while graphics are downloading. Most browsers load text first and then graphics. If a graphic at the top of your page takes up the entire screen, your users might not know that there is any text following for them to look at. The minimum video configuration on the Internet is typically 640 by 480 pixels with 16-color or 256-color support. We suggest that when you plan pages, you don't take up the first screenful of any page with a graphic.

DON'T DEPEND ON GRAPHICS FOR TEXT FLOW

Keep in mind the possibility that some of your users turn off the graphics capability of their browsers; if you have used graphics to help you position your text on the page, they will probably see something that doesn't look very good. See Figure 6-4 for an example of this. Directing text placement on a page can be handled with tables that are designed for this purpose.

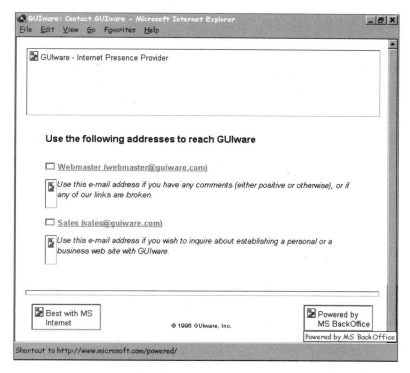

Figure 6-4. *This page was improperly formatted with graphics used to direct text flow. This is what the page looks like from a browser with the graphics turned off.*

Creating Content with HTML

So, if we didn't scare you away from creating your own Web pages by telling you how difficult it is to make compelling and professional content, you're still here, wanting to know how to put your information into a form that Web browsers can read. This section introduces you to *HTML*, the language used to develop Web pages. We will briefly tell you what HTML is, how it works, and point you to resources for learning the HTML language and creating HTML pages.

What Is HTML (Hypertext Markup Language)?

HTML is the language used to create Web pages that can be read by Web browsers. It's a script-based language, which means that it uses special sequences of characters called *tags* as commands. If you were using computers in the early days of word processing technology or if you've been a typographer, you've probably encountered scripting languages before. Basically, the tags that you attach to a certain piece of text dictate the style that the text will appear in. Tags can also be used to instruct the browser to load graphics in certain positions, and other tags can create links to other pages.

When a browser connects to a Web page, the HTML script is transmitted to the browser, which then renders the page described in the HTML. The entire representation of text and graphics on a page is processed by the client. The server transmits the HTML file blindly using HTTP (Hypertext Transport Protocol). Your Web server merely supplies the file. This allows your Web server to handle large numbers of clients.

How to Learn HTML

If you're at all intimidated by the thought of learning to use a "programming" language to develop your Web pages, well, don't be! The good news is that basic HTML is far easier to learn than a typical computer programming language. You don't need special compilers, and, although you can use special HTML editors to create HTML, you don't have to use them. You can use the text-based editor that comes along with Microsoft Windows NT Server if you want to.

The bad news is that we will not teach you HTML in this book. A lot of good books are already available that do a fine job teaching HTML. If you look around, you'll also find a multitude of courses available and many resources on the Web to teach you Web authoring. Some people find that a good way to learn HTML is by seeing the source code of a good Web page. You can see how a Web author coded certain styles and how the author achieved a certain effect. Viewing source code is simply a matter of selecting the View Source option in your Web browser. The way you choose to learn HTML is going to depend on the way you personally learn best.

NOTE: As a matter of Internet etiquette, it is not considered good form to completely plagiarize the HTML code from someone's Web page. Use the source code as a way to learn how an author handled certain techniques, but don't simply plug your material into someone else's code and then put your name on it.

HTML Editors

Since HTML is ASCII (American Standard Code for Information Interchange) text, you can use almost any text editor you want to create your files. Also, since HTML is an *interpreted* scripting language, there is no compiler to run the code through. You could choose to use something as simple as Notepad, the text editor that comes with Windows NT Server, to write HTML code, or you could use one of the many specialized HTML editors available on the market. Some tools now allow you to generate HTML code without actually writing it yourself.

American Standard Code for Information Interchange

ASCII is a standard for representing the English alphabet and other control characters, such as Tab and Return, over communication lines.

Microsoft produces several tools (discussed in the following sections) for creating HTML content. These reduce or eliminate the need for you to learn HTML. While these tools are great starting places, you might find that you soon outgrow their capabilities. To create more sophisticated Web pages, you probably want to make yourself an expert at HTML.

INTERNET ASSISTANTS

Microsoft has recently developed a suite of tools known as Internet Assistants for Office that allow you to use the Microsoft Office 95 products to create Web content. The Internet Assistants take your already existing files or documents from applications like Word, Excel, PowerPoint, Access, and Schedule+ and convert them into Web-readable pages. You can create a spreadsheet in Excel and save it as an HTML table. With PowerPoint, you can create a presentation or animation, and, with the addition of the new Microsoft Internet Explorer plug-in for PowerPoint, those presentations can be viewed on the Web. Access, the powerful desktop database system, can be used to publish your database on the Web. You can even use a beta of the Internet Assistant for Schedule+ that makes it possible for you to publish calendars or schedules on the Web.

The main advantage to the Internet Assistants is that they allow you to create Web content easily and without ever learning how to code in HTML. They are very useful, therefore, for getting a Web site up quickly. The main drawback to these tools is that since they support only basic HTML formatting, they won't generate truly original pages. If you want to be able to do exciting Web pages, you still need to learn HTML. A good use for Internet Assistants is in the creation of corporate intranets where you may care more about making information available quickly than having Web pages that are unique and interesting.

For more information about the Internet Assistants from Microsoft, visit Microsoft's Web site at *http://www.microsoft.com* and follow the links down the Internet Resource path.

MICROSOFT FRONTPAGE

Microsoft FrontPage is one of the most sophisticated Web authoring tools available. It not only contains an excellent text editor for creating HTML, but it also allows you to create and organize your entire Web site. FrontPage has wizards to help generate starter pages, and it has tools to help you manage the site as well. For beginners with HTML, FrontPage is a great product to start out with.

All Web Browsers Are Not Created Equal

In their constant quest to stay competitive, the companies that develop browsers each include support for different HTML tags. Basically, this means that the way one browser reads and displays your content could easily not resemble the way another browser displays it. As a matter of fact, some browsers support such completely different tags that you can end up with a finished product that on some browsers looks nothing like what you intended when you created the document.

In your travels through the WWW, you might have noticed that some pages have the logo of a certain Web browser somewhere on the page saying something like "Netscape Enhanced" or "This page best viewed with Microsoft Internet Explorer." This tells people which browser the page was created for and, therefore, which browser you should use to see the page in all its glory. Additionally, some older browsers still kicking around don't support graphics capability at all, and some people might choose to turn graphics off in favor of speed of downloading. Don't count on your pictures (as we said before) to organize or tell your Web site story unless, of course, pictures are the only story you're telling.

What does this mean for you? Well, you might need to make some tradeoffs. If you're creating your own Web pages, you need to consider how your Web pages will look on different Web browsers. (See Figure 6-5.) Maybe you avoid using new and snazzy tags that aren't supported all around. You won't have the latest cool features on your page, but your page will look good to most users.

So, should you make sure your Web pages look great no matter which browser your audience is using, or should you throw caution to the wind and use all the cool new features on one platform? This is completely up to you. But, no matter what, you should keep up with what is going on in browser technology to know who supports which HTML tags.

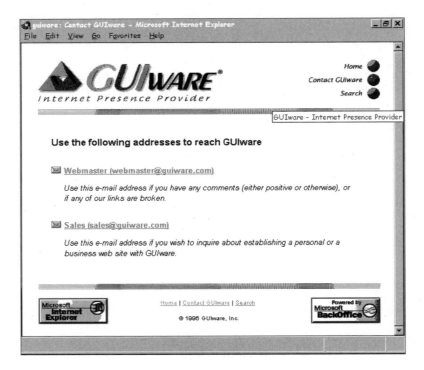

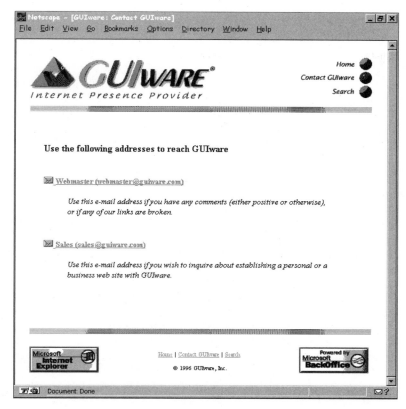

Figure 6-5. *One page as seen through Internet Explorer (on page 132) and through Netscape (above).*

NOTE: Not only can the browser make a difference in the way information is displayed, but also the hardware platform that your user has can have a large impact. Different operating systems handle graphics in unique ways so that even the same brand of browser running on different platforms can produce varied results.

Test, Test, Test

Before you go live on the Internet with your content, thoroughly test your Web pages on different browsers so that you know exactly what you are making available to people. It's also a good idea to test all the links in your Web site to ensure that they actually go to the correct places. You want to be the one who finds any errors on your site—better you than your users.

How to Structure Content on Your Disk

As a Webmaster, it will be your job to maintain the data on your Web server, which includes all the files that make up your Web site. Depending on the size of your organization, this can be a very challenging task. The simpler the directory structure you create, the easier your job as Webmaster will be. It's a good idea to set a standard structure for the different elements for your site. For example, in each directory that includes Web pages, you might create subdirectories for the various elements of the Web pages, such as HTML, images, sounds, video, forms, or anything else that might be on your pages. If you have a structure sorted this way, it is easy to keep track of any elements that might be missing.

Windows NT Server and Internet Information Server have very good methods for allowing you to create an easy-to-maintain structure. By spending a little time beforehand thinking about your directory structure and using features such as *virtual directories* and *virtual servers*, you can reduce the time it takes to administer your Web server by a significant amount.

Virtual Directories

Virtual directories can be a hard concept to grasp at first, but they are very simple and useful tools once you understand the way they work. See Figure 6-6. Virtual directories are merely pointers to other directories located in another place. They behave much like a call forwarding device on the telephone. If you are out of the office, you can activate call forwarding to point your telephone calls to your new location. When people call you, they don't need to know the phone number of your new location—they call your office number. Virtual directories do essentially the same thing. When you access a virtual directory, you are actually accessing a file that is located in another place; the virtual directory is pointing you to the real location of that file even though you don't know the name of *that* directory.

The physical directory that a virtual directory references can be on the same hard disk or on a different hard disk, on the same machine or even a hard disk on a completely different server. Also note that each Internet service (WWW, FTP, and Gopher) has its own set of virtual directories. So, the next question you might ask is why would I use a virtual directory?

Assume you have a directory called C:\WWWROOT, and this is the root directory for your Web server. You also have another directory called C:\DOCS that contains a bunch of files. You want to publish these files on the Web. You might think, well, that's easy, just copy those files into the directory C:\WWWROOT. This is certainly a possibility. But now assume that you have 100 people in your organization who have access to the C:\DOCS directory and whenever they create new files, they go into that directory. Every time someone created a new file, you would have to copy it into the root directory for the Web. To solve this problem, you could create a virtual directory from the Web root directory that points to the C:\DOCS directory but looks like C:\WWWROOT\DOCS. All you have done is place a marker in the directory structure where you want the files to appear that specifies the actual physical location of the directory. See the procedure set out on page 137 for how to do this.

This is the short answer for why you'd use a virtual directory. The following sections detail the full set of reasons to do it.

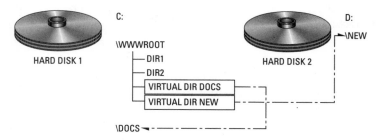

Figure 6-6. *Virtual directories.*

PORTABILITY

When you create a Web site, you probably have pages that link to other pages located on your own Web server. You must specify these links in terms of their locations on your server's hard disk. If the need arose to move the location of pages on your hard disk, you would have to edit all of your pages to change the URL that points to the actual location of each page. Using virtual directories, however, you can simply move the physical directory and then edit the virtual directory information to correctly note the location of the files. Your URLs will continue to be correct, since the virtual directory structure you use in your pages to reference the URLs did not change.

FLAT FILE SYSTEM MANAGEMENT

If you're an old command-line person like some of us, then you know that when you have complicated file directory structures, things can get messy when you have a lot of subdirectories. The more directory layers you have, the harder it is to keep track of where things are. If you have a very large Web site with a lot of content, you can end up with many layers of directories. You can make it easier to manage the file system and keep track of file locations if you place all your main content in different but same-level directories for easy access. However, on your Web site, you need the data to appear more hierarchically. You can create virtual directories for each of your top-level physical directories and have a structure that looks to the Web server like a hierarchy but really isn't.

USING MULTIPLE DISKS AND SERVERS

Have you ever installed a new computer thinking that you would have enough disk space to last a lifetime, only to run out of space in the time it takes to say "I love computers"? If you use virtual directories, you don't have to change your directory structure just because you have added new disk space. You can simply create a physical directory on the new hard disk and place the virtual link in the C:\WWWROOT directory, even though the new actual directory is located on D:\NEW. Virtual directories allow you to extend the virtual size of your Web server to the total disk space that Windows NT Server can handle, which, if you don't recall, is 32 terabytes. It is even possible to specify a directory on a completely different server if you want, although we don't recommend this as it can be confusing to keep track of.

SIMPLER URLS

If you create a directory structure in your Web server that has many layers of subdirectories under it, you could end up with URLs that are very long, making it difficult to test and debug your Web site. By using virtual directories, you can flatten your URL references and make it far easier to track down page-linking problems on your site.

REPLACING LEGACY SYSTEMS

You might be in a situation where you have legacy systems in place that require data to be in a specific location. If you want that data to be available on your Web site without having to replace the legacy system, you could set up a virtual directory on your Web server to point to that information.

GIVING ALL INTERNET SERVICES ACCESS TO THE SAME DIRECTORY

If you want to allow the different Internet services on your Web server to access the same directory, you must use virtual directories. For example, if you are an IPP with customers who want to modify their own Web pages, you could set up private areas in FTP for each customer to access data. Then you would create virtual directories in the Web server to access these private FTP areas.

SECURITY

If you want to encrypt specific information for transmission over the Internet using SSL, you must create a virtual directory for that information and specify that the virtual directory requires SSL. This is because SSL is an IIS-specific security setting and the only directories for which IIS keeps specific settings are virtual directories.

You also can set Read and Execute access to the virtual directory. Read access allows the server to display the contents to the end user, while Execute allows scripts to be run from the directory. Refer back to Chapter 5 of this book for other security issues related to virtual directories.

BECAUSE YOU WANT TO SET UP A VIRTUAL SERVER

If you want to set up one or more virtual servers (detailed below), you must create a virtual directory to represent that virtual server. We have no long explanation for this; it is simply the way the system works.

HOW TO SET UP A NEW VIRTUAL DIRECTORY

1. Launch Internet Service Manager, and double-click on the Internet service for which you want to create or modify a virtual directory.

2. Select the Directories tab.

3. Select the Add button, and enter the location of the actual physical directory.

4. Specify the name you want to give to the virtual directory.

5. If you want to use any security options, select them from the bottom of the dialog box. Please note that file-level security is set on the actual physical directory represented by the virtual directory.

6. Click the OK button when you are finished.

HOW TO MODIFY AN EXISTING VIRTUAL DIRECTORY

1. Double-click on the entry you want to modify.

2. Change the properties of the displayed virtual directory. See Figure 6-7.

3. Click the OK button when you are finished.

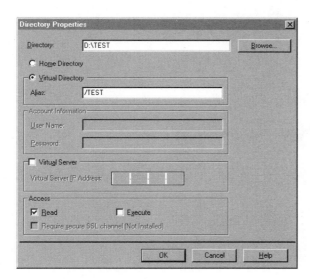

Figure 6-7. *Directory properties.*

Virtual Servers

A virtual server is a special kind of virtual directory that allows a single Web server to appear as though it is actually many different Web servers. If you maintain a number of domains, you might want *www.domain1.com* to open a different page than *www.domain2.com* does. Or suppose you are an IPP or an ISP and you manage Web sites for multiple domains. If you couldn't set up virtual servers, you would have to have a separate Internet server for each domain, or you would have to run the Web server as many times on the same machine as you have domains, using up valuable memory resources. Using virtual servers allows your server to make efficient use of its resources and provide the best possible performance for all the domains you manage. Setting up virtual servers makes this simple.

The ability to set up a virtual server is a big advantage that Windows NT Server has over other Web servers. Many of them don't support this concept, and the ones other than Windows NT Server that do are difficult to configure.

Only the Web service provides support for virtual servers. FTP and Gopher don't offer this feature.

HOW TO SET UP A VIRTUAL SERVER

To set up a virtual server, first you must register the new domain name with the InterNIC. You also must obtain an IP address for the virtual server. For each virtual server you have, you must have a unique IP address assigned to it. You can have as many IP addresses as you need on any Internet server provided that they are *valid* IP addresses on the Internet.

HOW TO ASSIGN A NEW IP ADDRESS TO YOUR INTERNET SERVER

1. Launch the Network control panel.

2. Select the Protocols tab, and double-click the TCP/IP option.

3. Click the Advanced button, and type in the new IP address for your computer. See Figure 6-8.

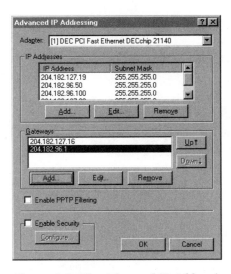

Figure 6-8. *The Advanced IP Addressing dialog box.*

HOW TO ADD IP ADDRESSES IF YOU ALREADY
HAVE FIVE OR MORE ASSIGNED TO YOUR SERVER

1. Choose Run from the Start menu. Type *REGEDT32* and click the OK button.

2. Open the HKEY_LOCAL_MACHINE registry window, and double-click on *SYSTEM*.

3. Double-click on CurrentControlSet.

4. Then double-click on Services.

5. Look for the name of the network adapter you are using. Note that the name in this list might not be the same as the name on the box; if this is the case, you should contact your adapter's manufacturer to find out the exact name you should be looking for. Beneath the adapter's entry in the registry, you'll see a second entry that has the same name with the number 1 appended. Double-click that entry.

6. Double-click the Parameters entry.

7. Click on the Tcpip entry. To the right, you will see a list of TCP/IP settings. See Figure 6-9.

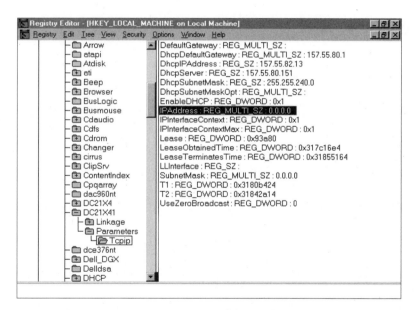

Figure 6-9. *The Registry editor, showing the TCP/IP settings for a network interface card.*

8. Double-click the IPAddress entry.

9. In the Multi-String Editor dialog box, enter all the IP addresses for this machine. Each IP address must be separated by a space or carriage return.

10. If the additional IP addresses have different subnet masks from the others, which is very unlikely, double-click the SubnetMask entry and match the order of masks with the order of IP addresses.

11. Make sure the DNS entry for WWW on the new domain points to the new IP address you assigned to your Internet server. (Refer to your ISP or DNS documentation for more help with this step.)

CONFIGURING A VIRTUAL SERVER

1. Launch Internet Service Manager, and double-click on the WWW service.

2. Select the Directories tab.

3. Follow the steps listed above for creating a virtual directory, but don't click the OK button. Instead, look for the Virtual Server option in the middle of the dialog box, and click it.

4. Enter the IP address you are using for this new domain in the space provided.

5. Click the OK button when you are finished.

TO MODIFY A VIRTUAL SERVER

To modify a virtual server, follow the same steps, listed on page 137, that you used to modify a virtual directory. See Figure 6-10 to see how a virtual server is defined.

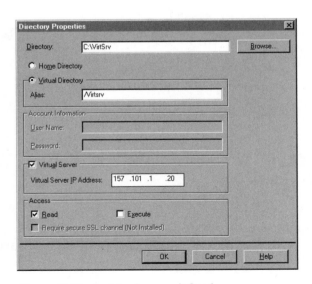

Figure 6-10. *A virtual server defined.*

Where to Develop Your Content

It's a good idea to keep a copy of your Web files in a directory different from where they are being used so that you can make changes to these files without directly editing your live content. If you edit live content, there is a possibility that a user will try to access a file while you are editing it, and this could cause problems. Also, if you make a mistake, you can easily recover without causing any damage to the live files.

Managing Version Control

One task associated with the management of your content that you might find particularly fun is keeping track of versions. Is the version of a file that is loaded on your Web site, in fact, the latest version of that file, or does it need to be updated? Version control can be particularly difficult if you have a large site, and especially if you have many people working on files. Any time you have two or more copies of a file, version control is an issue. If you want to edit a file, you need to be sure that you are editing a copy of the latest edition of the file so that other edits don't get lost. The methods used to keep track of version control can vary greatly depending on the size and needs of your organization.

VERSION CONTROL FOR A SMALL SHOP

Most small businesses with one or two people who manage the Web site can get by without special software to handle version control. More than likely, two people can establish a system to let each other know who is working on what. But you might choose to avoid letting two people work on the same files altogether. In this way, there is little chance that a "save collision" could occur which would over-write one person's changes with those of a second person.

LARGE SHOP

In a larger shop, or any organization that requires a greater level of sophistication for version control, tools are available to help maintain the active and developmental Web sites so that the authors don't have to keep track of versions manually. Microsoft has a tool called Visual SourceSafe (VSS) that was developed for this purpose. Although VSS was created originally to handle C/C++ code, it has been adapted to handle any kind of code, including HTML.

VSS keeps track of versions automatically. It makes sure that you are editing the latest version of a document, and if two people edit the same document, the tool merges the changes when the editors check their changes back into the system. The system works rather like a library. When you want to edit a file, you check it out, and when you are finished working with the file, you check it back in. If you try to check out a file that someone else already has, the system will inform you that the file is currently unavailable.

For more details on Visual SourceSafe, take a look at Microsoft's Web site. The documentation and release notes that come with VSS discuss how you use it with HTML.

How to Deal with FTP and Gopher Content

FTP and Gopher content is really easy to deal with. There is no special formatting or coding you have to do to develop or alter the files. All you have to do is place files for these services in the corresponding directory. Since FTP and Gopher both support virtual directories (although not virtual servers), you can manage content in the same way you do your Web content.

Announcing Your Web Site to the World

Once you have a Web site up and running, complete with content, and you have tested it carefully and thoroughly, it's time to announce the existence of your Web site to the rest of the world. One way to introduce your site is to get it listed with the various search engines. Most of them have a link on their home pages for this purpose. One quick warning to you: A number of services out on the Web offer to get you listed with the search engines for a fee. There is really nothing that they can do for you that you can't do for yourself.

You can also try to get other people to establish links from their page to yours. Contact organizations that are complementary to your site, and see if they would like to establish links. You can reciprocate by putting links in your page to theirs.

Summary

◆ Take the time to think about the organization of the content on your Web site, and make sure you create a logical way to navigate the site.

◆ Create individual Web pages that are eye-catching, fun, and interesting and that contain content your users are looking for. Keep your pages easy to navigate and as fast as possible to download.

◆ You can hire professional Web authors to create the content for your Internet site or you can learn HTML to develop the content yourself.

◆ Consider how your Web pages will look on different Web browsers and on different operating system platforms.

◆ Virtual servers and virtual directories are tools that can help you to efficiently organize your Web server and your directory structure.

◆ Develop your content in a different directory structure from where you keep your live Internet content.

◆ Visual SourceSafe can be a good tool for large organizations to use to manage version control of their Web pages.

7

Giving Your
Web Site a
Dynamic
Personality

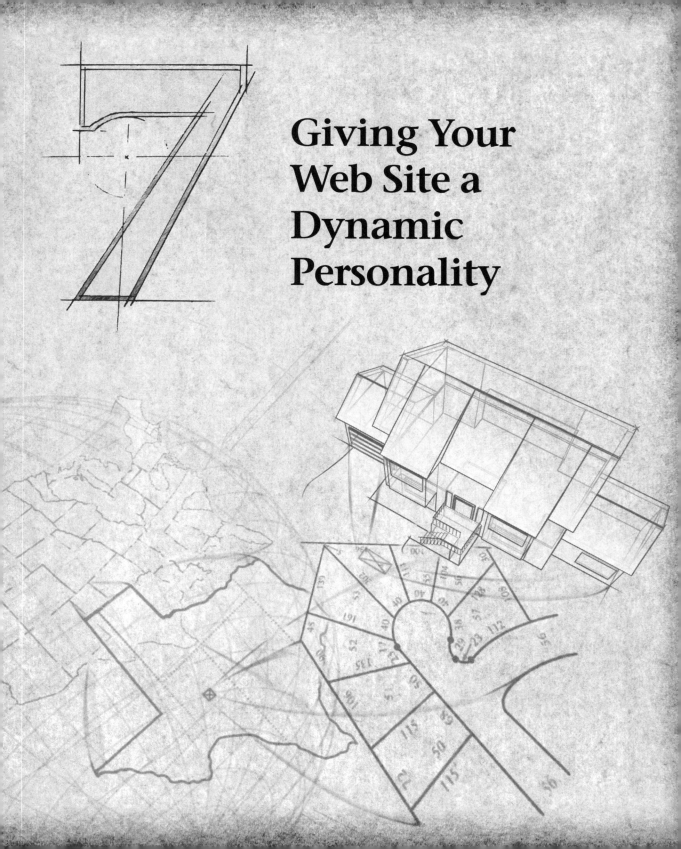

Now that we've told you what you can do with HTML, it's time to look at what you can't. As good as HTML is for Web authoring, it has its limitations. Web pages created with HTML are static, meaning that each time a user accesses these pages, they are exactly the same unless, in the meantime, the content has been updated or the HTML code changed. Also, HTML files by themselves cannot interact with other applications on your server. If you want your users to supply you with information to store in a database, you must use some other tool that is capable of this kind of interaction.

For those of you who just want to provide your users with information and plan to make changes to your site only periodically, the limitations of HTML will not be a problem for you. But if you want to make your Web site or parts of your Web site more interactive in nature, dynamically providing information to your users, or if you want to take information supplied by your users and use it as a trigger for some other action to occur, you must look beyond HTML to enhance your site.

As you've explored the WWW, you have probably come across some sophisticated Internet sites. You might have seen Web pages on which the advertising changes each time you access the site, or you've seen sites that have forms to fill out or sites where documents are generated as the direct result of user input. Your site could exploit numerous possibilities for dynamic features.

Dynamic Web pages can make your Web site much more enticing and powerful and, therefore, can make your site and your organization much more competitive on the Web. Here is a list of common features that a dynamic Internet site allows you. Of course, this list is incomplete. The only limit to the features you can have on a dynamic Internet site is your imagination.

◆ Custom home pages

◆ Communication with databases

◆ Image maps

◆ Transactions

◆ Fillable forms

◆ Subscription services

◆ Content rotation

- Daily advertisements

- Quotes or tips of the day

- Voting

Web authors of dynamic Internet pages must use more advanced-level programming than HTML to create this kind of interaction. To make these kinds of functions work on your Internet site, Web authors commonly use programs called *scripts* to process the information.

What Are Scripts?

Just as actors follow scripts to tell them how to behave, what to do, and what to say in a given situation, so do computers follow them. Scripts on your computer are programs that tell your computer how to behave when certain conditions are met. On your Internet site, scripts allow you to provide advanced features for your users. A script program usually executes as a result of an action performed by the client, such as direct input or a click of the mouse. One of the most common and useful functions a script can perform is to link your Web server to another of your applications, such as a database. See Figure 7-1 for a diagram of how this works.

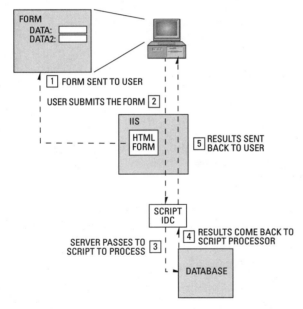

Figure 7-1. *The server sends a form to the client, which in turn submits the responses back to the server. The server passes that information to the script that communicates with the database. The script then sends the results back to the client through the IIS.*

The amount of programming skill required to create a script varies according to the tools that you use to create it. Scripts can be written using just about any programming language that you already know, or you can use one of the many scripting languages that were created specifically for this purpose. You can also find many scripts publicly available on the Internet that might meet your needs, although if you go this route, you might need to tweak these scripts a bit to have them work with your own HTML documents. The software industry for producing Internet scripts is growing swiftly. If you want to avoid programming altogether, this is a good time to jump ship and hire experts to handle this part of your Internet site.

Since this is not a programming book, we are not going to teach you how to write scripts in this chapter. As in the previous chapter of this book that discussed content creation using HTML, our goal here is to give you a basic understanding of what scripts can do for you and point you in the direction of tools that you can use.

Server Extensions

You can write or find scripts to extend the capabilities of both the client side and the server side of your Internet presence. We'll first talk about scripts used to extend the functionality of the server: these are referred to as *server extensions* or *server-side scripts*.

A server extension provides a method for the Web server to do more than simply pump HTML data onto the wire when a user requests it. Server extensions are what make it possible for your Web pages to communicate with a database, they can be used to customize the user interaction with the Web server, and they can even provide a search engine for your Web site. For one simple example of the benefits of server-side scripting, you could write a script to randomly select content to include in an HTML file, providing, this way, a different "Quote of the Day" each time your user accesses your site.

You can use many different tools to create server extensions. Some have been specifically developed for this purpose, and others have been adapted for this use. We discuss a range of tools, from interfaces to programming languages to APIs, that you can use to create server extensions.

Interface

An *interface* is a predefined method of communication between two different systems. In some ways, an interface is a lot like a protocol on the wire. Interfaces are constructed according to well-understood procedures for what "language" to use and how to communicate in it.

Internet Database Connector (IDC)

Just as its name implies, IDC provides a method for you to connect your Internet server to your database. See Figure 7-2. The IDC server-side extension comes with IIS and allows you to access any ODBC-compliant database engine, such as Microsoft SQL Server. As a scripting language, IDC is one of the easiest languages to use for processing forms with IIS.

ODBC (Open Database Connectivity)

ODBC is software that provides a standard interface to different database engines. It communicates with each database engine by means of ODBC drivers geared to a variety of databases. As a result, a program can access different types of database engines without changing the code in the program. ODBC acts as a translator between a program's own interface and various databases.

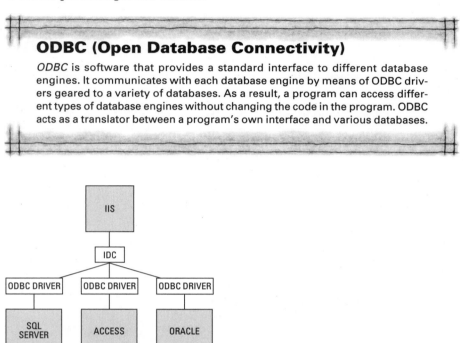

Figure 7-2. *IDC uses ODBC to access different database engines. ODBC has special drivers to handle the communication to the specific data stores.*

If you have any information stored in a database that you want to share with your users, or data that you want to collect from your users, IIS needs to be able to access your database. You can also create IDC scripts that can dynamically display the information. For example, if you want to provide Web access to sales data, such as who the current top sales associate is, the top-selling product, or the highest-volume region, you could create an IDC script that queries the accounting database and displays the results. Some other uses for database access are handling customer lookups, providing subscription services, providing ordering systems, and enabling surveys. IDC scripts specify the database you want to access, the action to perform with the database, and input to any required fields. If you are looking for ways to improve customer usability, adding SQL Server with IDC to your Internet site can give you many ways to enhance your site.

Setting Up IDC for SQL Server

Since IDC comes along with IIS and connecting with SQL Server can greatly extend the possibilities for your Internet site, we'll run through the steps for setting up the IDC for SQL Server. The setup is relatively easy. First, you need to make sure that you have IDC installed on IIS. Run the IIS Setup program to see if the check box for ODBC is selected. If it is, IDC is installed. If not, select it and start the installation.

Once you are certain that you have IDC installed, follow three basic steps to set up IDC for SQL Server. The first thing you need to do is create an ODBC data source. Second, you create an IDC script file, and, third, you create an HTX file. More specific instructions for accomplishing these tasks follow.

CREATING AN ODBC DATA SOURCE

A *data source* defines the ODBC driver and database location to use and associates them with a name to reference in your IDC file. Here's how to create it.

1. Launch the ODBC control panel.

2. Choose the System DSN button.

3. You next see a list box. From it, select the ODBC driver for your data source. In this case, select SQL Server.

4. Enter a name for the data source. This will be the name you refer to in your IDC file. See Figure 7-3.

5. Enter the name of the SQL server that you want to use. (If SQL Server is installed on the same machine with IIS, select Local.)

6. Click the Options button, and enter the name of the specific database on the SQL server you want to use.

7. Click the OK button, and you are finished.

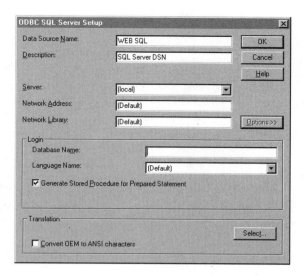

Figure 7-3. *Creating a data source name (DSN).*

CREATING AN IDC SCRIPT FILE

IIS uses the script file you create to specify the fields you are interested in and the user account IIS uses to log on to SQL Server. Please refer to the IIS documentation for details about the format of this file.

CREATING AN HTX FILE

The HTX file is a template used by IIS to format the output or results from SQL Server. The output is converted into HTML using the template from the HTX file so that results can be displayed by the browser.

ActiveX

If you follow the news in the computer industry, you might have recently heard about Microsoft's new ActiveX technology. ActiveX refers to a suite of component technologies that are used by both clients and servers for different Internet-related functions.

ACTIVEX SERVER-SIDE SCRIPTING

ActiveX server-side scripting allows you to create dynamic content using Visual Basic script commands and expressions. The server processes these, and the output is integrated into the HTML files, which are then sent to the user's browser. The format for ActiveX server-side scripts was designed to resemble native HTML as closely as possible to make it easier to use for those who are already familiar with HTML.

ActiveX server-side scripting has many uses. For example, you might want a Web page that users can customize to suit their own needs or on which you can randomly change content. ActiveX server-side scripting can be used in place of IDC if you want to perform some process on the data prior to its transmission to or from the server. For instance, you might want to validate, modify, or confirm data before it goes to the database. Or when you pull data from a database, you might want to provide summary data rather than the raw data.

ACTIVEX SERVER CONTROLS

Controls are prepackaged pieces of code you can use to perform common tasks. They save you the trouble of writing the code yourself; you merely integrate the controls into your ActiveX script. A server-side control extends the functionality of server-side scripting by providing an interface to specific tasks. For example, if you want to use server-side scripting to communicate with a database, you must use the database server control to gain access. Other controls perform tasks such as sending mail, working as search engines, generating surveys, and automatically identifying users. New controls can be acquired and installed at any time. For more detailed information, refer to the Internet Resource Center in the Microsoft Web site.

ACTIVEX SEARCH ENGINE

On your travels through the Web, you might have noticed some larger Web sites that have searching capabilities, allowing you to post queries to find content within the site. You can provide this capability to your users with the ActiveX search engine, a special control developed for the purpose of searching. Once you install the search engine, all you have to do is create an HTML search form with which the user posts the query search. This search engine knows how to index your entire Web server and follow all your virtual directories. Index files are created automatically.

ISAPI (Internet Server Applications Programming Interface)

IIS includes a programming interface known as ISAPI. ISAPI is both an API and an interface to the IIS. You need to know how (or know someone who knows how) to write programs to exploit this interface. ISAPI works similarly to the way server-side scripting works, except that your program can be more specialized, will probably be faster, and can have more advanced features. If you can write out what you want to do on paper, in detail, you can create or have created for you an ISAPI-based server extension to do whatever you want. ISAPI allows a server extension to run as part of the IIS instead of separate from it.

IDC, ActiveX server-side scripting, and the ActiveX search engine are built using ISAPI. Because of this, they are able to perform significantly faster and provide more functionality than server extensions written using CGI (described in the next section).

API (Application Programming Interface)

An API is a set of functions that are provided by a vendor to allow programmers to do a set of tasks without having to write the code for common tasks themselves.

Common Gateway Interface (CGI)

CGI is software that provides an interface between the Web server and other programs operating on the same server and also provides a defined method of passing information from one program to another. At this time, CGI is being supplanted by ISAPI. However, a large number of existing programs use CGI. Until there are ISAPI replacements for these programs, you might choose to run them on your server. But because CGI programs must run as separate processes from IIS, they tend to be slower, take up more memory, and use more system processing power. For new applications that you might write, we recommend you use ISAPI or ActiveX server-side scripting.

Practical Extraction and Report Language (PERL)

PERL, a language commonly used for writing scripts, is the predominant scripting language on UNIX systems. It has evolved over time to become very powerful, but it is also very difficult. PERL is available for Microsoft Windows NT in the Windows NT Resource Kit and on the Microsoft FTP server. You can find many existing PERL scripts to extend the functionality of your Internet site. If you create a PERL script, it must follow the CGI conventions.

We recommend ActiveX scripting over PERL for performance and security reasons. Since PERL scripts interface with the Web server via CGI, they are slower and use more memory. Also, a hacker who has experience with PERL could pose a security risk by sending rogue PERL commands to your processor.

Client-Side Extensions

In some situations, it is more efficient for the client to handle the processing of content than for the server to do it. Unlike server-side extensions, where the server creates a dynamic document to be sent to the client, client-side extensions allow the client to dynamically change what is displayed on screen without further input from the server. It takes less processing power for the client to handle dynamic data when the data is based on actions by the user at the client. Because the server transmits only a small piece of code, interaction with the specific Web page is significantly faster.

Client-side extensions might be used, for example, for placing orders on line with a pizza delivery service. It saves the server processing power if the client handles part of the ordering process. As you choose the items you want on your pizza, a client-side extension could be used to take the order and keep a running total of the cost. In this way, if you are having an indecisive day and keep changing your order, or if you find that the extra cheese you've ordered costs more than you have in your piggy bank, all the changes you make happen on the client side and don't affect the server's resources. If the client's connection is not fast, it also speeds the use of the Web page if processing is done on the client side. Your order is not processed by the server until it is complete.

Another way client-side extensions could come in handy is if you want to display a chart representing some dynamic data stored on the server. Without client-side extensions, you would need the server to generate dynamically a graphic for the chart and then transmit that graphic to the client. With client-side extensions in place, you could simply send the client the raw data and let the client's computer create the graphic. This saves in two places. The processing on the server is reduced significantly, and the traffic across the network is lessened.

There are two main client-side extension standards that you should consider: ActiveX and Java.

ActiveX Client-Side Extensions

ActiveX client-side extensions allow you to create highly interactive and entertaining Web pages to be displayed on the user's browser without putting an extra burden on your Web server. This is accomplished by embedding small pieces of code in the HTML document that direct the browser software to do some task. ActiveX client-side extensions can give you not only the added functionality of displaying a Web page on the clients computer but also the use of the client's processing power. The client's computer can handle a task that would otherwise need to be done by the server or could not be done at all.

ActiveX client-side extensions integrate many different components. The scripting language used for ActiveX is Visual Basic Scripting (VBS), but ActiveX controls are available from almost any other programming language. ActiveX controls are loaded on the client's computer and provide the building blocks on which to create your extended pages. With a little imagination and some programming skill, there is nothing you can't accomplish on your Web site if you and your clients are using ActiveX.

For more information about ActiveX client-side extensions, take a look at the Developer and Internet sections on Microsoft's Web site.

Java

Java is a scripting language developed by Sun Microsystems. It was originally created to control set-top boxes for an interactive television project, but developers soon found that Java was useful for creating scripts on the Internet as well. Java allows you to extend the client- or server-side extensions of your Web site by embedding the programming language in your HTML documents.

Comparing ActiveX and Java

ActiveX is a combination of different technologies. The ActiveX controls, the building blocks for your client-side extensions, are compiled for each user's computer platform, making the controls more efficient and allowing them to take full advantage of the features available on that platform.

Java is an interpreted scripting language, meaning that the code is transmitted to the client's computer and then a process on the client's computer converts it into a working program. This takes a little more time to process and also limits some of the possibilities, since different clients have different capabilities. One advantage this gives Java is its portability to many different platforms.

Before deciding to use one technology over another, you should do some further research comparing the technologies to determine which will work better for you and your Web site.

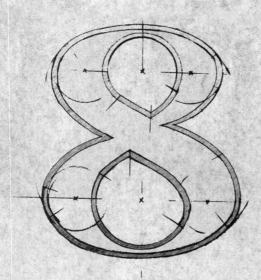

8 Becoming an Internet Service Provider

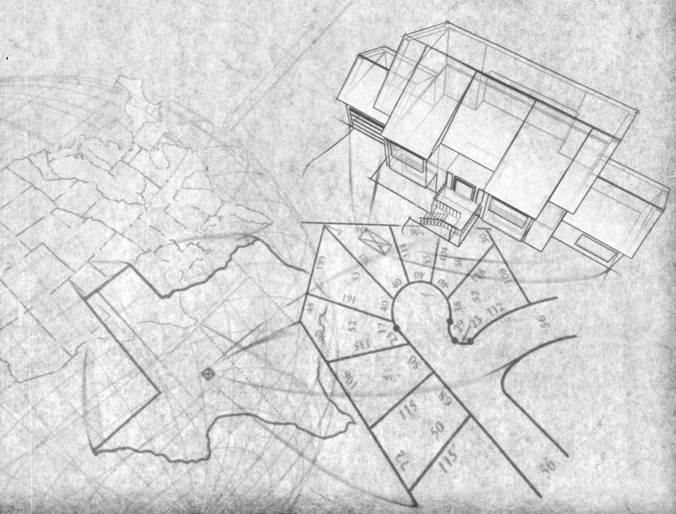

The growth of the Internet is spawning many new business opportunities. Those who have the ability to publish on the Internet can become Internet presence providers by selling Internet publishing services and renting server space to others. As we discussed in Chapter 2, an Internet business opportunity that requires similar expertise is that of Internet service provider (ISP). To this point, we have been teaching you how to set up a server to publish on the Internet. This chapter is specifically geared toward those of you who might be interested in becoming ISPs.

Internet service providers have specific hardware and bandwidth requirements in order to provide dial-in service to their customers. We'll discuss these requirements and walk you through the steps of configuring Microsoft Windows NT Server for dial-in. We'll also go over some of the other services that ISPs can offer and some of the business issues associated with this kind of venture.

What Exactly Is an Internet Service Provider?

First and foremost, an ISP offers its customers dial-up access to the Internet—a gateway through which customers can connect to the Internet for their own use. In essence, becoming an ISP is like starting up a small version of the Internet access departments of MSN, AOL, AT&T, or any of the other companies that are currently providing Internet access. OK, we know what you're thinking now. Can I really compete with behemoth companies like that? Well, if we didn't think opportunities exist, we wouldn't be writing this chapter.

Many small ISPs have viable and profitable businesses providing Internet access and other Internet-related services. To be completely honest, however, some skeptics think that the small Internet service providers out there will be eventually swallowed up by big companies. Our opinion differs. We think that you can compete with these companies if you can offer competitive services and prices and if you offer top-rate customer service, an area where the large companies often fail miserably.

In addition to Internet access, you can offer your customers many other services. You can provide mailboxes for e-mail, communications services like IRC, and access to Usenet newsgroups through NNTP. (See discussions of these services on page 163.) You can also increase the service level that you provide to customers by offering the same services that an IPP can offer: Internet publishing and content creation. Offering a complete range of Internet services can really help distinguish you from the big companies and gives your customers the convenience of being able to purchase all of their Internet services from the same place.

Providing Dial-in Access

In order to connect your customers to the Internet, you must provide them with dial-in access to your network. Your customers will typically use either standard telephone lines or ISDN lines to connect to your server, and then your server will route them onto the Internet over your high-speed connection. In order to offer dial-in access to other people, you will obviously have more demanding hardware and bandwidth needs than those we discussed in Chapter 3. Modems and/or ISDN adapters, telephone and/or ISDN lines, and additional serial ports will be needed in order for your customers to connect to your server. Also, you must consider whether the bandwidth of your current Internet connection can handle the increase in traffic.

How to Set Up the Dial-in Service

In order for your customers to be able to connect to your server for their access to the Internet, you will need additional telephone lines for them to dial into. The number of additional lines that you should order depends primarily on the number of customers you have and the kinds of service contracts you have with them. For instance, you may have customers who want to pay for full-time dedicated connections or customers who are only occasional users and will be paying for their connections on an hourly basis. Contact your local telephone company to order standard telephone or ISDN lines.

The dial-in phone or ISDN lines your customers use connect to modems or ISDN adapters. See Figure 8-1. The modems and most ISDN adapters are connected to your computer via serial ports. A standard personal computer can support up to four serial ports. For numbers beyond that, you need to use an enhanced multiport serial device. Look to the Windows NT Server hardware compatibility list to choose an enhanced serial device so that you are sure to get one with a driver for Windows NT Server. Once you connect your modems to your server, you will be ready to configure your system for dial-up access and set up shop.

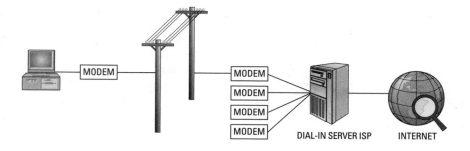

Figure 8-1. A customer dials in for access to an ISP and from there to the Internet.

The Dreaded Capacity Question

Figuring out the capacity that you will need for dial-in access, specifically the number of lines and modems you need, is a difficult problem. Many variables affect your needs. It probably isn't economical for you to have a modem and phone line for each customer unless those customers are specifically buying private service and paying a premium. To be able to offer competitive rates to your customers, you need to come up with a ratio for the number of customers per modem, with the types of services that you offer and the usage habits of your customers affecting this ratio.

So how do you determine how many users per modem? Since there is no formula that will work in all cases, we suggest that you either consult a psychic friend for advice or start out with something like one phone line for every five customers and be prepared to make adjustments if necessary. You will have to rely on customer feedback to find out how well this works. If your customers are constantly complaining that they can't get a connection, you need to scale up. Windows NT Server has been tested using up to 256 modems on a single computer, so there is plenty of growth potential available on each server. If your needs grow beyond the capacity of 256 modems, you'll probably need to add a second server.

Hunt Group Service

It's more convenient for both you and your customers if you can give out a single telephone number that will access all the lines that you have. Telephone companies offer a service called *hunt groups* that allows you to do this. If you have a hunt group, a call made to your number causes the telephone system to hunt for and connect your user with the first open line it finds. If your needs change, additional lines can always be added to your hunt group.

Bandwidth Considerations

Before you can offer Internet access to your customers, you need to consider whether the bandwidth of your current connection is able to support additional users. Since the primary business of an ISP is to provide dial-up access to the Internet, having sufficient bandwidth available is critical for the success of this business; you should connect to the Internet using a permanent high-speed connection, either frame relay or a leased line. We recommend a T1 leased-line connection. The total bandwidth you need is dependent on traffic and the services that you will be offering. The more users you have connected to your dial-in service at one time, the higher your overall bandwidth needs will be.

As we discussed in Chapter 3, calculating bandwidth needs is imprecise. If you are an ISP, you need to consider bandwidth needs for both access to the Internet and access from the Internet, depending on the services that you are providing. If you are an ISP offering access to the Internet only and no Internet publishing services, you should add together the maximum data-transfer rate for each of your dial-in devices to estimate the total bandwidth you need. If you are also providing Internet publishing services, don't forget to add those bandwidth needs to the calculation of your total. Recall from Chapter 3 that your bandwidth needs for Internet publishing are based on your best guesses as to the number of people who will access your site.

Configuring the Operating System for Dial-in Access

Before you can configure Windows NT Server for dial-in access, all your serial ports, adapters, modems, and phone lines must be installed. The installation process will differ depending on the manufacturer the devices came from, so we won't walk you through the installation steps. Follow the instructions that came along with your specific hardware.

INSTALL AND CONFIGURE REMOTE ACCESS SERVICE (RAS)

RAS is the software that supports dial-in access for your customers.

1. Launch the Network control panel from the Control Panel.

2. Click the Services tab, and select Add if Remote Access Service is not already in the list. If RAS is already in the list, double-click its entry to go to step 4. See Figure 8-2.

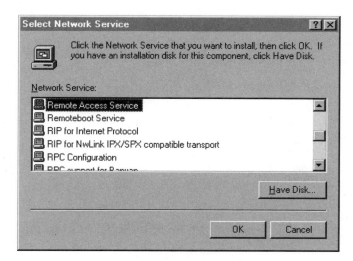

Figure 8-2. Network Service list.

3. Follow the prompts to install Remote Access Service from the Windows NT Server CD-ROM.

4. After Remote Access Service is installed, you need to install your various modems. RAS prompts you to pick the devices you want to use. If you have no devices currently defined, RAS prompts you to install new devices. Click Yes to configure your new modems or ISDN adapters.

5. Repeat the process of adding new devices until all your modems and ISDN adapters are configured.

6. Click the Configure button for each of your modems or adapters while each is highlighted. Choose either dial-in support or both dial-in and dial-out support to allow RAS to answer incoming calls on these devices. See Figure 8-3.

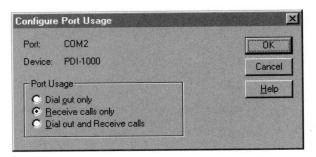

Figure 8-3. *The Configure Port Usage dialog box.*

7. Then click the Network button, and make sure that TCP/IP is selected as at least one of the protocols on the list. For ISP service, the only protocol that you must have is TCP/IP. You don't need to select the other protocols unless you know that you have a specific need for them. See Figure 8-4.

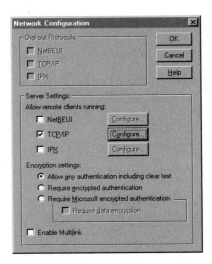

Figure 8-4. *Network configuration for RAS.*

8. Click the Configure button for TCP/IP, and make sure that the IP addresses for each modem or ISDN adapter come from either a DHCP server or from a static pool of valid Internet addresses. See Figure 8-5.

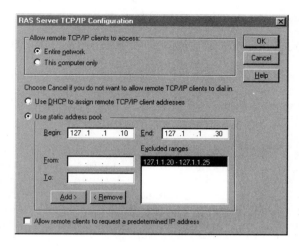

Figure 8-5. *RAS Server TCP/IP settings.*

9. When you are finished with the network settings, click the OK button, and Windows NT Server will configure itself and ask you to let it reboot. Upon completion of the reboot, your server will be ready to take calls.

Setting Up RAS Users

User Manager for Domains is used to add user accounts for each of the users who will dial into your system. When you set up user accounts, pay particular attention to security. Make sure you assign only the minimum access to your system that each user needs. Permission for dial-in access can be granted in either User Manager for Domains or in Remote Access Admin. Normally, you will give a user access to your RAS system, and you won't configure any other settings. One option that you might want to consider, however, is *callback*. When callback is enabled, each time your customers are verified on the RAS system, RAS hangs up and calls them back to make the connection. Callback is sometimes used for security reasons or when you want to pay for your customer's toll charges. We recommend that you not enable callback unless you absolutely need it.

How Does Your Customer Connect?

As an ISP, you will have to instruct your customers on configuring their computers to be able to dial into your system. Users connecting to a RAS system first need to have dial-out support using *Point-to-Point* protocol (PPP). Microsoft Windows 95 and Windows NT Workstation have this protocol built in, so as long as your customers are using one of those operating systems, they will simply use dial-up networking to connect to your system. If your customers are using any other operating system, such as Apple Macintosh, UNIX, or Microsoft Windows for Workgroups, they will need to find a third-party TCP/IP-capable PPP dial-in software package. Often this software can be obtained free of charge, but not always. Your customers should contact their operating system vendor for information regarding this software. Once your customers have PPP software installed, then all they have to do is configure it with the username, the password, and the phone number that you give them for access. If your customers are using Windows NT Workstation or Windows 95, you also must provide them with the domain name for your Windows NT domain structure.

Remote Access Admin

Remote Access Admin is a program installed with RAS on Windows NT Server and used to manage your RAS system. You use the Admin program to configure a user's dial-in access to the system and to check the status of the modem and ISDN ports on your system. You can see whether a port is currently in use and who is using it, reset a port that is not functioning correctly, and even disconnect a user you don't want on line. Remote Access Admin is a very handy tool to use when trying to maintain control of a dial-in server.

Services to Offer as an ISP

Once you have the ability to provide dial-in access to your customers, you have the potential to offer a greater range of Internet services to enhance your business. The service that will likely bring you the most business is e-mail, but you can also offer access to chat groups through IRC and to newsgroups through NNTP. We briefly discuss these services, but since setting them up depends on the specific software that you choose, we don't go into great detail.

E-mail

E-mail is probably the most important service that you can offer as an ISP. Customers who have mailboxes on your server access your server regularly to send and receive their mail. Having a user's mailbox tied to your mail system can make it harder for the user to leave you for another ISP.

Many vendors have e-mail systems available for use with Windows NT Server. You probably want to shop around for prices and features. If you are looking for a basic system limited to inbox and outbox services, you might consider the MAILSRV program that is available with the Windows NT Resource Kit. For a more advanced system that includes features like public folders, mail-routing rules, and server message store, Microsoft Exchange is a very good choice.

IRC (Internet Relay Chat)

Internet Relay Chat (IRC) is a popular service that allows users to interactively chat with one another via the Internet. You might want to provide access for your customers to one of the public IRC networks, or you could set up a private IRC server. Lately, IRC has been getting so popular that it can be difficult for people wanting to join a chat session to actually find a free server to connect to. By having an IRC server on your system, your customers can more easily connect to an IRC because you've provided them with a dedicated server for access. You can also set up a private IRC server that is not connected to a public IRC network and use it for chats between users of your own service.

Several third-party products on the market allow Windows NT Server to act as an IRC server. More than likely, these won't impose any additional hardware or bandwidth requirements over what you already have as an ISP to run IRC.

NNTP (Network News Transfer Protocol)

Another service that ISPs often offer their customers is network news or Usenet (NNTP). This service enables customers to access the vast network of bulletin board–like discussion groups that exist on the Internet. Providing your customers with access to an NNTP server that you maintain can allow them to have faster access to the data. With NNTP, there is no significant increase in bandwidth needs, but the amount of disk space required is quite large. Every day more than 150 MB of new information travels across the NNTP network. Unless you think it will be useful to your customers or will give you a great competitive advantage, we don't recommend running a full NNTP server.

You might want to provide a local-only NNTP server that covers your own private discussion group topics, such as new policies for your customers, surveys, and feedback. Many third-party products handle both NNTP and links to allow access to those NNTP groups from a Web server. Microsoft is also working on an NNTP server that will be released as an add-on to Microsoft Exchange Server.

Business Issues

Setting up a business as an ISP is a significant venture that can't be run part-time. An ISP business is very competitive, service oriented, maintenance intense, and time and effort consuming. If you are currently an IPP who has a customer base and is familiar with Internet technology, you can gradually expand your business to provide dial-up access to the Internet relatively easily. We advise those who are starting out as an ISP to do a lot of research in advance, into both the technology and general business issues, especially if you have never run your own business before. Some areas that you may want to give careful consideration to as an ISP are how you market your services, how you price them, and how you conduct customer service. Smart marketing, good services offered at good rates, and responsive customer service can help fend off the competition from large companies.

Marketing Your Services

If you are offering many different services, consider bundling some of these services together and offering your customers package deals. For your customers, package plans can be more economical. For you as an ISP, package plans allow you to sell more services at a time, can simplify billing, and might improve your competitiveness.

Offering a large range of services to your customers can tie your customers more closely to you, at the very least by making it more difficult for them to switch to another service provider. This strategy becomes increasingly important in the ISP community as competition heats up and the larger companies begin offering lower rates and possibly higher speed of access. Customers often need more incentive to move than marginally lower prices if they have all of their (in this case, Internet) needs taken care of by a single company. It could be more costly for them to change the e-mail address on all of their business cards and stationery than the savings they would realize through another provider.

Keeping Your Rates Competitive

Currently, no standard billing methods have been defined for ISP services. Some companies offer flat-rate service; others charge an hourly usage fee. In the competitive Internet market, it is important to stay on top of your competition and be aware of your rates in comparison to theirs. If you are going to handle time-based billing, some new third-party software systems allow Windows NT Server to handle this kind of tracking.

Customer Support Issues

To be perfectly plain about it, becoming an ISP will be *very* customer-support intensive. You must be prepared for this. Because an ISP is the gateway or connection to the Internet for its customers, small technical problems on either your end or theirs will not easily be forgiven. At the slightest hint of trouble, you can expect that your users will start calling. Users will turn to you as both the cause and the fixer of their problems.

Before you embark on the process of setting up as an ISP, you want to make sure you have a customer-service system in place and that you are prepared to handle this kind of service. Many of your customers will expect 24-hour-a-day, 7-day-a-week customer service. Getting a user connected to your server via dial-in access is complicated by variables such as the type of operating system and the software that the customer uses and the user's general level of knowledge. You need to have a strong base of technical knowledge yourself and the ability to be responsive to your customers' needs.

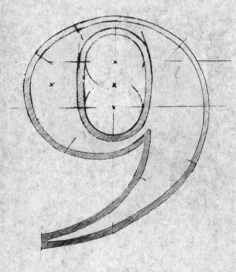

Keeping Your
Server Healthy
and Happy

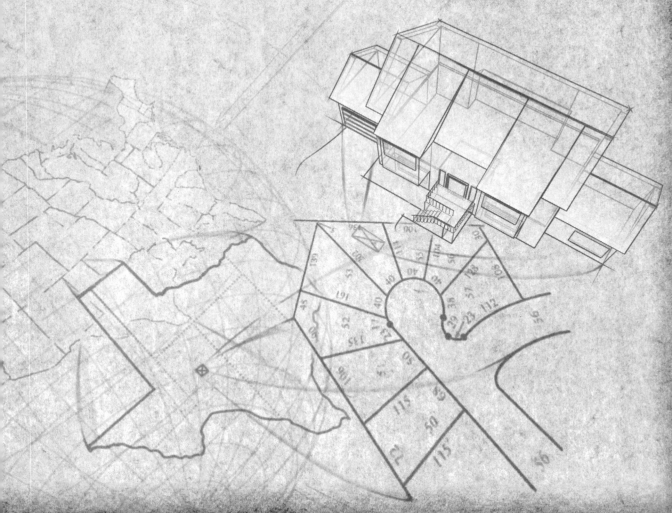

We wish we could tell you that you've done all the work now that your Internet server is up and running, but that's not the case. As with any other computer system, you can't just set up your Internet server, walk away from it, and expect it to happily do its thing. You need to perform regular maintenance to keep your system in good working order. To keep your server in top form, you need continually to manage and maintain your hardware, software, and content. This chapter is about how to manage and maintain it all well.

Using Event Logs to Track Your System

Event logs are used to track various occurrences in your system, mostly unusual events and errors, but some logs track usual events too. An event might be as ordinary as a service starting or quitting, or it could be an error in the system, such as a controller card that times out while trying to write to the hard disk. Windows NT Server gives you the option of maintaining three event logs for tracking system events, and the Internet Information Server has its own log for tracking use of the Internet Server.

Windows NT Server Event Logs

Windows NT Server has three event logs that track various areas on your server. The System log tracks hardware and core-system, software-level services. The Application log is used by the software running on your system to log application-specific errors. The Security log tracks the users of services for security purposes.

One word of warning: Many of the event log messages can be described as cryptic, at best. In some cases, the information that you find in the logs won't be very useful to you. You should be looking primarily for repeated errors that happen in fast succession or critical disk errors. Detailed explanations for each error message can be found in the Microsoft Windows NT Resource Kit, where they are thoroughly documented.

Often when there is an error in one part of your system, it causes a cascade of events, where one problem will cause more problems, leaving a chain of entries in the event log. When you open Event Viewer to look at a log (see Figure 9-1), you want to determine what the original error is. For example, assume that the interrupt isn't correctly configured on your network card. In this case, the network card driver doesn't initialize, the protocol TCP/IP can't find the card, and then there is no protocol for the server to use for communication. In a chain reaction like this, each of these systems logs an error.

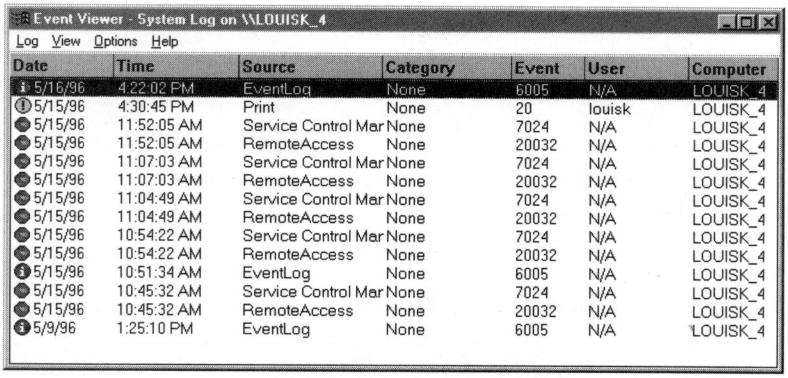

Event Viewer - System Log on \\LOUISK_4

Log View Options Help

Date	Time	Source	Category	Event	User	Computer
5/16/96	4:22:02 PM	EventLog	None	6005	N/A	LOUISK_4
5/15/96	4:30:45 PM	Print	None	20	louisk	LOUISK_4
5/15/96	11:52:05 AM	Service Control Mar	None	7024	N/A	LOUISK_4
5/15/96	11:52:05 AM	RemoteAccess	None	20032	N/A	LOUISK_4
5/15/96	11:07:03 AM	Service Control Mar	None	7024	N/A	LOUISK_4
5/15/96	11:07:03 AM	RemoteAccess	None	20032	N/A	LOUISK_4
5/15/96	11:04:49 AM	Service Control Mar	None	7024	N/A	LOUISK_4
5/15/96	11:04:49 AM	RemoteAccess	None	20032	N/A	LOUISK_4
5/15/96	10:54:22 AM	Service Control Mar	None	7024	N/A	LOUISK_4
5/15/96	10:54:22 AM	RemoteAccess	None	20032	N/A	LOUISK_4
5/15/96	10:51:34 AM	EventLog	None	6005	N/A	LOUISK_4
5/15/96	10:45:32 AM	Service Control Mar	None	7024	N/A	LOUISK_4
5/15/96	10:45:32 AM	RemoteAccess	None	20032	N/A	LOUISK_4
5/9/96	1:25:10 PM	EventLog	None	6005	N/A	LOUISK_4

Figure 9-1. *Event Viewer displaying an event log.*

The System log probably contains the most useful information for you. Generally, if an error occurs during the boot-up sequence or during the normal operation of your server, an event with some details shows up in the System log and might clue you in as to what is going on. The information that you find in the System log can help you track down and repair the cause of the problem.

The Application log contains events that typically apply to server applications. For example, if you are running Exchange, you usually find messages about the status of the Exchange server in the Application log. If you suspect errors in your applications, you should definitely check the Application log, but it's also a good idea to check the System log, as well, because there is a bit of randomness concerning which errors are written to which logs.

The Security log keeps track of the users who use specific services and resources. In Chapter 5, we advised you not to turn on the Security log in favor of system performance and to rely on the IIS logs instead. If you followed this advice, no events will be written into the Security log.

MANAGING EVENT LOGS

As time goes on, the log files can get quite large and difficult to wade through. To keep the logs smaller and easier to read and to free up disk space, clear your event logs occasionally, maybe every week or so. It is not possible to selectively delete entries from the logs. The only option you have is to choose the Clear All Events menu option in Event Viewer, eliminating all the entries at once. If you want to keep a record of the entries, you can archive the event log data to a file before deleting them.

EVENT LOG SETTINGS

The event logs can be configured to help you manage their growth. The Event Log Settings dialog box (choose Log Settings from the Log menu) lets you set the maximum size for the log. (See Figure 9-2.) The default is 512 KB, and, unless you can think of good reasons to change it, we recommend you leave this setting as is. Once you have set the log size, you have to determine what will happen after the log reaches that size. The first option is to Overwrite Events As Needed, and this is the option that we recommend. After the log has reached capacity, the oldest events are automatically overwritten with new events. The other options are Overwrite Events Older Than *x* Days and Do Not Overwrite Events. If you choose not to overwrite events, you could have a situation where serious events happen without your knowledge.

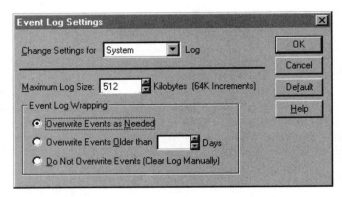

Figure 9-2. *The Event Log Settings dialog box.*

CRYSTAL REPORTS FOR WINDOWS NT SERVER

Crystal Reports is a tool that comes with the Windows NT Resource Kit that you can use in place of Event Viewer. For most single-server Internet hosts, Event Viewer will meet your needs, but for more advanced users or for those with multiple servers, Event Viewer is limited. It supports only one level of filtering or sorting, allows you to view events for only one server at a time, and does not allow for analysis. Crystal Reports has more advanced features than Event Viewer, allowing complex analysis of the log files, and it offers an unlimited set of reporting options.

IIS Logs

IIS maintains a set of logs separate from the event logs maintained by the operating system. IIS logs can provide a wealth of information about the users of your Web site and the pages they access. The IIS logs keep a list of access events that tell you the IP address through which a user accessed the server, the IP address of the user, the objects the user accessed, and the time and the date of that access. The data that you get from the IIS logs is very useful, but it comes in a very raw format. In order to make this information more useful to you and easier to analyze, you probably want to invest in an analysis tool to use when you review your IIS log files. Analyzing the IIS logs can give you even more useful information, such as which of your pages gets the most hits, peak usage times, the kinds of resources your users are accessing, and the operating system and the Web browser software your users are using. A number of analysis tools are on the market.

On a popular Internet site, the IIS logs can get very large, so pay close attention to the management of these files by either archiving or deleting old logs. Additionally, you can specify how often IIS logs are created by going to the Logging tab in Internet Service Manager and configuring settings there. We recommend that you configure the log files to be broken out by week or by day so that the files are smaller and easier to manage.

Preventative Maintenance

Much of the regular maintenance you'll need to do to keep your system running well is preventative. Some areas of your system are more likely than others to give you problems. You need to be aware of likely problems to keep them from happening in the first place, and you need to anticipate and plan for the future needs of your Internet server.

Don't Forget to Back Up

I bet you thought we wouldn't mention backup again in this book.... Wrong! Backup is the single most important maintenance task you should perform. Too many people don't worry about backup until after the first disaster occurs, and then it's too late. Make sure that you back up your system at least once a week in order to prevent possible heartache and probable headache for yourself. In Chapter 3, we recommended that you invest in a SCSI tape backup drive. Although tape backups are slow, the technology is very reliable, and you can store vast amounts of information on tapes.

Make Sure Your Hard Disk Is Healthy

Be careful to monitor the amount of hard-disk space that you have available. Windows NT Server will place an event in the system log when it senses that available disk space has reached a critically low level, but, to avoid any problems, you should be aware of your status before it reaches this point. Periodically open the My Computer icon and select Properties for your hard disk to see how much space you have. If you find you are running low, either go through your system and clear unneeded stuff from your hard disk or add new hard disks to your system.

You should also get into the habit of checking your disk for problems about once a month or so. To do this, you can run the CHKDSK utility. Make sure that you are on the disk you want to check, and then enter the command *CHKDSK /F* at the command prompt. CHKDSK processes the command at the next reboot, so you must reboot your system. Checking the disk allows the system to clean up the hard disk in order to keep serious problems from occurring. If you notice bad sectors showing up and they continue to get worse, you have a clear indicator that the hard disk in question is going bad and should be replaced as soon as possible.

Reboot Your Server Monthly

It's a good idea to reboot your server at least once a month just to take care of any problems that might exist and that have not made their presence known to you yet. If you are running CHKDSK monthly as we suggest, you will be rebooting anyway, and you can take care of these two measures at the same time.

Monitor for Performance

Part of the regular maintenance of your server is the work of performance monitoring. Tuning your server for the best possible performance can be a continual task. You can tweak and refine your system and find many utilities to help you do this. Like piano tuning, the tuning of your server is an artful science and also a very complex subject—a bit too much for this book. For a detailed source of information about performance tuning along with some good and useful utilities, we recommend that you turn to the Windows NT Resource Kit.

Check Modems and Phone Lines (If You Support Dial-in)

Windows NT Server attempts to keep your modems in good working order, but sometimes, for some strange reason, a modem will get confused and refuse to work. You can use Remote Access Admin to check the status of each modem you have and reset it if you need to. Sometimes when a modem is acting up, cycling its power (turning the modem off and on again) will fix the problem. Any time you cycle a modem's power, you must make sure that RAS reinitializes itself for that modem. To do this, go to Remote Access Admin and, for the serial port that corresponds to the modem, press Reset.

If the phone line that your home telephone is connected to goes dead, you are likely to notice it before long. With a phone line connected to your Internet server, though, especially if it is just one of many phone lines, a problem can go unnoticed for quite some time. You should check all your phone lines occasionally for dial tones, just to make sure that they are working. If you think you might be having a problem, you should report it to the telephone company.

If you notice that you're not getting calls into your system on a particular line, you should dial that number and try to connect. If you can't, check the modem, the phone line, and all the connections between them.

Do Continual Capacity Planning

In Chapter 3, we talked at length about capacity planning. It's not until you actually get your server up and running that you'll be able to see how it performs under the loads you are placing on it. If you find that the server is continually busy and slow to respond, you should consider increasing the resources for that server. Some possible remedies for a poorly performing server are to add more memory or to move to a faster processor. If your customers complain about having a very slow connection or they regularly have a difficult time connecting at all, you might have a problem related to the bandwidth of your link. If you suspect a link problem, you probably need to increase the speed of your connection. As we have said before, capacity planning is not an exact science. The only sure thing that you'll find out about capacity planning is that it's the one job that never ends.

> **NOTE:** If you currently have ISA (Industry Standard Architecture) network cards, you might consider switching to PCI (Peripheral Component Interconnect) cards if your computer supports it. PCI is a much faster architecture for adapters, allowing much faster throughput. If you are seeing performance degradation, this switch could help increase the performance of your server and would very likely make your connection faster.

Check Your E-mail Accounts Regularly

If you have created a Webmaster e-mail account and referenced that e-mail address on your Web pages, getting e-mail from your users can be a great way of monitoring problems on your server. Check your Webmaster e-mail regularly for user feedback related to system problems that you might be having, links that might be broken, or other general comments about your site. Users do a very good job, as a rule, reporting problems, and this can save you from having to test every permutation of your system over and over again. One thing to keep in mind when reading user feedback is that not everyone in the world is tactful. Some people will write furious, obnoxious e-mail if they come across a problem with your Web site. If you encounter this kind of flame mail from customers, we suggest that you take into account any problem they may point out and ignore the manner in which it was reported. Make sure you provide a timely response to every reasonable e-mail message sent to your account because this reflects the level of concern that you have for your users.

How to Deal with Upgrades

Software has bugs, and bugs can cause problems for your system. This isn't earth-shattering news—it's just the nature of software. In order for some of the problems with your system to be fixed, you might simply have to wait for the next release of the software and upgrade to it. Software companies generally try to fix bugs in their programs between releases. Of course, new versions bring both new features and new bugs, but it is definitely worth your while to upgrade to the latest technology. Theoretically, each new upgrade of software should perform better than the last one and will include significant innovations.

In between releases of new versions of software, manufacturers often release service packs, which are basically patches for the current version of the software. These include bug fixes and, sometimes, new features. Service packs are *not* new versions of the software. If you acquire a service pack, we recommend that you give it some shake-out time, perhaps as much as a couple of weeks, before you install, just in case the service pack you get ends up causing significant problems. For Microsoft software, service packs are made available on Microsoft's FTP site, or you can find other ways of acquiring them by calling Microsoft Product Support Services. Contact the manufacturers about service packs for other software.

In order to upgrade software on your system, you need to shut down your Internet server. The best time to do the upgrade is one that affects the least number of users. You can consult your IIS logs and determine from them when the off-peak times are for your server. If you have an intranet site that you must shut down to upgrade, you can warn these users in advance that the system will be down for a certain period. It's also wise to do a complete backup of your system before you do any kind of upgrade, regardless of whether you are upgrading hardware or software.

Common Problems

If you've worked with computers before, you know that no matter how much you do to prevent problems, you will still have occasional bits of trouble to resolve. The following section tells you how to deal with some common situations that you might encounter with your Internet server.

What Do You Do When an Application Displays Flaky Behavior?

Occasionally, when you're running an application, you encounter a problem that just doesn't seem to go away. Maybe you've triggered a bug in the program or somehow done something to confuse your computer. (Yes, this happens.) The best method for handling this kind of situation is to just shut down (if you can) and restart the server. Most annoying little problems will go away after a reboot. If the problem returns, then you've probably found something bigger that you should try to fix. Look to your event logs to see if there is any unusual activity. Common causes of many of these kinds of problems are the device drivers of network adapters and video cards. These drivers, especially if they are not on the Windows NT Server compatibility list, can be buggy and cause problems.

What to Do in a Low Disk-Space Situation

If you find yourself in a situation where you are almost out of disk space, you want to work very quickly to fix this situation. Some server applications create temporary files on the disk while they are in operation. If the disk space is not available when the application needs it, unexpected behavior of the application could occur. For example, a script file that reads a database and displays results to a user will store the results in a temporary file before sending the information to the user. If your disk has no space for the temporary file, no results will be sent. You can solve the problem of low disk space by either "cleaning house" on your hard disk or by installing a new hard disk.

To clean up your hard disk, you need to go through your files, identify the ones on your disk that are no longer needed, and delete or archive them. It is possible to find a significant amount of disk space by clearing out old log files, old content, and anything else useless and outdated.

Since the cost of hard disks has dropped dramatically over the past year or so, and this trend appears to be continuing, the purchase of additional disk space is a very attractive option that offers more advantages than simply the additional storage space. Once a system gets two or more disk drives, it can write out data across multiple drives at the same time, which can increase performance across the overall system.

If you are going out to purchase a hard disk, make sure you know what kind of hard disk to purchase before you go to the store. Check your computer manual to find out whether you have an IDE or SCSI hard-disk controller or something else. If you use IDE, you can have only two disks per IDE channel. SCSI controllers can handle at least seven devices on one channel. Hard disks are not difficult to install, but you will have to shut down your server. Make sure, as we advised before, to do a shut down at an off-peak time to minimize disruption for your users. Follow the installation instructions that come with your new hard disk.

How to Deal with a Power Failure

In the case of a power failure, an uninterruptible power supply (UPS) usually buys you enough time to do a proper shutdown of your system. If, for some reason, you are not able to shut down before the UPS runs out, or the UPS fails to kick in fast enough to keep the server running (a rare occurrence), problems can happen and data can be lost. If such a situation occurs, when the power has reliably returned, you should boot up your machine normally and thoroughly check out your system. You might want to manually run a CHKDSK /F just to be certain that nothing really bad happened. In most cases, Windows NT Server is able to resume gracefully after an improper shutdown. Nonetheless, because of the potential for lost data, you should do anything you can to prevent this kind of shutdown.

How to Deal with the Blue Screen of Death

When Windows NT encounters an unrecoverable error that causes the operating system to fail, a message on a blue background reporting some information about that problem will show up on your screen. This condition has been fondly dubbed *the blue screen of death.* Blue screens are rare occurrences, especially if you are using hardware listed on the HCL. In most cases, they are caused by adverse conditions like poorly written device drivers, bad memory, the inability to find the disk where the operating system lives, or, in rarer cases, buggy software. Whatever the cause, you need to see if you can recover from a blue screen. If you followed our advice in Chapter 4 for configuring your system, you will have enabled the option to reboot automatically after a crash. If the system does not reboot itself, try restarting manually. If you can get your system restarted, check the event logs immediately to see whether you can determine what the problem was. If, however, you can't get restarted or the system repeatedly displays blue screens, record the error information found on the screen and contact Microsoft Product Support Services for further assistance. It's possible that you need to reinstall Windows NT Server. If this is the case, then Setup will attempt to retain your system settings where it can.

Content Maintenance

As with the regular maintenance you must perform for your hardware and software, you must also keep up your server's content. Fresh and updated content is just as important as an operational system. Having a regular schedule for updating content can help you to keep on top of this work. You can make your users aware of your update schedule so that they know when to check for new information; this also gives you incentive to stick to your schedule.

If you have a *What's New* section on your Web site, make sure that you update it regularly. Remove material from your site that's no longer relevant, and store it in an archive. Make sure you get any new information on line as soon as possible. Stale information will not keep users coming back and will probably give them a poor perception of your organization.

Test Your Links and Scripts

We've mentioned this before, but we think it's worth repeating. You should periodically test the links on your site to make sure that they are still active. Checking links is especially important if you have links to locations that are not on your own server. Users don't like to see an error message in their browser window when they click on a link, and it might cause them to leave your site altogether.

If you have any scripts running on your Internet site, you should periodically test them to make sure they're in working order. The best way to check your site is to connect through Internet Explorer, just as if you were a user. Browsing your own site is your best diagnostic tool to make sure that your users' experience of your site is what you intended.

Be Responsive to Customer Feedback and Requests

Users will occasionally send you suggestions or requests for things to include on your site. A lot of this feedback will be useful, and you might want to act on it, while some of it will be useless. It's a good customer relations policy to, at the very least, acknowledge all feedback and requests. Even if you won't be implementing a customer's idea, you should thank the user for his or her interest. If an angry user reports an error that you can't seem to reproduce, ignore the anger and let the user know that you can't find the problem. It's important to let your users know that you are listening to them. Responding to your users can take a bite out of your day, but since many of your users will come because they heard good things about your site, it's important to do whatever you can to keep your users happy with you and with your site.

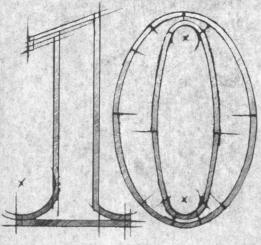

10

Here Today, Gone Tomorrow

Change in Internet Technologies

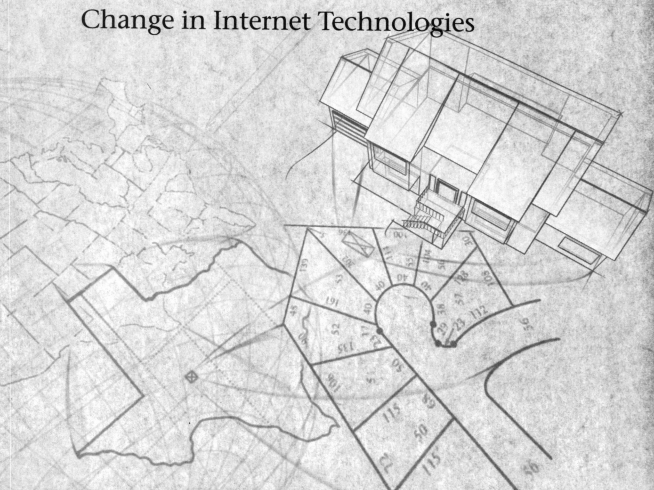

Technological developments in the computer industry have been moving at what seems like light speed for the last several years, and we don't assume that the pace of these changes will slow in the coming years. You can buy a brand-new, top-of-the-line computer one day and find out the next that a faster processor has already been developed. At the same time, individuals and businesses have been wholeheartedly embracing the Internet to reach an extended audience and market, and all indications suggest that Internet technology will significantly influence the direction of hardware and software development. All the large computer companies are devoting resources to the development of Internet technologies, and other industries, such as media and telecommunications, are rapidly incorporating the Internet or Internet technology into their business plans.

All these swift changes make it truly difficult to plan. Not only do you need to know which technological changes have occurred, but also you need to determine which will be lasting. In this chapter, we look through our crystal ball and share with you our vision of the future of Internet technology. We discuss some of the short-term and long-term changes in the Internet and its technologies that we expect to see, some of the new technologies and services that are already arriving, and the direction of the industry in general.

NOTE: Just to settle down your expectations, we hasten to say that we are not going to preannounce new products or technologies. Any specific technologies that we discuss have been announced previously or are already in existence; we confine our talk to how we see these technologies moving the Internet forward. Any predictions that we make for the future of Internet technology are based on our experience and knowledge of the current industry.

Keeping Up with Technological Developments

Competition is responsible for driving the fast pace of changes in technology. Companies within the computer industry are constantly working to add new features to their current products or to develop new technologies with which they'll keep or give themselves an advantage over their competition. With the emerging importance of Internet technologies, many new and "old" companies are working to win the hearts and souls of Internet and intranet communities. Netscape and Microsoft are currently battling for dominance in the Internet browser and server arenas, pushing these technologies rapidly forward.

Ultimately, in the technology wars, the consumer wins. The fierce competition among vendors generally leads to the swift production of better technology at lower prices. In the short term, however, consumers can experience some pain as different, often incompatible technologies scramble for the dominant position. As a consumer, you want to be careful that you don't get stuck in dead-end technology. It takes a certain amount of talent and research to know when to implement a new technology. You don't want to be too late using it, but you also don't want to waste your time on something that isn't going to last. In the computer industry, this dilemma is known as living on the "bleeding edge" of technology.

The fact is, new technology or a new version of software always comes along to replace some existing technology. But it's not a good idea to wait to implement a new technology simply because another one is on its way. The experience you gain using technology that's currently available will put you in much better shape to deal with new technology that replaces it, and you'll be working effectively in the meantime.

What Is the Future of the Internet?

You can still find skeptics lurking around almost every corner thinking that the Internet will fade into oblivion. You need only look around with your eyes open to recognize the shortsightedness of that view. The Internet has become an indispensable tool for multitudes of businesses and individuals, for communication within and outside organizations, as an information gathering tool, as a means to sell and advertise products and services, and, not least, as a source of entertainment. We think the continued adoption of the Internet, along with the emergence of new technology, will make the Internet an even more pervasive tool and a necessary part of every home and office. In short, the Internet will be (actually, it might be already) the most powerful tool you can use to extend the capabilities of your computer.

Keep in mind, however, that the Internet itself is just a network, a pipe that carries information from one place to another. The services and technologies that surround and permeate the Internet are what will evolve the most and are bound to influence the industry. The Internet itself will show the changes primarily by becoming bigger and faster. Increasing bandwidth will be very important in order to move greater amounts of information around, allowing the Internet to support an increasing user base and more advanced services.

The new technologies that will be developed for the Internet will serve to empower your computer. In the future, plugging into the Internet will enable your computer to act like a supercomputer that can perform tasks your computer alone would never be able to handle. Your computer will no longer be limited to the speed of your processor or the amount of RAM you have but will have access to almost limitless CPU cycles on the Internet, not merely to bring you data but also to analyze it.

Convergence of Technologies

With old Internet technologies going out of favor so rapidly and the instantaneous adoption of new technologies, identifying trends to help you decide where to devote your resources is difficult. An apparent trend is that new technologies are being developed to work inside the framework of the Web, and older technologies are gradually being retrofitted to work within the Web framework. A benefit of this convergence of technologies is a consistent user interface. If this trend continues, and we expect it will, HTML and the Web will become the glue that holds many different Internet technologies and services together. Over time, you will find that more useful services and technologies on the Internet are accessible from the Web and will have a consistent user interface.

Internet Enhancements to Desktop Operating Systems

We see the client side of Internet computing changing very quickly. Web browsers as we know them are disappearing and gradually becoming integrated with the operating system. Future enhancements to desktop operating systems will make access to the Internet increasingly easy and eventually invisible. These changes to client-side computing will merge the way users view their local data with the way they view data across the Internet. In other words, the way you access and view a document located halfway across the world on the Internet will be no different from the way you access and view a document located right on your own computer.

The Future of Internet Technology for Small Businesses

Large businesses have embraced the Internet at a dizzying rate. It's hard to find a large company that doesn't have a Web site or doesn't use e-mail. Most large companies have the human and monetary resources necessary to establish an Internet presence. The majority of businesses, however, are smaller, and most have yet to join the electronic revolution of the Internet.

The good news for small-business owners is that software companies are finally starting to recognize their unique needs and are starting to develop software with them in mind. Software companies are also beginning to think about viable and easy ways to get small businesses on the Internet. Software companies are recognizing that many small businesses either don't want to or don't have the resources to hire a team of experts to install systems for them and get them on line. We expect to see increasing numbers of products especially designed for small businesses that will help users easily set up their software and hook up with an Internet service provider. Software for small businesses will also make it easier for them to get their content on the Web, putting them on more equal footing with the bigger businesses on the Net.

Content Creation

Creating content and Internet applications is the software design of the future. Rather than monolithic applications, software designers will build components that plug into the Web. The tools that exist for content creation today, such as FrontPage and the Internet Assistants, are rather basic and probably will be for some time. The tools for content creation are based on technologies such as HTML, ActiveX, and Java, which are still evolving at a rapid pace. As a result, tools written for these languages and technologies are outdated rapidly. Writing tools for content creation today is like trying to build a house while the foundation is still wet. However, great strides are being made on both the client and server sides to make it possible for anyone to produce good content and Internet applications, and once the technologies on which content creation tools are based settle down, people will be able to build intelligent tools to help construct reasonable Internet applications and content without having to be an expert in the technologies.

HTML, THE LANGUAGE OF THE WEB

As a result of the Microsoft and Netscape battle for the browser market, HTML is becoming extended with the development of new tags (keywords that specify how the text appears to the user), moving HTML along at a fast pace. HTML *will* stabilize, and all new development will focus on content creation tools and other technologies that use HTML as their base. HTML is going to become more of a background language. It will be the binding agent between scripts and applications.

THE FUTURE OF SCRIPTING LANGUAGES

Scripting languages, used to extend the functionality of Web servers and browsers, are in their relative infancy and are growing in importance. You need only go into your local bookstore and see the number of titles on Java alone to be convinced of that fact. Developments are being made on both the server and the client side to enhance the scripting capabilities available. As languages such as Java and Microsoft Visual Basic, Scripting Edition, mature and technologies such as ActiveX grow to encompass all the different Internet services, such as chatting, video, audio, and e-mail, we'll see a rich set of applications spring up that will perform functions that currently require operating-system–specific and processor–specific software to be compiled for the platform. Sophisticated scripting languages will be able to create powerful scripts that will be executable across all platforms. Scripting languages will eventually enable processing power to be distributed across the Internet.

Video, Audio, and Telephony over the Internet

Some people believe that the Internet could replace existing communications technology, such as the telephone and television. We believe that this is one of the reasons that the telecommunications and cable companies are vesting their interests so heavily in the Internet. The beginnings of the technology for video, audio, and telephony over the Internet are evident now, but, at this time, the quality is pretty rough. As the bandwidth on the Internet increases, though, and compression technologies get better, the quality of transmissions over the Internet will certainly improve dramatically.

The cost of entry into the Internet broadcast medium is relatively low and, as with most technology, will decrease with time. The uses of this kind of technology, however, are limitless. It is currently possible to connect to the Internet by calling a local number, then chat on line for hours with someone in a distant country. You can use Internet Radio to listen to thousands of radio stations all over the world. Broadcasting video over the Internet could come close to, if not equal to, the current quality of television, although this innovation will be the longest in coming. If you have a business, you could use this technology in many ways. You could offer your customers training courses over the Internet, audio- and perhaps video-capable technical support, or conference calling. You can probably think of a multitude of other uses.

MULTIMEDIA STREAMING

Multimedia streaming of information refers to the real-time transmission of video and audio. Many companies are devoting resources to these technologies to make many different functions possible across a network, such as telephone calls, video conferencing, and broadcasting. To date, most of the work done in this area has been in audio applications. Video is lagging behind because it entails the transmission of much more data over a limited bandwidth. The technology that is leading the way in this area so far is RealAudio by Progressive Networks. RealAudio is already in use on the Internet, and with it you can listen to sports broadcasts from ESPN, news broadcasts from TV networks, and real-time radio broadcasts, among other things. To check out what RealAudio can do, take a look at their Web site at *http://www.realaudio.com*.

IP PHONE

IP Phone is a service that allows live interactive voice communication over the Internet. If you have IP Phone software and compatible sound hardware, you can "call" another person with the same setup over the Internet. The quality of these calls is not quite up to telephone company standards at this point (actually, it's kind of like using a CB radio—remember those?), but because you need only connect to your local service provider to make the call, you can have limitless long distance telephone conversations for the cost of your Internet connection. As a greater number of homes get on line with the Internet and the bandwidth increases, we expect that many people will use their computers and the Internet to communicate with friends, family, and business contacts. No wonder the telephone companies are getting into the Internet game!

CU-SEEME

Like IP Phone, CU-SeeMe is a service that makes communication possible over the Internet. The difference is that CU-SeeMe provides both an audio and a visual way to communicate. People who use CU-SeeMe have small cameras aimed at themselves and connected to their computers. During a CU-SeeMe session, the camera transmits the user's image over the Internet so that the person or people the user is talking to get to see him or her on their screen. (See Figure 10-1.) In effect, making a CU-SeeMe connection is like having a video-telephone conversation. This is a fairly new technology on the Internet, and, frankly, at this stage the audio capabilities are poor, but you have the option to "talk" using your keyboard as you would in a chat session.

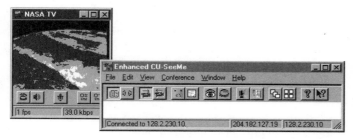

Figure 10-1. NASA broadcasts a 24-hour-a-day series of programs known as NASA TV over CU-SeeMe.

Like IRC, CU-SeeMe could have wide application for business as a tool for customer service and support. Once the connection to the Internet is established, CU-SeeMe is much less expensive than talking on the telephone, and the ability to actually see the "caller" makes the conversation much more friendly. This technology could ease problems with the impersonal nature of the Internet and of e-mail, especially as the audio technology improves. To see what CU-SeeMe can do for you, visit the White Pine Software home page at *http://www.wpine.com*.

How Do I Keep Up with the Changing Technology?

If you're establishing a presence on the Internet, you should spend some time keeping up with developments in technology and the direction of the computer industry. As we said before, with the pace of the changes today, this can be a never-ending job, but there are many resources to help you keep up. One way to stay on top of the technologies is to surf the Web. You can use the news services on sites such as Yahoo to look for breaking stories on technology, or you can visit the Web sites of various companies in the computer industry to get the news firsthand. Many corporate sites have demos of new technology, and some of them make free software available for you to download. There are also news services that will filter the information for you. For a small monthly fee, they will e-mail you news stories concerning topics that are of interest to you.

Browsing the computer and Internet sections of your local bookstore can also give you a lot of information; if you are really interested in a particular topic, you'll probably find a book already written about it. (Believe us, it's difficult to find a topic on which there's not been a book written!) Our recommended reading list in Appendix C points you toward books that can further your knowledge about creating Internet sites. Magazines about communications and the Internet are also great ways to keep up with the technology, at least at a general level.

If you ever get a chance to attend any, industry trade shows are great for learning about new technologies. Companies like to save up their new products and demonstrate them at trade shows where they are guaranteed a huge and interested audience. They also provide a good forum for you to have specific questions answered.

If you don't have the time or desire to do all this work yourself and you have some extra money to spend, you might want to hire a consulting firm to keep up on the technology for you.

The Last Word

The Internet is not going to disappear; in fact, it has already been around for decades. What is in question, though, is the kind and extent of its uses. You've probably been hearing for years that computers are going to be just as commonplace in homes as televisions and telephones are today. We believe that the Internet and associated technologies are going to make this shift possible. Furthermore, we think that it is very likely that the computer and the Internet will eventually replace your TV and your telephone.

These kinds of predictions are really not extremely far-fetched when you consider where computers are today with respect to where they were just several years ago. Who would have thought 20 years ago while running her Apple II that in such a short time such a large number of people could afford to buy for their homes computers that have the capabilities we are used to today? Taking into consideration the fact that technology is changing even faster today, just try to imagine all the things people will be able to do with computers connected to the Internet in the next 20 years!

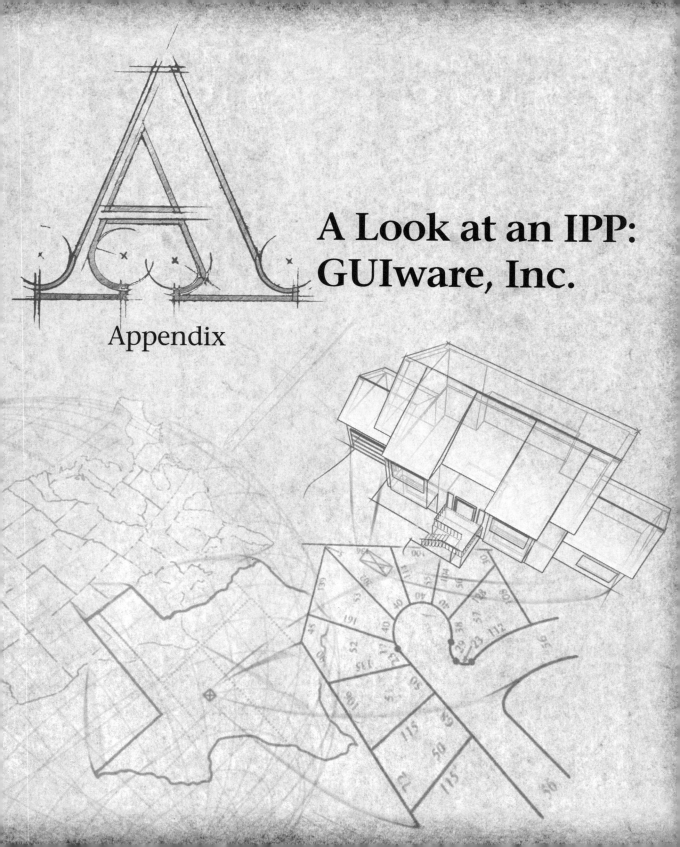

A Look at an IPP: GUIware, Inc.

Appendix

For those of you who might be interested in starting an Internet business venture, here is a look at GUIware, a small but growing company that provides Internet services and consulting. GUIware's primary business as an Internet presence provider is the design, implementation, hosting, and maintenance of Web sites. At the present time, the company has a staff of two, but demand for people with Internet design and development skills is increasing, and GUIware needs to hire more staff to keep up with a recent surge in demand.

GUIware's Business

GUIware's largest source of revenue, accounting for about 80 percent of its business, comes from the custom design and implementation of Web sites. GUIware contracts with a number of companies, designing both Internet and intranet sites. Each project is time-consuming and unique because it depends on the particular needs of the customer proposing each Web site. Some Web authoring is just a matter of designing a simple Web page to convey a message using HTML. Other customers require the design of more complex sites involving interaction with a database and more complicated programming with scripting languages.

Hosting and maintaining Web sites has become a secondary business for GUIware, providing steady revenue for relatively low-maintenance work. Individuals and organizations who use GUIware's servers to host their Internet sites are charged a monthly fee for this service.

GUIware's entire network operates using Windows NT Server as the platform for all the services GUIware offers, including routing, dial-up connections, Web services, e-mail, FTP, Gopher, and DNS. Clients who publish their Web sites on GUIware's servers have the option to update their own content directly via FTP.

How Did GUIware Begin?

GUIware grew out of an experiment to see whether Internet services could be provided using nothing but Windows NT Server and applications designed for Windows NT. In the beginning, many people in the Internet community scoffed at the idea that Windows NT Server could replace a UNIX server to handle the kind of traffic that exists on the Internet. This skepticism was just the challenge that GUIware's founder Louis Kahn needed to get motivated. He hooked up a modem to a Windows NT Server and arranged dial-up access to the Internet with a local service provider. Although this initial setup was slow, it did provide a good testing ground for experimentation at a fairly low cost with all the different Internet services.

At about the same time, Louis's partner, Mark Walter, was looking to make a career change using his skill in Web design and HTML programming. Recognizing an increasing demand for Internet hosting and Web authoring services, the pair merged their skills and GUIware was born. Immediately, they upgraded their communication lines to a frame relay connection and went about setting up a real network system to handle the level of traffic a professional IPP would have.

The business started off small as a moonlighting venture for both founders, with clients mostly coming from family and friends. After about six months, demand for GUIware's services began to increase and Mark realized that he could consistently make more money running GUIware full-time than staying with his current job. Since then the company has continued to be successful and grow.

Hardware and Software

The first server GUIware set up was on a 486/66 PC with 80 MB of RAM and a 2-GB hard disk. A 28.8-Kbps modem was hooked up to the serial port, and an Ethernet card connected the server to a small local area network with three other computers on it. A dedicated dial-up account was set up with a local ISP, and the 486 PC was configured to route traffic between the dial-up connection and the local network. At that time, IIS was not available, so GUIware used the EMWAC Web server from the Windows NT Resource Kit. See Figure A-1 for an illustration of GUIware's original setup.

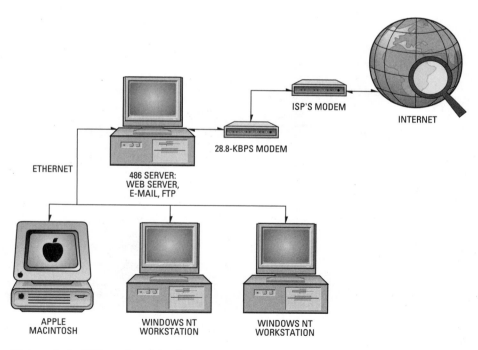

Figure A-1. GUIware's original setup.

After they were confident of the connection working with a dial-up line, GUIware's owners ordered a frame relay line from the local telephone company and worked with their ISP to upgrade their connection to the Internet. The switch to frame relay made it necessary to acquire a frame relay card that was compatible with Windows NT Server. Once the telephone company installed the frame relay line, GUIware connected the line to the frame relay card and started routing traffic over the frame relay network.

When IIS became available, GUIware installed it on their Web server. GUIware now has multiple servers: three Web servers, two DNS servers running Microsoft's DNS server software, two FTP servers, one Gopher server, a dedicated e-mail server, and a dedicated communications/routing server. (This last machine handles dial-in access and routing between Ethernet, the dial-up lines, and the T1 line.) GUIware also has a LAN with Windows NT, Windows 95, and Power Macintosh computers that are used by GUIware employees for their day-to-day work. See Figure A-2 for an illustration of GUIware's present server arrangements.

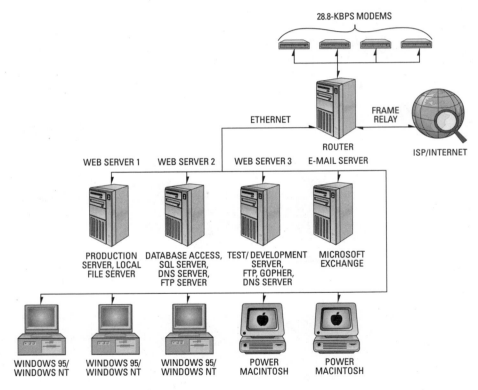

Figure A-2. GUIware's present setup.

GUIware maintains a test/development server used to stage new content either for its own or for its customers' Web sites. This server allows GUIware to test new content and scripts to see the way they will actually look and behave on a real server. This also allows GUIware to access content from many different platforms.

GUIware tests its content using Internet Explorer for Windows and the Macintosh, and Netscape for Windows and the Macintosh, as platforms. Occasionally, GUIware tests on a Lynx browser as well.

The major part of GUIware's content and graphics are produced on Macintosh computers. Windows NT Server allows GUIware to easily support cross-platform development of content. Posting content to the server from the Macintosh is done easily using drag and drop.

Most of the Web authoring work done by GUIware on the Macintosh is accomplished using a simple text editor, BBEdit, that has HTML extensions. Adobe Photoshop, Adobe Illustrator, and Adobe Gallery Effects are used to create complex graphics and edit pictures to fit the specific goals of the project. Other tools are used to create and edit movie and audio files. For script development, GUIware most often uses a Windows NT workstation to create, edit, and debug those systems.

Managing the System

Overall, GUIware's computer system doesn't require a great deal of maintenance, and Windows NT Server makes most of the regular maintenance easy. GUIware regularly monitors disk space, checks for viruses, and analyzes the log files. The biggest maintenance task is backup. To prevent loss of information, GUIware performs backups at least every other day and more often on days in which significant changes have occurred. To avoid disruption of service, GUIware tries to keep maintenance timeouts to a minimum. The owners use analysis tools with the data from the IIS logs to determine the lowest usage times on their servers (usually on the weekend and in the late evening) and use those times to make any changes that require taking the server off line.

GUIware has problems sometimes, however. Recently, two hard disks crashed on a primary computer within minutes of each other. Although there were moments of panic, the situation was easily rectified by replacing those disks with new ones that GUIware keeps on hand for just such an emergency. Data was restored from backup tapes, so only a half-day's work was lost.

GUIware's Future

GUIware's business has been growing steadily, with advertising performed solely by word of mouth and its own Web site. Currently, GUIware is planning to expand its business by advertising in more traditional media and by offering a greater range of services to its customers. GUIware also plans to offer specialized software to help users build and test Web pages for their Internet or intranet sites.

GUIware's long-term goal is to be able to offer its customers complete Internet services under one roof (so to speak). To do this, GUIware needs to expand its services to providing Internet access. Because of the competition in the Internet access business, GUIware doesn't believe that providing Internet access will be a significant way to generate revenue by itself but rather sees Internet access combining with the other services to provide a complete Internet package for customers who want to deal with only one company for all their Internet needs.

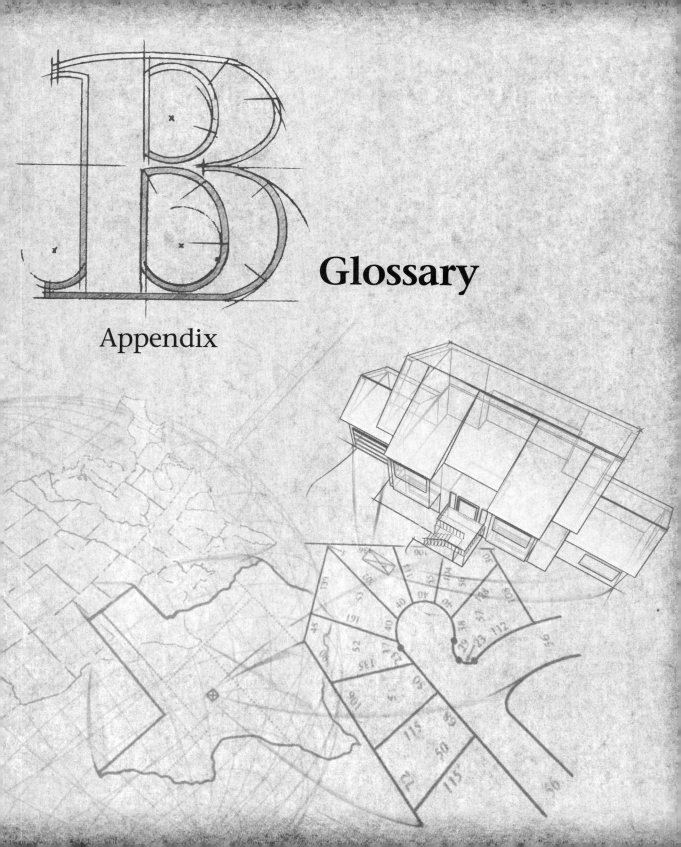

B

Appendix

Glossary

ActiveX A suite of Internet-related technologies that can be used to extend the capabilities of applications and Internet content.

API Application programming interface; provides a precoded set of functions for software developers to use to achieve a specific task.

authentication The process by which a computer confirms the identity of a user or other computer trying to gain access to a set of computer files. Authentication is usually accomplished by checking a username against its corresponding password.

backbone A high-speed, large-bandwidth network that connects local area networks and individual computers over long distances.

backdoor A secret password or generally unknown method for gaining access to a computer system that bypasses the security system in place. *See also* security loophole.

back up A process by which you copy important data from your hard disk to alternative media.

bandwidth In computer terms, the amount of data that can be transmitted over a network connection at a given time.

baud The number of level transitions per second of a communications device (such as a modem). Often (erroneously) used as a synonym for bps.

bps Bits per second; refers to the transmission of data over a communications line or network.

CGI Common Gateway Interface; an older method of allowing a Web server to communicate with another application on the server. *See* ISAPI.

client A computer that uses resources provided by another computer. *See also* server.

client/server technology A method of taking a task and splitting its function across multiple computers.

client-side extension Code that adds additional functionality to an Internet browser on the client computer.

DHCP   Dynamic Host Configuration Protocol; provides a method for dynamically distributing and maintaining IP configurations on multiple computers.

dial-up networking   Allows a remote computer to use a modem or an ISDN connection to access the local network as though the computer were connected directly to the network.

disk mirror   A specific kind of fault tolerance where a second disk is set up to automatically mirror another disk, preventing loss of information.

DNS   Domain Name System; an Internet service that converts people-friendly server names to numeric IP addresses that computers can read. DNS databases are distributed, meaning that they are located in servers throughout the Internet.

domain   In Windows NT Server terminology, a logical grouping of computers all running Windows NT. An Internet domain is not the same thing as a Windows NT domain, although they can both be configured for the same set of machines. *See* domain name.

domain name   In the Internet world, a name for a group of computers that are part of one organization. The computers don't necessarily have to be part of the same network.

Domain Name System   *See* DNS.

Dynamic Host Configuration Protocol   *See* DHCP.

e-mail   Familiar term for electronic mail, which allows people to exchange messages with any other person who has access to e-mail.

encryption   A process used to allow the safe transmission of data by making the data unreadable as it is sent across a network.

Ethernet   A commonly used technology for connecting local area networks. *See* LAN.

fault tolerance   A quality of a computer capable of withstanding (and even continuing to work during) a hardware or software failure. Fault tolerance is achieved by various means, such as disk mirroring.

File Transfer Protocol   *See* FTP.

firewall   A device that isolates one network from another.

frame relay   A communications service available from telephone companies that provides a dedicated high-speed connection between computers.

FTP   File Transfer Protocol; allows the transmission of files from a server to a client computer.

Gopher   A text-based service for document retrieval over the Internet.

HTML   Hypertext Markup Language; the specialized programming language used to create content for the WWW.

HTTP   Hypertext Transfer Protocol; used to transfer HTML documents from server to client.

Hypertext Markup Language   *See* HTML.

Hypertext Transfer Protocol   *See* HTTP.

IDC   Internet Database Connector; a system used to provide database access for Web pages.

IIS   Internet Information Server; a Web, FTP, and Gopher server designed specifically to take advantage of Windows NT Server.

Internet address   *See* IP address.

Internet Database Connector   *See* IDC.

Internet Explorer   Microsoft's Web browser.

Internet Information Server   *See* IIS.

Internet presence provider (IPP)   An organization that provides any combination of Internet services, such as Web site hosting, domain name resolution, content creation, and other Internet-related services *except* dial-up access to the Internet.

Internet Relay Chat   *See* IRC.

Internet service provider (ISP)   An organization that provides dial-up access to the Internet for its customers as well as any of the services that can be provided by an Internet presence provider.

InterNIC   The organization that is charged with managing Internet IP addresses and the top-tier domains for *gov, mil, org, net, edu,* and *com.*

interoperability   The ability of software and hardware to communicate over many computers despite differing platforms or vendors.

IP *See* TCP/IP.

IP address The unique 32-bit address that is assigned to each host computer on the Internet. Transmission of data on a network is not possible unless every host uses the same addressing scheme.

IP gateway *See* router.

IRC Internet Relay Chat; a global chat system that provides a way for people to have real-time conversations on the Internet.

ISAPI Internet Server API; provides a way for software developers to extend the functionality of the IIS using their own software.

ISDN Integrated Services Digital Network; a high-speed telephone line that can be used with dial-up networking.

Java A scripting language used to extend the functionality of a client or server computer.

LAN Local area network; a high-speed network that spans a limited geographic area. Ethernet is often the network technology used to connect the computers in a LAN.

leased line A high-speed dedicated line directly connecting two locations.

local area network *See* LAN.

Mbps Megabits (1024 bits) per second. *See* bps.

modem Contraction of modulator-demodulator; a device that connects a computer to a regular telephone line and allows the transmission of data.

name resolution The process of mapping a name into a corresponding address. Specifically, on the Internet, name resolution refers to DNS, where domain names are matched to their IP addresses.

newsgroups A specific discussion on the NNTP system. *See* NNTP.

NNTP Network News Transfer Protocol; allows a client to participate in discussions in a public forum (known as Usenet) similar to a bulletin board system.

ODBC Open database connectivity; provides a common interface for accessing many different database engines.

packet A unit of data transmitted over a communications line.

PCT Private Communications Technology; an enhanced version of the SSL technology. It allows for much stronger authentication than the standard SSL allowed by the U.S. Government. *See* SSL.

PERL Practical Extraction and Report Language; a programming language that can be used to extend the functionality of the client or server.

Ping A program that transmits a packet to a remote destination and back to determine whether there is a communications problem and the amount of time the round trip takes.

protocol The formal set of rules that govern data transmission, allowing computers to exchange information.

PPP Point-to-Point Protocol; provides an efficient means of allowing a remote computer to connect to a network and use multiple protocols remotely.

RAS Remote Access Service. *See* dial-up networking.

router Can be either a dedicated computer or software that connects to two or more networks and routes information from one network to another. Routers decide which path a packet traveling on the Internet will take to reach its destination. Internet routers are commonly referred to as IP gateways.

scripting Using a programming language to extend the functionality of a server or client computer.

SCSI Small Computer System Interface; a high-speed architecture for connecting peripheral devices to a computer.

search engine A system that allows a user to find specific resources on a network based on user-supplied criteria.

Secure Sockets Layer *See* SET and SSL.

security loophole A hole in a computer's security system created by overlooking or not considering all possible security relationships. *See also* backdoor.

serial port A low-speed (one bit at a time) interface for connecting a peripheral device to a computer.

server A computer accessible to users via a network that makes resources available to users as though these resources originated at the users' own workstations. *See also* client.

server extension   A script or application that extends the functionality of a server.

SET   Secure Electronic Transaction; provides a way for two parties to transact business using a financial clearinghouse as the go-between.

SLIP   Serial Line Internet Protocol; an older method of allowing a remote computer to dial into a network using the IP protocol only. SLIP is being replaced with PPP. *See* PPP.

SSL   Secure Sockets Layer; a data encryption protocol that allows secure transmission of data to and from a server.

subnet mask   Used with TCP/IP to direct packets traveling on the network to their appropriate destinations. A subnet mask is used to determine whether the destination of a packet is on or off the local network.

T1 connection   A type of communications service that provides very high-speed connection between two points. The speed of a T1 connection is 1.5 Mbps.

T3 connection   The fastest communications service available today, providing a connection speed of 45 Mbps.

TCP/IP   Transmission Control Protocol/Internet Protocol; a suite of protocols that, working in combination, make it possible to transmit data across the Internet.

Telnet   A protocol and an application used for logging onto a computer remotely using TCP/IP. A Telnet session allows the user to issue commands on the remote computer as though the user were logged on locally. Telnet uses a command line interface; there is no graphic interface.

UNIX   A registered trademark of X/Open Company, Ltd. The name UNIX refers to one of many operating systems built on a common code base.

UPS   Uninterruptible power supply; a device that allows a computer to continue operating during a power outage.

Usenet   *See* NNTP.

virtual directory   A pointer to a physical directory that allows IIS to use the physical directory as though it were in a different location.

virtual server   A method by which a single Web server can look like multiple servers.

virus   A program that inserts itself into other programs and periodically replicates. Viruses are usually meant to be destructive or, at the least, annoying.

WAN   Wide area network; a network that spans a large geographic distance. Also referred to as a long-haul network.

Web   *See* World Wide Web.

Web browser   Software used on a client computer to view and interact with Internet resources.

Webmaster   A person who is responsible for maintaining a Web server. Usually, the Webmaster is responsible not only for the server hardware and software but also for the content.

wide area network   *See* WAN.

World Wide Web   The total collection of all servers that make Web content available on the Internet.

WWW   *See* World Wide Web.

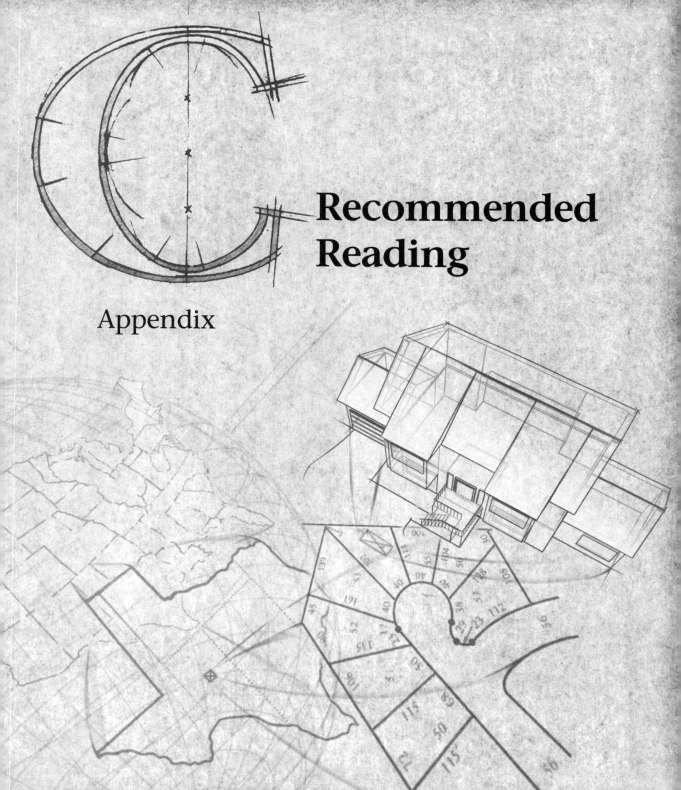

Recommended Reading

Appendix

Your average bookstore these days devotes an astounding amount of shelf space to Internet-related books. (Ten years ago you would have been hard-pressed to find a single book about the Internet in many bookstores.) The following reading list is intended to help you wade through the new mountains of material in the bookstore.

We have divided our list into subject categories and chosen a selection of books that we think are very good sources in their respective areas. Besides screening these books for subject matter, we also chose them for their organization and readability. We have included extra notes for some titles that we thought required further explanation or for books that really impressed us as being excellent in their categories.

You can also find a lot of great information on Internet-related topics on the World Wide Web, so we have included a list of some Web sites that you might find particularly useful. Happy reading!

Content Creation and Web Authoring

Fry, Andrew, and David Paul. *How to Publish on the Internet*. New York: Warner Books, 1995. This is a very friendly, well-written book that concentrates as much on the good design of a Web site as it does on HTML programming.

Graham, Ian S. *HTML Sourcebook*, 2nd ed. New York: John Wiley and Sons, Inc., 1996.

Lehto, Kerry A., and W. Brett Polonsky. *Introducing Microsoft FrontPage*. Redmond, WA: Microsoft Press, 1996.

Lemay, Laura. *Teach Yourself Web Publishing with HTML in a Week*, 2nd ed. Indianapolis, IN: Sams.Net Publishing, 1995. This is an excellent source for learning to code HTML and design Web pages.

Morris, Bruce. *HTML In Action*. Redmond, WA: Microsoft Press, 1996.

Weinman, Lynda. *Designing Web Graphics*. Indianapolis, IN: New Riders Publishing, 1996. A very nice book that concentrates on the graphic design possibilities for Web sites.

DNS

Albitz, Paul, and Cricket Liu. *DNS and BIND*. Sebastol, CA: O'Reilly and Associates. Although very technical and somewhat dry, this is the DNS bible. It explains the database format for DNS and how DNS works.

Internet Business

Ellsworth, Jill H., and Matthew V. Ellsworth. *The New Internet Business Book*. New York: John Wiley and Sons, Inc., 1996.

Resnick, Roslind, and Dave Taylor. *The Internet Business Guide*, 2nd ed. Indianapolis, IN: Sams.Net Publishing, 1995.

Sterne, Jim. *World Wide Web Marketing*. New York: John Wiley and Sons, Inc., 1995.

Internet General

Catapult Inc. *Internet Explorer 3.0 Step by Step*. Redmond, WA: Microsoft Press, 1996.

Glister, Paul. *The New Network Navigator*. New York: John Wiley and Sons, Inc., 1995.

Jaffee, Tom and Keith White, Winstruct Inc. *Learn! Windows 95: Internet and the Online World*. Redmond, WA: Microsoft Press, 1996. (Video only.)

Nelson, Stephen L. *Field Guide to the Internet*. Redmond, WA: Microsoft Press, 1995. Even though this is a Windows 95–specific book, it's a very good reference for Internet fundamentals.

Pfaffenberger, Brian. *Introducing the Internet*. Redmond, WA: Microsoft Press, 1996.

Internet Security

Atkins, Derek, and others. *Internet Security Professional Reference*. Indianapolis, IN: New Riders Publishing, 1996.

Garfinkel, Simson. *PGP: Pretty Good Privacy*. Sebastopol, CA: O'Reilly, 1995.

Loshin, Pete. *Electronic Commerce*. Rockland, MA: Charles River Media, Inc., 1995.

Lynch, Daniel C., and Leslie Lundquist. *Digital Money: The New Era of Internet Commerce*. New York: John Wiley and Sons, Inc., 1996.

Intranets

Eckel, George, and William Steen. *Intranet Working*. Indianapolis, IN: New Riders, 1996.

Scripting and Server Extensions

Davis, Stephen R. *Learn Java Now*. Redmond, WA: Microsoft Press, 1996.

Gulbransen, David, and Kenrick Rawlings. *Creating Web Applets with Java*. Indianapolis, IN: Sams.Net Publishing, 1996.

Mezick, David, and Scot Hillier. *Inside Microsoft Visual Basic Script*. Redmond, WA: Microsoft Press, 1996.

Tyma, Paul M., Gabriel Torok, and Troy Downing. *Java Primer Plus: Supercharging Web Applications with the Java Programming Language*. Corte Madera, CA: The Waite Group, Inc., 1996.

Server Applications

Benage, Don, and others. *Special Edition Using Microsoft BackOffice*. Indianapolis, IN: Que Corporation, 1996.

Gerber, Barry. *Mastering Microsoft's Exchange Server*. San Francisco: Sybex, 1996.

Microsoft Corporation. *Internet Information Server Training Kit*. Redmond, WA: Microsoft Press, 1996.

Solomon, David, and others. *Microsoft SQL Server 6 Unleashed*. Indianapolis, IN: Sams Publishing, 1996.

TCP/IP

Comer, Douglas E. *Internetworking with TCP/IP*. 3 vols. Englewood Cliffs, NJ: Prentice-Hall, Inc., 1991. If you want to know how the Internet works at a very detailed and technical level and don't mind reading a college-level text, these books will teach you everything you wanted to know and more about TCP/IP.

Windows NT Server

Microsoft Corporation. *The Windows NT Server Resource Kit*. Redmond WA: Microsoft Press, 1996. The Windows NT Server Resource Kit provides an extensive supplement to the Windows NT documentation. It also includes extra software and utilities to increase the functionality of the operating system.

WWW Sites for Content Creation

The National Center for Supercomputing at the University of Illinois in Urbana/Champagne has an online HTML primer that provides a very good and thorough guide for learning to program in HTML. To view this site, point your Web browser to *http://www.ncsa.uiuc.edu/General/Internet/WWW/HTMLPrimer.html*. You can find another site at NCSA, offering *Guides to Writing Style for HTML Documents*. This can be found at *http://union.ncsa.uiuc.edu/HyperNews/get/www/html/guides.html*. (The URLs for these Web sites are case-sensitive.)

Carnegie Mellon University's School of Computer Science has a page called *Composing Good HTML*. The URL for this site is *http://www.cs.cmu.edu/~tilt/cgh/*.

D

Appendix

About the Software That Comes with This Book

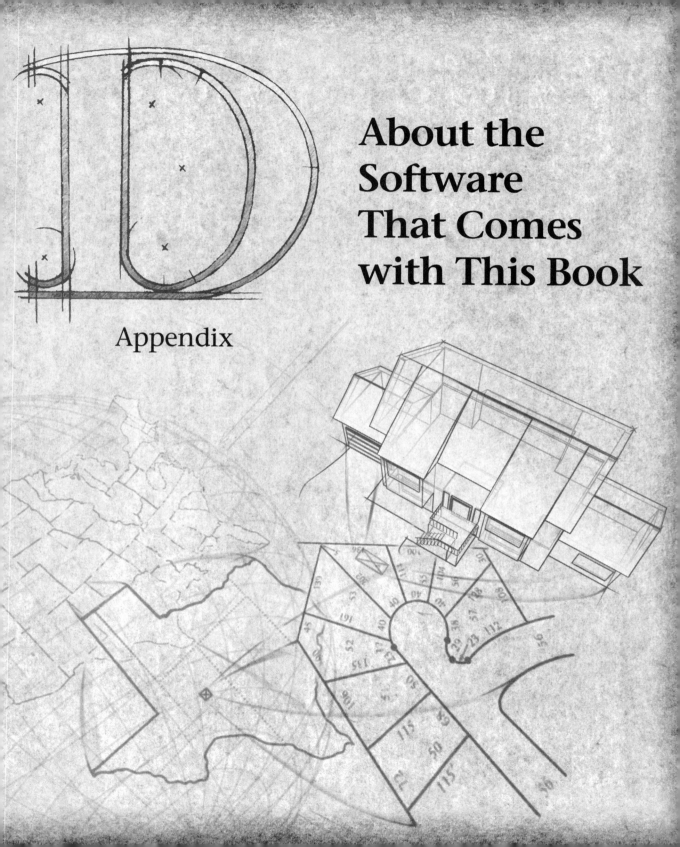

The CD-ROM that accompanies this book contains software tools to help you in the creation and maintenance of your Web site. Each tool is in its own directory on the CD and has its own setup process. Much of this software is also available for downloading from the Internet. You might want to check the Net to see whether a newer version has been released since the printing of this book.

NOTE: At the time of this writing, we were still in the process of gathering software and utilities to include on the CD so the list in this appendix might not be complete. Please see the README.TXT file on the CD for information and details about all the software on the CD.

The Web Media Publisher

Publisher is a text editor that has been specialized to handle HTML and to make it easy for someone with little or no knowledge of HTML to create Web pages. It works in much the same way as most word processor programs—you highlight a section and then apply a style to it—but in this case, the correct HTML code is applied. As well as making the creation of Web pages easier and quicker, Publisher allows you to create forms and tables and to integrate Java applets into your Web pages.

To install Publisher from the CD, run the SETUP.EXE program from the Publisher directory and follow the prompts.

WebTrends

WebTrends is a log analysis tool that you can use in conjunction with the information your IIS log gathers to determine many useful facts about your Web site. You can use WebTrends to discover your Internet site's most active and least active times of day and days of week, which of your Web pages are the most popular, the number of users who have accessed your pages, and much other valuable information that will help you to better manage your site. For anyone who runs a professional Web site, having a good analysis tool is critical. WebTrends should supply you with all the information you need.

Internet Assistants for Microsoft Office

The Internet Assistants for Microsoft Office are a group of programs that can be added onto the Microsoft Office suite of products. The Internet Assistants allow you to leverage your preexisting files and documents by enabling you to convert them into HTML very quickly. With the Internet Assistants, you'll be able to produce simple Web pages based on HTML 2.0 tags. They are not intended for producing complex HTML pages or for taking advantage of new HTML 3.0 tags.

Internet Assistant for Word

The Internet Assistant for Word allows you to save any Word document as an HTML document. Admittedly, the look and feel of these documents isn't all that great yet, but if you have a large amount of existing content that you want to convert quickly to HTML, this tool is a very good option. All you must do to convert a document to HTML is to open it and select the Save As option under the File menu. Then you choose HTML as the document type to save it to.

To install the Internet Assistant for Word from the CD, first make sure that Microsoft Word is already installed on your computer. Then launch the program WRDIA20Z.EXE from the IA directory.

<aside>
Note:

This version of Internet Assistant for Word works only on Windows NT or Windows 95 with Word 7 or Office 95.
</aside>

Internet Assistant for Microsoft Excel

The Internet Assistant for Microsoft Excel allows you to save a spreadsheet as an HTML table. If you have lots of existing spreadsheets you want to publish on the Web, this tool makes quick work of it.

The Internet Assistant for Excel has no installation program. To install it from the CD, simply copy the file HTML.XLA in the IA directory to the appropriate directory. (See the sidebar about location depending on version of Excel.) Inside the Excel directory is a subdirectory named Library. The HTML.XLA file needs to be placed inside this subdirectory. After the file is copied, launch Excel, go to the Add-Ons option under the Tools menu, and select the Internet Assistant Wizard.

To use the Internet Assistant for Excel, highlight the range of your spreadsheet that you wish to convert and select the Internet Assistant Wizard from the Tools menu.

Where the MS Excel Library Directory Is

The Internet Assistant for Microsoft Excel add-in file, HTML.XLA, should reside in the Microsoft Excel Library directory. The path to this directory varies depending on which version of Microsoft Excel you are running.

For stand-alone Excel 5, you will find the Library directory immediately under the EXCEL directory (for example, C:\EXCEL\LIBRARY on a Microsoft Windows system and My Computer:Excel:Library on an Apple Macintosh system).

For Microsoft Office 95 and Excel 7, you will find the Library directory under the MSOFFICE and EXCEL directories (for example, C:\MSOFFICE\EXCEL\LIBRARY).

Internet Assistant for PowerPoint

The Internet Assistant for PowerPoint will transform your PowerPoint slides into HTML pages that you can publish on the Web by simply selecting Export As HTML in PowerPoint 95. Your layouts, designs, and graphics will be maintained, and links are automatically set up to connect related slides or Web pages.

To install Internet Assistant for PowerPoint, run the IA4PPT95.EXE program in the IA\PPT subdirectory.

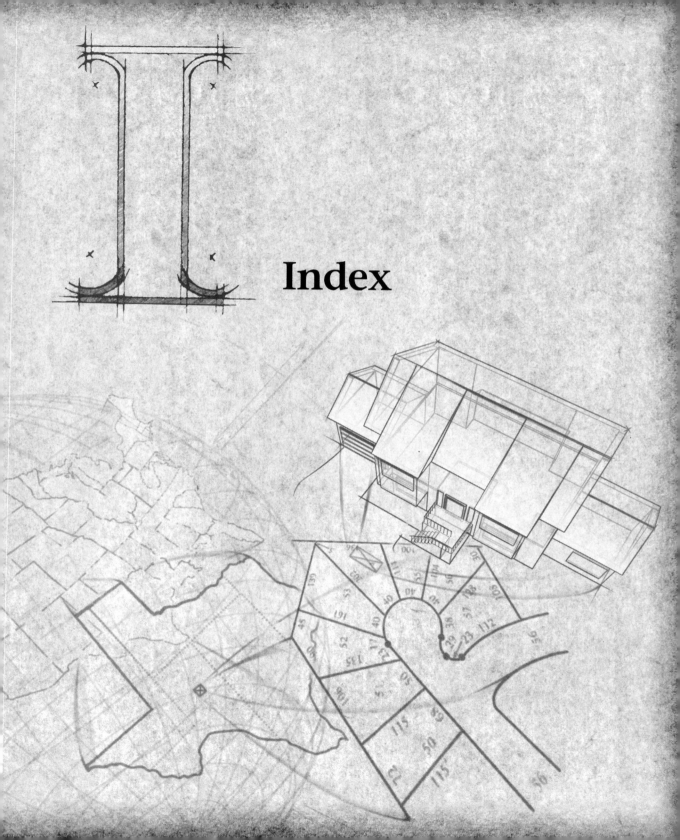

Index

Special Characters

14.4 rule, 127–28

A

access. *See* connections, Internet; dial-in access
access permissions, 105–13. *See also* accounts; security
   glossary, 110–11
   for non-Internet files, 109–10
   for private Internet files, 112–13
   protecting non-Internet files from IIS accounts, 109
   for public Internet files, 111–12
   setting, with Windows NT Server, 106–9
account lockout, 100
accounts. *See also* identification and authentication
   Administrator, 95–96
   checking e-mail, 171
   file and directory access (*see* access permissions)
   groups, 96–97
   Guest, 99
   selecting user account names, 103
   user, 97–99
ActiveX technology, 149–50
   client-side extensions, 152–53
   Java vs., 153
   server controls, 150
   server-side scripting, 150
adapters, ISDN, 42–43
addresses
   IP, 15, 138–40
   site, 8, 14, 136
Administrator accounts, 95–96
API (Application Programming Interface), 151
Application log, 166, 167
application problems, 172
Application Programming Interface (API), 151
Archie search engine, 18

ARPANET, 5
ASCII text, 130
asynchronous connections, 81–83
audio, 182–83
audit logs, 105
authentication. *See* identification and authentication

B

backbones, 6
backup domain controllers, 52
backup systems, 84–87
   disk mirroring, 39–40, 85, 86–87
   fault tolerance and, 40–41
   installing, 84, 85–86
   preventative maintenance and, 169
   security and, 118–19
bandwidth, 36
   capacity planning and, 37–38
   dial-in access, 158–59
   recommendations for ISPs, 45–46
bindings, 66
block allocation, 52
books. *See* reading, recommended
boot partition mirroring, 87
browsers, Web, 8–9, 131–33
businesses
   costs (*see* costs)
   finding sites for certain, 14
   future Internet technology for small, 180–81
   GUIware example (*see* GUIware, Inc. (company))
   information publishing for, 23–25
   interactive sites, 25–27 (*see also* dynamic Web pages)
   Internet (*see* Internet businesses)
   intranets (*see* intranets)
   manufacturing, 26, 27
   service-oriented, 26
   supporting, with Internet sites, 23
   version control and, 141–42
   virtual storefronts, 27–28

C

callbacks, 161
capacity planning, 36–38, 158, 170–71
CD-ROM software, 206–8
CERN, 8
certificates, SSL encryption, 115–16
CGI (Common Gateway Interface), 114, 151
charitable organizations, 25
chat services, 13–14, 163
checklists
  security, 119
  Windows NT Server installation, 54–55
CHKDSK utility, 169
clients, 9
client/server technologies, 9
client-side extensions, 152–53
Common Gateway Interface (CGI), 114, 151
communications. *See also* connections,
    Internet
  devices, 62–64, 71, 170
  security, 115–16
companies. *See* businesses
computers. *See also* hardware
  machine security policies, 100–102
  recommendations, 38–39
connections, Internet, 41–44
  checking, 84
  configuring, 62–66, 81–84
  dial-in access (*see* dial-in access)
  download times and, 127–28
  frame-relay, 43–44, 84
  ISDN, 42–43, 81–83
  leased-line, 44, 84
  modem dial-up, 42, 81–83
content, Internet site, xiii–xiv, 4–5
  finding (*see* search engines; services and
    technologies, Internet)
  future of, 181
  information publishing and, 23–25
  maintaining, 174–75
  reading recommendations, 200
  Web site (*see* Web pages; Web sites)
controls, ActiveX, 150
costs
  connections and, 41
  hardware and bandwidth, 36
  registering domain names, 49
  site, 22–23
  Web site listing, 142
crackers, 93
crashes, operating system, 41
Crystal Reports for Windows NT Server, 168
CU-SeeMe, 183
customer feedback, 175
customer support, 164
CyberAtlas (company), 4

D

database services, 67–68, 88, 112, 147–49
data sources, 148–49
Defense Advanced Research Project Agency
    (DARPA), 5
developments. *See* technological
    developments
devices. *See* hardware
DHCP (Dynamic Host Configuration
    Protocol), 53
dial-in access, 157–62
  bandwidth considerations, 158–59
  capacity planning, 158
  configuring Windows NT Server for,
    159–61
  connections, 42, 81–83
    (*see also* connections, Internet)
  customer configuration, 161–62
  hunt group service, 158
  managing RAS, 162
  setting up, 157
  setting up RAS users, 161
dictionary attacks, 94
directories. *See also* disks; files
  FTP and Gopher, 142
  Microsoft Excel Library, 207
  publishing, 68
  recommended structure for Internet files,
    111–12
  security (*see* access permissions)
  structures for Web sites, 134–40
  URLs and, 14
  version control and, 141–42
  virtual, 134–36
  virtual server, 137–40
Disk Administrator, 40
disk mirroring, 39–40, 85, 86–87
disks
  backups (*see* backup systems)
  checking, 169
  directories (*see* directories)
  emergency repair, 59
  file systems, 51–52 (*see also* files)
  mirroring, 39–40, 85, 86–87
  partitioning and formatting, 56
  size recommendations, 38–39
  space problems, 172–73
  using multiple, 135–36
DNS (Domain Name Service), 14–15.
    See also domain names
  reading recommendations, 201
  registering domain names and, 49
  Windows NT Server, 53
  WWW servers and, 32
domain controllers, 52

hardware
- capacity planning and, 37–38, 158, 170–71
- client and server, 9
- communications devices (*see*
  communications, devices)
- computers (*see* computers)
- disks (*see* disks)
- Internet connections (*see* connections,
  Internet)
- as Internet platform, xiv
- network cards, 171
- recommendations, 38–41
- reliability and fault tolerance, 39–41
- servers (*see* servers, Internet)
- setting up network, 50–51
- Windows NT Server and, xvii, 41–42

Hardware Compatibility List (HCL), 41–42,
   50, 84, 157
hierarchical organization of Web sites, 124
home pages, Web, 122, 123. *See also* Web
   pages
- design guidelines, 126
- personal or family, 25, 26

HTML (Hypertext Markup Language), 129–33
- editors, 130–31
- future of, 181
- learning, 130
- Web browsers and, 131–33

HTTP (Hypertext Transfer Protocol), 8, 14
HTX files, 148, 149
hunt groups, 158
hypertext, 6–7
Hypertext Markup Language. *See* HTML
   (Hypertext Markup Language)
Hypertext Transfer Protocol (HTTP), 8, 14

I

IDC (company), 4–5
IDC (Internet Database Connector), 147–49
identification and authentication, 99–103
- choosing user account names, 103
  (*see also* accounts)
- rules for choosing passwords, 102–3
  (*see also* passwords)
- setting user properties, 100–102

IIS (Internet Information Server)
- authentication, 100
- configuring, 72–78
- event logs, 168–69
- FTP server, 54
- FTP settings, 76–78
- Gopher settings, 78
- installing, 60–62, 67–69, 71
- protecting non-Internet files and, 109
- setting up IDC for SQL Server, 148–49

IIS (Internet Information Server), *continued*
- SSL and, 114, 115–16
- WWW settings, 72–76

information publishing, 23–25. *See also*
   content, Internet site
Integrated Services Digital Network (ISDN),
   41, 42–43, 81–83. *See also* dial-in access
interactivity. *See* dynamic Web pages
interfaces, 146
Internet, 2–19
- this book about, xvii–xviii
- businesses (*see* Internet businesses)
- as communication network and
  technology, 2
- connections, 41–44 (*see also* connections,
  Internet)
- contents and users, 4–5 (*see also* content,
  Internet site; users)
- evolution of, 5–6
- future of (*see* technological developments)
- hardware (*see* hardware)
- protocols, 3–4 (*see also* protocols, Internet)
- reading recommendations, 201
- servers (*see* servers, Internet)
- services and technologies (*see* services and
  technologies, Internet)
- sites (*see* sites, Internet; Web sites)
- software (*see* software)

Internet Assistants for Office, 131, 206–8
Internet businesses
- IPPs (Internet Presence Providers), 30
- ISPs (Internet Service Providers), 30–31
  (*see also* ISPs (Internet Service Providers))
- reading recommendations, 201
- selecting services, 31–32
- turning Internet sites into, 29–31

Internet Database Connector (IDC), 147–49
Internet Explorer, 8–9, 132–33
Internet Information Server. *See* IIS (Internet
   Information Server)
Internet presence providers (IPPs), 30–31, 32
Internet Protocol. *See* TCP/IP (Transmission
   Command Protocol/Internet Protocol)
Internet Relay Chat (IRC), 13–14, 163
Internet Server API (ISAPI), 114, 150–51
Internet service providers. *See* ISPs (Internet
   service providers)
InterNIC, 45, 48–50, 138
intranets
- definition, 28–29
- Internet sites vs., 29
- reading recommendations, 202
- security, 118

IP. *See* TCP/IP (Transmission Command
   Protocol/Internet Protocol)
IP addresses, 15, 138–40. *See also* DNS
   (Domain Name Service)
IP Phone, 182

Microsoft Windows NT Server installation,
  continued
  installing Internet-related software, 87–89
  Microsoft SQL Server database software,
    68, 88
  modifying, 69–71
  network configuration, 59–66, 69–71
  preparing for, 51–54
  prerequisites for, 54–55
  selecting file systems, 51–52
  selecting protocols, 51
  selecting server roles, 52, 58
  selecting services, 52–54
  text-mode, 55–57
  Windows NT Resource Kit, 89
Microsoft Windows NT Server security,
    95–103. *See also* security
  Administrator account, 95–96
  directory and file access permissions, 51–52,
    105–13
  drop boxes, 113
  glossary of directory and file settings,
    110–11
  guest accounts, 99
  identification and authentication, 99–103
  IIS settings, 114
  logging systems, 105
  maintaining user accounts, 99
  managing multiple users, 96–97
  removing remote management
    capabilities, 103–4
  scripts and, 114
  selecting passwords, 102–3
  selecting user account names, 103
  user accounts for access from Internet,
    97–99
  user and machine policies, 100–102
Microsoft Word, Internet Assistant for, 207
mirroring, disk, 39–40, 85, 86–87
modem connections, 41, 42, 81–83, 170.
    See also dial-in access
modems, ISDN, 42–43
multimedia streaming, 182

N

names, domain. *See* domain names
National Science Foundation (NSF), 5
NetBEUI protocol, 51
Netscape browser, 132–33
Network News Transfer Protocol (NNTP),
    12–13, 14, 163
networks
  backbones, 6
  cards, 171

networks, *continued*
  checking communications devices, 71
  configuring, for Windows NT Server, 59–66,
    69–71
  connections (*see* connections, Internet)
  hardware setup, 50–51
  Internet as, 2
  intranets (*see* intranets)
  optimizing performance, 81
  protocols, 51, 61 (*see also* protocols,
    Internet)
  routing and, 54 (*see also* routers)
news services, 12–13, 163
NNTP (Network News Transfer Protocol),
    12–13, 14, 163
nonprofit organizations, 25
NSFNET, 5–6
NTFS (Windows NT File System) files, 51–52

O

ODBC (Open Database Connectivity), 67–68,
    147
online magazines, 24
Open Database Connectivity (ODBC), 67–68,
    147
operating systems
  crashes, 41
  Internet enhancements, 180
  UNIX vs. Windows NT Server, xiv–xvii
    (*see also* Microsoft Windows NT Server)
optimization. *See* performance
organization of Web sites, 123–26
organizations. *See* businesses

P

packet analyzer, 94
packets, 3
pages. *See* Web pages
partitions, disk, 56, 87
passwords, 73, 82. *See also* identification and
    authentication
  dictionary attacks, 94
  recommendations, 101–2
  rules for selecting, 102–3
  setting, 100–101
PCT (Private Communications Technology)
    protocol, 116
performance, 79–81
  capacity planning and, 37–38, 158, 170–71
  connections, 41
  monitoring, 170

software
- antivirus, 117
- backup, 85–86
- this book's CD-ROM, 206–8
- client and server, 9
- Crystal Reports, 168
- e-mail, 88, 162
- HTML editors, 130–31
- as Internet platforms, xiv
- Internet-related, 87–89
- operating systems (*see* operating systems)
- security risks and, 94
- upgrades, 171–72
- version-control, 141–42

speed. *See* performance

spoofing, 94

SprintNet, 6

SQL Server, Microsoft, 68, 88, 112, 148–49

SSL (Secure Sockets Layer) protocol, 114, 115–16

stand-alone servers, 52

storefronts, virtual, 27–28

support, business, 23

support, customer, 164

synchronous connections, 84

system crashes, 41

System log, 166, 167

system performance, 79–80.
- *See also* performance

systems. *See* hardware; operating systems; servers, Internet

T

tags, HTML, 129

tape backup systems, 41, 84, 85–86, 118–19

TCP/IP (Transmission Command Protocol/ Internet Protocol), 3
- addresses, 15, 138–40
- configuring, 62–66, 70
- DHCP and, 53
- firewalls and, 104–5
- installing, 61
- network performance and, 81
- reading recommendations, 203
- selecting, 51

technological developments, 178–84
- content creation and, 181
- convergence of technologies, 180
- CU-SeeMe, 183
- future of Internet, 179–84
- HTML, 181
- Internet enhancements to operating systems, 180
- IP Phone, 182
- keeping up with, 178–79, 183–84

technological developments, *continued*
- multimedia streaming, 182
- scripting languages, 181
- small businesses and, 180–81
- video, audio, and telephony over Internet, 182–83

technologies. *See* services and technologies, Internet

telephone communication, 182–83

telephone lines. *See* connections, Internet

testing Web pages, 133, 174

text-mode Setup, 55–57

time requirements
- registering domain names, 50
- setting up Internet servers, 48
- Web page download, 126, 127–28

tokens, 105

Transmission Command Protocol. *See* TCP/IP (Transmission Command Protocol/ Internet Protocol)

U

Uniform Resource Locators (URLs), 8, 14, 136

uninterruptible power supplies (UPSs), 41, 173

UNIX operating system, xiv, xv–xvi

unrecoverable errors, 173–74

upgrades, software, 171–72

UPSs (Uninterruptible Power Supplies), 41, 173

URLs (Uniform Resource Locators), 8, 14, 136

Usenet, 12–13

User Manager, xv–xvi

users
- account names, 103
- accounts, 97–99
- Internet, 4–5
- managing multiple, 96–97
- RAS, 161
- setting security policies, 100–103

V

VeriSign (company), 116

Veronica search engine, 18

version control, 141–42

video, 182, 183

virtual directories, 134–36

virtual servers, 136–40

virtual storefronts, 27–28

viruses, 116–17

Visual Basic Scripting (VBS), 152

Visual SourceSafe (VSS), 141–42

voice communication, 182–83

W

WAIS (Wide Area Information Service), 11
Web. *See* WWW (World Wide Web)
Web browsers, 8–9, 131–33
weblike organization of Web sites, 125–26
Web pages, 122. *See also* Web sites
   content maintenance, 174–75
     (*see also* content, Internet site)
   creating, with HTML, 129–33
   design and creation, 30
   design guidelines, 126–29
   dynamic (*see* dynamic Web pages)
   graphics and, 127–29
   home pages, 123, 126
   maintaining, 174–75
   personal and family home pages, 25, 26
   testing, 133, 174
   Web browsers and, 131–33
Web sites, 122–64. *See also* sites, Internet;
     WWW (World Wide Web)
   announcing, 142
   for content creation, 203
   content maintenance, 174–75
     (*see also* content, Internet site)
   designing, 123–29
   designing and implementing, as business,
     186
   disk directory structures, 134–40
   FTP and Gopher content, 142
   hierarchical organization, 124
   interactive, 25–27 (*see also* dynamic Web
     pages)
   linear organization, 124–25
   organization, 123–26
   pages, 126–29 (*see also* Web pages)
   reading recommendations, 200
   servers (*see* servers, Internet)
   services, 31–32
   terminology, 122–23
   version control, 141–42
   virtual directories, 134–36
   virtual servers, 137–40
   weblike organization, 125–26
WebTrends tool, 206
Wide Area Information Service (WAIS), 11
Windows Internet Naming Service (WINS),
     53–54
Windows NT Challenge/Response, 100
Windows NT Resource Kit, 88, 89, 162, 203
Windows NT Server. *See* Microsoft Windows
     NT Server
WINS (Windows Internet Naming Service),
     53–54
Word, Internet Assistant for, 207

WWW (World Wide Web), 6–9
   bandwidth recommendations, 45
   browsers, 8–9, 131–33
   hardware recommendations, 39
   IIS settings, 72–76
   search engines, 16–17
   sites (*see* Web pages; Web sites)
   URLs, 14
   users, 4–5

Y

Yahoo search engine, 17

About the Authors

Louis Kahn started playing with computers when he was four years old and has never stopped. He began writing software at the age of twelve and was named Young Entrepreneur of the Year in 1986 by Atlanta's Association for Corporate Growth after forming a software design and computer consulting company. Currently a Program Manager on the Windows NT team at Microsoft, Louis also devotes time to his five-year-old Internet services company, GUIware. When not busy working, Louis enjoys movies, cooking, and Internet chat sessions. He can be reached at *louisk@microsoft.com* or *louisk@guiware.com*, and his Web site is *http://www.guiware.com*.

Laura Logan received her B.A. in English at the University of Waterloo in Canada in 1987. Having been desensitized by exposure to Waterloo's extensive computing facilities, Laura accepted a proposal from a computer geek and moved to Redmond, Washington in 1989 so that her new husband could pursue a career with Microsoft. While awaiting work permission, she kept herself busy with volunteer work, scuba diving, and by acting as an unofficial software beta tester. Laura squeezes her writing career in between being full-time caretaker of her three-year-old daughter Anya, who already enjoys surfing the Net with Mom.

The manuscript for this book was prepared and submitted to Microsoft Press in electronic form. Text files were prepared using Microsoft Word 7.0 for Windows 95. Pages were composed by Microsoft Press using Adobe PageMaker 6.0 for Windows 95, with text in Stone Serif and display type in Univers. Composed pages were delivered to the printer as electronic prepress files.

Cover Graphic Designers
Greg Erickson
Robin Hjellen

Cover Illustration
Philip Howe

Interior Graphic Designers
Pam Hidaka
Kim Eggleston

Interior Graphic Artists
Michael Victor
Lori Campbell

Desktop Publishers
E. Candace Gearhart
Sandra Haynes

Principal Proofreader/Copy Editor
Devon Musgrave

Indexer
Lynn Armstrong

IMPORTANT—READ CAREFULLY BEFORE OPENING SOFTWARE PACKET(S). By opening the sealed packet(s) containing the software, you indicate your acceptance of the following Microsoft License Agreement.

MICROSOFT LICENSE AGREEMENT

(Book Companion CD)

This is a legal agreement between you (either an individual or an entity) and Microsoft Corporation. By opening the sealed software packet(s) you are agreeing to be bound by the terms of this agreement. If you do not agree to the terms of this agreement, promptly return the unopened software packet(s) and any accompanying written materials to the place you obtained them for a full refund.

MICROSOFT SOFTWARE LICENSE

1. GRANT OF LICENSE. Microsoft grants to you the right to use one copy of the Microsoft software program included with this book (the "SOFTWARE") on a single terminal connected to a single computer. The SOFTWARE is in "use" on a computer when it is loaded into the temporary memory (i.e., RAM) or installed into the permanent memory (e.g., hard disk, CD-ROM, or other storage device) of that computer. You may not network the SOFTWARE or otherwise use it on more than one computer or computer terminal at the same time.

2. COPYRIGHT. The SOFTWARE is owned by Microsoft or its suppliers and is protected by United States copyright laws and international treaty provisions. Therefore, you must treat the SOFTWARE like any other copyrighted material (e.g., a book or musical recording) except that you may either (a) make one copy of the SOFTWARE solely for backup or archival purposes, or (b) transfer the SOFTWARE to a single hard disk provided you keep the original solely for backup or archival purposes. You may not copy the written materials accompanying the SOFTWARE.

3. OTHER RESTRICTIONS. You may not rent or lease the SOFTWARE, but you may transfer the SOFTWARE and accompanying written materials on a permanent basis provided you retain no copies and the recipient agrees to the terms of this Agreement. You may not reverse engineer, decompile, or disassemble the SOFTWARE. If the SOFTWARE is an update or has been updated, any transfer must include the most recent update and all prior versions.

4. DUAL MEDIA SOFTWARE. If the SOFTWARE package contains more than one kind of disk (3.5", 5.25", and CD-ROM), then you may use only the disks appropriate for your single-user computer. You may not use the other disks on another computer or loan, rent, lease, or transfer them to another user except as part of the permanent transfer (as provided above) of all SOFTWARE and written materials.

5. SAMPLE CODE. If the SOFTWARE includes Sample Code, then Microsoft grants you a royalty-free right to reproduce and distribute the sample code of the SOFTWARE provided that you: (a) distribute the sample code only in conjunction with and as a part of your software product; (b) do not use Microsoft's or its authors' names, logos, or trademarks to market your software product; (c) include the copyright notice that appears on the SOFTWARE on your product label and as a part of the sign-on message for your software product; and (d) agree to indemnify, hold harmless, and defend Microsoft and its authors from and against any claims or lawsuits, including attorneys' fees, that arise or result from the use or distribution of your software product.

DISCLAIMER OF WARRANTY

The SOFTWARE (including instructions for its use) is provided "AS IS" WITHOUT WARRANTY OF ANY KIND. MICROSOFT FURTHER DISCLAIMS ALL IMPLIED WARRANTIES INCLUDING WITHOUT LIMITATION ANY IMPLIED WARRANTIES OF MERCHANTABILITY OR OF FITNESS FOR A PARTICULAR PURPOSE. THE ENTIRE RISK ARISING OUT OF THE USE OR PERFORMANCE OF THE SOFTWARE AND DOCUMENTATION REMAINS WITH YOU.

IN NO EVENT SHALL MICROSOFT, ITS AUTHORS, OR ANYONE ELSE INVOLVED IN THE CREATION, PRODUCTION, OR DELIVERY OF THE SOFTWARE BE LIABLE FOR ANY DAMAGES WHATSOEVER (INCLUDING, WITHOUT LIMITA-TION, DAMAGES FOR LOSS OF BUSINESS PROFITS, BUSINESS INTERRUPTION, LOSS OF BUSINESS INFORMATION, OR OTHER PECUNIARY LOSS) ARISING OUT OF THE USE OF OR INABILITY TO USE THE SOFTWARE OR DOCUMENTATION, EVEN IF MICROSOFT HAS BEEN ADVISED OF THE POSSIBILITY OF SUCH DAMAGES. BECAUSE SOME STATES/COUNTRIES DO NOT ALLOW THE EXCLUSION OR LIMITATION OF LIABILITY FOR CONSEQUENTIAL OR INCIDENTAL DAMAGES, THE ABOVE LIMITATION MAY NOT APPLY TO YOU.

U.S. GOVERNMENT RESTRICTED RIGHTS

The SOFTWARE and documentation are provided with RESTRICTED RIGHTS. Use, duplication, or disclosure by the Government is subject to restrictions as set forth in subparagraph (c)(1)(ii) of The Rights in Technical Data and Computer Software clause at DFARS 252.227-7013 or subparagraphs (c)(1) and (2) of the Commercial Computer Software — Restricted Rights 48 CFR 52.227-19, as applicable. Manufacturer is Microsoft Corporation, One Microsoft Way, Redmond, WA 98052-6399.

If you acquired this product in the United States, this Agreement is governed by the laws of the State of Washington.

Should you have any questions concerning this Agreement, or if you desire to contact Microsoft Press for any reason, please write: Microsoft Press, One Microsoft Way, Redmond, WA 98052-6399.

097-000-680